MARBLE, GRASS, AND GLASS

MARBLE, GRASS, AND GLASS

B. Sham Moteelall

Library of Congress Control Number:		2021916328
ISBN:	Hardcover	978-1-6641-8947-8
	Softcover	978-1-6641-8473-2
	eBook	978-1-6641-8472-5

Print information available on the last page.

Rev. date: 08/18/2021

To order additional copies of this book, contact:
Xlibris
844-714-8691
www.Xlibris.com
Orders@Xlibris.com
826043

CONTENTS

INTRODUCTION

This writing is the result of many years of searching and investigating. It centers on East Indian indentured servants who were shipped to various parts of the world in the 1800s and early 1900s to work on various British sugar plantations and other colonial entities.

The focus is on the country of Guyana, once British Guiana, located on the northern coast of South America. The indentured process for Guyana started in 1838 and continued until 1917, resulting in Guyana receiving some 240,000 Indian subjects. They were recruited as contracted indentured servants. It is estimated that the total number of Indians shipped to various parts of the world totaled 1.2 million. Some estimates claimed that number to be 1.5 million. Initially, the early recruits were largely men. However, as a result of early protests and the demand of men themselves, women were included as part of the quota of recruits. Because of the mandate, women had to be secured by any means, including kidnapping.

My ancestors were among those people who were sent to a colonial British Guiana in various ships during the indentured process. I am a Guyanese by birth and immigrated to the USA alone over fifty years ago to attend college. I have always been curious about my ancestral migrations. Because of such curiosity, some forty years ago, I embarked upon a preliminary search to gather further detailed information on this subject. It has been a slow and difficult process.

I collected narratives from various individuals, talking, telling, and discussing particular family members and friends from long ago. The intent was to piece together and recreate the varied stories of migration that we told each other.

The extended family of diverse individuals are now scattered in various parts of the world, and with each passing generation, descendants are being engulfed into different cultures, not knowing about their roots. Many families had similar faiths. For all such families, this writing can partially fill some curiosity about what happened to all our ancestors. This is not a history book. It's a book based on several true stories told about people who lived a long time ago in far-away places.

First I went in search and found bits and pieces that verified the accuracy of some of those long-ago stories. That was encouraging, but further investigations on some individuals came to sudden dead ends. Many names were known, but for those dead-end searches, names had to be invented in order to bridge the gaps. To add to the confusion, many of those people were given at least two names. One name was given by the Hindu priests or pundits after consulting astrological and other documents. The second and more popular name was given by the family. In addition, nicknames were popular. It therefore made it difficult to know what name was used for a particular individual. Many of the astrologically derived names were not known to some family members, especially to later generations. Spelling created other obstacles, because English translators had to spell and document Hindu and Muslim names. Finally, some people wanted to change and elevate their Hindu caste, which resulted in names being modified.

The indentured process to Guyana started after slavery was abolished in 1834. However, the African slaves continued working as apprentices at the plantations until 1838. Growing and processing sugar cane into sugar, rum, and other by-products required a relatively large labor force, especially in the fields. Those sugar establishments (estates) were owned and managed by wealthy English entities like John Gladstone, who became paranoid about losing the African field laborers after their emancipation. For that reason, the indentured system was enacted on a contractual basis. Workers were recruited from various countries, and eventually the people of choice came from India.

The two main reasons for that choice were, first, the Indians tolerated the tropical climate better than people of other nationalities. Secondly, it was during that period when the British East India Company had gained substantial control of sections of India. That control process could have simplified the legality and cut through some red tapes and accelerated the indentured system. Nepotism was not uncommon, and the buddy system prevailed. Bribes and incentives were common practices. Needless to say, that the venal recruitment process included many lies and deceptions. It was costly to have the ships anchored at the harbor for any extended period. That is why the recruiters, called Arkathies, were pressured to ensure a full complement of passengers on all ships. The math was simple: more recruits meant more profits for everyone except the recruited, who were referred to as coolies. Simple translation for coolie is manual labor.

The indentured Indians (coolies) left their home country for various reasons. Some returned and some stayed in Guyana. For various reasons, none of my ancestors returned. This is their story. It is an attempt to document the family history and our ancestral survival in a strange land. Some survived better than others. Some died young and tragically. Some suffered severe abuse while bound to the plantations. Many died as a result of those abuses. Some were murdered. Some died from diseases unknown to them. Children died from malnutrition. Women had frequent miscarriages. Many babies were stillborn because of nonexistent prenatal care. A large percentage of babies died, and mothers were blamed for their poor maternal skills. Women were forced and subjected to repeated sexual abuses, and some died in shame, the shame for which they had no control. There were infanticides largely because such births were results of brutal rapes and the mothers wanted no reminders of such violations. Even if the mother wanted to keep the baby, direct and extended family members had other ideas. Their collective anger was vented on innocent newborns.

Some stories are good; others are horrible. There could be some inaccuracies, mistakes, and exaggerations, for this is just a messenger trying to resurrect a picture from a puzzle with missing pieces. But after forty years of searching, this is my story to tell. Although it deals with a particular family, many families dealt with similar issues. For those descendants of global Indian indentured process who do not know details of their respective ancestors, this writing is universal. It is our story. It applies to all descendants of East Indians indentures regardless of what part of the globe became their final destinations. It is also a story for and of the human race.

My hope is that you will find this writing interesting regardless of your ethnic background. It creates clarification and an understanding of what really happened to the 1.2 million (or more) Indians around the world placed in a glorified system of slavery to enrich the British planters. It's a little-known atrocity that started with and continued with lies, deceptions, and surreptitious practices. No matter who we are, we do know that right is right and wrong is wrong. Many of those people were woefully wronged and died without justice. That's the gist of this story. The story of a servitude contract that resulted in life sentences for many. An atrocious system that reinvented and redefined slavery.

To be fair, it should be noted that many were rescued from desperate situations in India. It gave them an excuse to elevate their caste, escape from spousal abuse, escape from political persecutions, escape high taxes, leaving prostituting habits behind, to seek and find better partners in life and to have new beginnings. Many tolerated and endured the punishments and took advantage of the opportunities offered to them and, through frugality, hard work, and sacrifices, created a good life that offered peace and tranquility. Some were opportunistic and devised various "get even" schemes. Whatever their situation, many created and later enjoyed much better lifestyles and prosperity for themselves and their descendants. For them, we celebrate. For the less fortunate, we honor by remembering their stories. For the dead, we mourn. For the survivors, we are the answers to their prayers and live to tell their collective stories. It is an honor to tell their collective stories in this book called *Marble, Grass, and Glass.*

Good reading.

PROLOGUE

After Columbus rediscovered the western hemisphere, European countries engaged in a series of treaties and battles to claim and occupy territories in that part of the globe. One factor that escalated such tension was the demand for and the production of sugar. As the sugar industry grew, so did the need for field laborers. That created the slave trade that lasted for many decades where African slaves were kidnapped and sold into slavery in the western hemisphere. However, emancipation was enacted over a period of time, which left the wealthy planters starved for an adequate labor force. One such colony was British Guiana, now Guyana, where slavery was abolished in 1834. After an apprenticeship period, the colony was starved for adequate labor.

The colony of British Guiana changed hands a few times. Sugar production started there in 1658 by the Dutch and was supervised by Nova Zeeland Company. The British took control of the territory in 1781. Dutch regained control in 1784. Finally, the British regained their control in 1796, which lasted until 1966 when the colony gained independence. Guyana continues to produce good-quality sugar that is still being sold under the brand name of demerara sugar.

Sir John Gladstone of Fasque, first baronet, a member of British Parliament, father of future prime minister William Gladstone, was one of those British plantation owners in Guyana. He desperately went in search of a new and suitable labor force to work his sugar cane fields.

On January 4, 1836, John Gladstone wrote a letter to Gillanders, Arbuthnot & Co. of Calcutta, India, investigating the possibility of acquiring a suitable workforce from India. On June 6, 1836, the reply from Gillanders, Arbuthnot & Co. to John Gladstone gave approval to the inquiry. That initiated the 1838 process of Indian indentured servants going to Guyana, on a contract basis, to work on the various sugar plantations.

That enactment evolved into a glorified slavery system that resulted in a corrupt and venal process that lasted until 1917. It was a system of servitude that reinvented and redefined slavery. John Gladstone and his lobbying cronies created the following system:

- Where affluence superseded human dignity. Money and power talked and people suffered.
- Where physical and sexual abuses were acceptable practices. People were beaten and raped.
- Where wealth and power, the plantocracy, a West Indian lobbying group controlled the system, including politicians. Venality became standard.
- Where the perception existed that not all people were created equally.
- Where fraud and nefarious practices became the norm.
- Where cats were in charge of guarding the bowls of milk.
- Where atrocities existed in the face of blinded eyes. They saw, but refused to notice.
- Where truth sayers were ethically, morally, and financially ruined. They were out casted.
- Where many bad things happened to good people and evil was tolerated.
- Where bad foods and poor nutrition, coupled with stress and exhausting physical labor, killed many.
- Where in one colony in one year over 60 percent of babies died and mothers were blamed for their poor maternal instincts.
- Where abuse and shame were too painful to tell and many tragic secrets got buried with victims' bones.

The stories of those indentured servants must be told before they are forgotten forever. The victims should be understood, the brave should be praised, and the aggressors must be condemned. The following pages reveal some real stories of a family that is representative of all families who descended from such atrocious system. This is their story.

MARBLE, GRASS, AND GLASS—THE BOOK

CHAPTER 1

The Village

The sun was slowly inching its way down into the western horizon. Tall shadows created by the evening rays stretched eastward, canvassing the almost-flat landscape over that little village in India called Arijela. Occasional gentle breezes waved the branches of the mango and eucalyptus trees in the neighborhood, causing the elongated shadows to dance in confused harmony. Their gentle, periodic gestures acted as if they were waving a parting signal to the setting sun as it continued its punctual and slow decline, leaving the landscape to darkness and extending invitations to nocturnal creatures that patiently awaited their respective moments.

While that orange ball was sinking to rest, a village farmer named Punit was busy feeding his cattle. He had no concept of helium or hydrogen. He did not understand the planets or the solar system. He couldn't care less if supernovae existed or if gravitational forces created black holes. But he knew that nightfall was inevitable and that the evening chores had to be done in his universe before darkness arrived. He worked continuously and encouraged his two sons to get their work done and not be so engaged in their usual boyhood games.

Those two boys were always playing practical jokes on each other. Instead of feeding the cattle, Desai would tease his little brother, Dashrath, who, in boyish anger, would occasionally hurl dried cow pies like Frisbees at his teasing older brother. They chased each other around the cattle pen and occasionally engaged in mild wrestling bouts. They were young boys about twelve and fifteen years old and behaving accordingly. They had fun together and entertained themselves on their family farm.

The cattle were bellowing as Punit encouraged his two sons to hurl their feed of freshly cut grass over the wooden fences. Those fences leaned slightly outward as a result of constant bombardment from the herd. An occasional support post was planted to prevent the entire structure from collapsing.

They could see the smoke rising from the house just a short distance away. They could faintly smell the familiar sizzling spices of masala that notified them that supper would soon be ready. As they were hungry teenagers, that was all the incentive they needed to move into overdrive. The outside chores had to be completed, or there would be no supper for them. They had no light except that from a homemade lantern. So that evening, like every other evening, the race began to get all the outdoor work done before that orange ball disappeared over the Gangetic plains and into the western horizon.

Arijela was in the province of Agra in Uttar Pradesh. The year was about 1894. The Punit family had lived in that village for many generations. According to their Hindu caste system, they were Ahirs, which defined them to be cattle herders and farmers. This rigid caste system did not permit them to participate in trades other than raising livestock and some small-scale farming. The food they produced was for domestic consumption, for sale at the local market, and for bartering with the neighbors. That was the world of the Punits. It was all they knew of life, and that was how they survived one generation after another.

In that society, roles were well-defined. The men performed the outdoor agricultural duties while the women were in charge of domestic chores. Girls were trained to become good homemakers and to ensure that the men were properly attended to. Boys were the prized members of a family, for they continued the family name and traditions.

When Punit and his sons finished their daily chores, they expected supper to be ready. Laced with sweat, dirt, and manure, they walked barefoot down the dusty trail toward the little brick-and-wood house. Hungry stomachs and the aroma of fried curry spices quickened their pace as they turned off the dusty cattle trail, past the vegetable garden, and toward the back door of the house. At the bottom of the steps, they were greeted by the usual buckets of water for washing up, especially for the remnants of the dried cow dung that they had been hurling around. Of course, Desai teased Dashrath about his dirty manure hands, so Dashrath hurled the half-empty pail at Desai. It was Desai's speed and agility that kept him from being drenched. They all laughed as Father called into the house for someone to bring out some more water.

The Punit family lived in their little house that Punit had built shortly after marrying his childhood bride. It was surrounded by trees and slightly rolling hills that interrupted the flatness of the landscape. They had an excellent herd of cattle, mostly buffalos that were locally referred to as *bhise*. Some of the animals came from the family as Punit's inheritance. One fine cow came from his in-laws as a marriage dowry. The rest had been raised by that immediate family. Punit had a keen eye for cattle. Over the years, through selective breeding and some savvy bartering, his herd became the envy in their neighborhood.

Being Hindus, the family was forbidden from eating beef. Those animals, nevertheless, provided numerous benefits to the family. The family drank the cows' milk. Some of the milk was sold or bartered. The rest was converted into various dairy products, like butter, ghee, cheese, and yogurt. Male calves were sold to local butchers. There was a demand for beef from non-Hindus, like Muslims and the recently arrived British. Those British subjects relished beef and paid premium prices for choice cuts. Previous to such arrivals, some of those animals had aimlessly wandered about and become nuisances to the neighborhood.

The Punit family kept select heifers as breeding stock. The castrated bulls were used as oxen. They pulled the plow and other farm equipment. They also pulled the wooden wheel carts that provided the family with a mode of transportation. Occasionally, the boys entertained themselves by challenging each other at calf rodeos at home and at the annual bull-riding events held during the village festivals. Well-trained oxen were ridden bareback by the village boys. Girls were strictly prohibited from riding, for it was considered unladylike.

Because the cattle provided so much, the Punits, like all true Hindus, considered them sacred. The Punit family could never ever consider butchering a cow for their own consumption. Their food came from various sources. There was no need to even consider beef as a food source. But they had no issues selling it to others. It was part of their livelihood, especially at the premium prices paid by the British subjects.

In the kitchen, Ms. Soba Punit (short for Subhadra) and her two daughters cleaned and washed the vegetables. They could hear the bellowing cattle outside and Punit's voice directing the operation. Soba minced and pulverized the spices using stone pieces carefully carved for such purposes. With folded legs and cotton dress properly secured, she sat on the floor, added drops of water to the mix, and ground away in a rhythmic rocking motion. As she did the grinding, her two daughters carried the wood and started the cooking fire. They had a cooking station that allowed most of the smoke to escape. And as Punit encouraged the boys outside, she directed the cooking routine.

Rice pudding, or *kheer*, was their favorite dessert, so as Soba worked on the spices, the girls maintained the fire and got the kheer started. Then the three of them finished making the evening meal.

Preparing a meal was a full-time job. The rice had to be ground and sifted into flour. The vegetables had to be picked and cleaned. They had to gather wood. Pails of water had to be carried from the community well located down the dusty road some distance away. There was no electricity. For light, the women filled little clay pots called *deeiah* with ghee and dipped cotton wicks into them. Those, when lit along with the cooking fire and the occasional homemade lantern, provided the only sources of light in the Punits' house.

It would be disrespectful for the men to enter a somewhat-dark house and not to have their food ready, so the women hurried in their hot, smoked-filled little kitchen. They could hear the men washing up and Punit calling for more water. They could not comprehend such a request, for it was hard work carrying pails of water down the dusty road, but like obedient Hindu farm girls, they did not question it. A pail of water was respectfully delivered to the men, who washed up, marched up the stairs, and sat on the floor, leaning their weary backs on the wooden wall. They expected to have their meals served. Father always sat in the middle to ensure that the boys could not get into mischievous food fights. With burning eyes caused by the mingling smoke and steam, the women did their customary duties, ensuring that the men were once again properly fed. They generally ate after the men finished their meal. Then they washed the pots and pans and all the dishes and left them to air-dry.

Soon, it was time for bed, and all the Punit children were nestled away and lost in dreamland, knowing that the next day they would have the same routine duties to perform. It was during those times that Punit and Soba had the world to themselves. In their night attire, they lay on their homemade bed, talked about whatever was important to discuss, and snuggled together under cotton sheets as a happily married couple.

Morning came fast and was promptly announced by the proud rooster that ruled the roost. Desai and Dashrath could hear their father's calls from outside, but in typical teenage manner, they could not leave the warmth and comfort of their cotton sheets and grass-filled mattresses. They could hear the pounding and clanging in the kitchen. They heard the bellows of cattle outside. They could see the rays of the morning sun shining through the cracks of the wooden windows. But only a stern yell from Mother could propel the two young men into motion as the sisters laughed at their lethargic morning motion. Yes, it was time to face another day at the Punit farm in that little Indian village.

After breakfast, Punit kept busy milking cows as the boys in their usual playful manner attended to their respective morning duties. Desai's job was to harness the team of oxen and get them ready for plowing, while Dashrath took care of the goats and chickens. The women kept busy with food preparation and fetching water from the community well.

The tall, handsome Desai, with his long black hair, conveniently harnessed the pair of oxen close to the main road. From such a strategic point, he could admire the village girls as they walked by to the community well. His sister, with water pail in hand, leaned on the outward leaning fence. That gave her the opportunity to escape housework and to visit with Desai while she waited to join the village girls on their way to the well. He enjoyed the teasing from the group of young girls, especially from the tall, shapely one with a long black curl of hair down her back. They were both about fifteen years old. He had great admiration for that girl. She was beautiful.

His gaze and admiration would be interrupted by his father, who came to take the oxen for the morning tillage session. Punit did the plowing while Desai took the herd off to grassy areas where he kept watch as the herd meandered about and grazed. He usually drove them down to the local canal where they drank. Usually, he got on the back of his favorite old ox and marched the herd to the designated pastures and to various grazing areas. They were adamant about rotational grazing. Sometimes the animals meandered along the banks of the canal in search of good grazing. His old ox was well trained, like a cutting horse, to head off any suspected deserters. As the old ox plodded along, Desai had intoxicating visions of that tall, beautiful girl he so admired. Such dreams helped time to pass as the sun reached upward and compelled shadows to obey. On occasion, the picture would be interrupted by passing clouds. Rainy days were less desirable, but farmers there would say that a little bit could get wet, but a lot more would grow.

At lunchtime, Desai's sister, Beti (meaning daughter), came along. As she walked along barefoot, she felt the uneven grass gathered around her feet. Always cautious about biting insects, she was especially careful where she stepped, knowing that a herd of cattle left piles of evidence in their grazing paths. She carried a little homemade bamboo basket lined with a piece of cotton. In the basket, she brought their lunch, which consisted of whatever they had prepared, along with some warm sweetened tea and generally some yogurt. Beti would unfold and spread a sheet under a nice shade tree, and together they would eat lunch and watch the herd continue its slow pace in search of fresh morsels of grass and other vegetative treats that cattle preferred.

Desai and Beti treasured those moments. It broke up the monotony and allowed them to share thoughts and ideas with each other. He could talk about things other than cows and farming. He especially liked to inquire about that tall, pretty girl with the long black curl down her back and a wiggle in her walk. Beti did not encourage that conversation for fear that that girl might not be the one chosen for him. For her, it was a time away from routine domestic chores of cooking, cleaning, gardening, and hauling water. It was time to enjoy the outdoors further from the house and to spend time with her favorite older brother, who was one year her senior. Occasionally, Desai would let her ride on the old ox even if it was forbidden by the elders for girls to ride. He particularly enjoyed her laughs and giggles as the old ox would sometimes be dragged into a slow trot, and she got bounced around, trying to keep her cotton frock in place while maintaining her balance. It was their fun time, bound together by youth and innocence in a remote land ruled by traditions and a caste system. It was the best time of the day for both of them.

It was always sad when she had to leave. But on schedule, she would gather up her lunch basket, fold the cotton sheet, and slowly meander home. She played on the way, skipping rocks in the canal and occasionally dropping a larger rock into the water to watch the ripples gently crash into the reeds. Sometimes, she stood in solitude and dreamed of things that most teenage girls dream about. Then she would continue at the slow pace, kicking pebbles with her bare feet. She had no desire for shoes. She treasured nature and admired the diversity that surrounded her. And as she plodded along, she gathered wildflowers to be used for decoration and in their periodic evening prayer rituals.

*   *   *

Desai would again be left alone to face the solitary afternoon with the herd. He did whatever had to be done and spent most of the time daydreaming about the future. He entertained himself in the typical boyhood manner. He knew that one day he would have to claim his childhood bride and start a family of his own. He speculated that his bride was the tall goddess with the wiggle in her walk and the black curl down her back. He was very excited about that idea. He knew where his house would someday be built and where his cattle pen would be located. He even had a spot picked out for a garden.

His thoughts and dreams were his companions for the rest of those days. Occasionally, he swam in the canal. He enjoyed swimming, and after years of long-distance swimming, he developed visible muscles in all the right places. Sometimes he climbed into the trees in search of wild fruits. He did whatever he could to pass the time as his cattle inched their way along the ditch bank, competing for the best blades of grass.

Finally, the sun would position itself in that part of the horizon that told Desai that it was time to start heading home. The tall tree shadows that extended eastward confirmed the time of day. He had no watch, but he could guess time quite accurately by the sun's position and the obedient shadows. With great enthusiasm, he would get on the back of the old ox and start the roundup. The ox understood his duty well and was always willing to help gather the herd and start the journey home. Another day would pass for Desai on the bank of that familiar canal as the herd was driven homeward in the same manner that his ancestral youths had done for many generations before him.

*   *   *

At home, Dashrath took care of the animals that were left behind, such as cows with young calves, oxen, goats, and chickens. Punit stayed busy plowing and cutting bundles of grass from a nearby meadow while the women worked in the vegetable garden. They were all on the lookout for the cloud of dust and listening for the thundering hooves of the bellowing herd as it approached home. Then all got busy. With sticks in hand, they steered the cattle into the wooden pen and closed the gates. The animals hurried through the gates because they knew that handfuls of freshly cut grass would be hurled over the fences for them to enjoy.

Once again, the race began to finish the evening chores before the darkness gathered and invited creatures of the night. Soon, the men would smell the sizzling supper and be greeted by the buckets of water at the bottom of the steps; they would eat supper, enjoy the kheer, and nestle themselves among the cotton sheets in search of Dreamland. Tomorrow, the routine would start all over again as it did for many generations before.

Saturdays were no exception to working. On that day, Punit would get an early start. He would hitch up the old ox to a wooden wheel cart, load up some produce, and drive to the local farmers' market. There he sold eggs and vegetables. With the cash, he bought supplies like salt and spices. It was also an opportunity for him to socialize with his neighbors, get informed of the happenings in the area, and keep up with the discussions of the week. It was a good place to meet potential buyers looking for choice beef.

The children patiently awaited his return, as he always brought candy and treats for them. So when they heard the clattering and squeaking of the cart coming down the lane, they dropped whatever they were doing and, in typical kids' manner, ran to climb on the cart and enjoy a short ride back to the house, smothering their father with hugs and enthusiasm until the treats emerged. Then, they would sit on the old wooden wagon and slowly devour the sweets as the old ox groaned to haul the extra weight. At home, Punit and his wife talked about the conversations that had taken place at the market. Then Soba would put the supplies away and resume her domestic routine. She always stashed some treats for Desai to enjoy when he returned with the herd.

Soba was a somewhat stoic woman. According to tradition, she and Punit were married as babies by their respective parents. Punit claimed her when they were teenagers, and by the time she was thirty, she was the mother of four children, two sons and two daughters. Desai was her firstborn and was the pride of her life. She truly loved that boy and occasionally complimented herself for bearing such a handsome specimen. She was a mother, and most likely, she overlooked any minor deficiencies associated with the lad.

The years passed, and the family survived in their traditional manner. The children grew, and the herd improved. Day by day, Desai stood by the road and admired his goddess with her sexy dimples and million-dollar smiles. He knew that it was just a matter of time for him to claim her as his bride so they could start their life together. He spent all his spare time cleaning up his future home site and forking up his garden plot. He was creating earthly heaven for a woman who was a goddess in his perception. He was especially thankful for one thing: that he would not have to claim the short, chubby, giggly girl who lived down the lane. He utterly despised that girl and her silly habits.

As the children were coming of age, Soba approached her husband one day to discuss a somewhat serious matter. Their daughter had come of age, and she must be married. His fatherly duty was to approach the parents of the boy to whom she was promised. It was time for Beti's husband to come and claim her. There would be a wedding, and Desai's sister would be married.

It was shocking news to Punit that his daughter had grown up. It did not seem possible that the child could have grown up so fast. He knew that the day would come, but not that soon. To him, she seemed like a child. Nevertheless, tradition must prevail, and it was time for him to give the bride away. So off he went to meet with the father of his son-in-law and discuss the wedding details. Together, they went to the local pundit to pick a suitable date as dictated by their scriptures.

As the weeks passed, the final arrangements were made. Then there was the wedding. Friends and neighbors gathered as the pundit read from his holy books and performed all the rituals necessary for the process of holy Hindu matrimony. Then the pundit gave his usual speech to the bride and groom about living as a happy couple should and defined their respective roles as husband and wife. At last, he collected his fees, pronounced them man and wife, and sent the bride to her new home with her husband.

Desai watched as his little sister, the bride, walked past him all dressed up in a beautiful sari and nice jewelry. She looked so pretty and grown up that it suddenly made him realize what a lovely lady his sister had become. She stopped, stared at him, and bowed down to his feet. He quickly picked her up, dried her tears, and hugged her. Then he congratulated the groom with a firm handshake and a hug and sent them along their way to their new life together.

With the wedding over, the family resumed their daily chores. The only difference was that now there was one less person in the Punit household. The daughters in Arijela obviously did not stay with their parents for long. But many did not go very far. Most of them stayed in the surrounding villages and grew up to become the next generation of adults. Hence, the Punit family continued with the routine.

Punit resumed his field duties, and Desai took care of the cattle. The one thing that Desai missed was the daily luncheon visits with his sister. Now his younger sister brought his lunch out to him. They ate together under a tree as he used to, but he missed the gossip and Beti telling him bits and pieces about the girl he so admired. Now, he quietly ate his lunch, drank his tea, and gave the little girl strict orders to go straight home.

With Beti gone, Desai felt a greater void for female conversations. He spent more and more time thinking about the one with the long black hair curled down her back. He spent as much time as possible along the dusty road to see that lovely creature as she walked past to the well. As she returned, she carried a large, brasslike container filled with water. She carried the vessel on her head with arms reaching up to hold it in place. She would walk past Desai smiling, her dimples sinking into her cheeks. His heart would race uncontrollably, his gaze fixed upon her every move. But he went absolutely crazy as she walked past, and he gazed at her from the rear. With her arms reaching up, she walked with more of a wiggle. That brought great joy to his teenage eyes as the black curl of hair swung from hip to hip in perfect harmony with every graceful step she took. The only thing that would spoil his mood was when he heard the annoying giggles of the girl he absolutely hated. Her shrieking voice and high-pitched giggles were painful to his ears as she stomped past him homeward. In fact, Desai once joked to his friends that a woman like that would be eternal punishment to the man who had to spend his life with such an obnoxious being. He hated her. She was short and chubby with unruly hair that blew about her face.

*   *   *

As parents, Punit and Soba were somewhat concerned about their son's admiration for the girl with the curl down her back. They could not help seeing his obvious gaze as she walked past every day, hauling water for her family. But Punit assured his wife that if young boys did not act in that manner, it would be of greater concern. He instinctively knew that something must be done but decided to have faith in his son not to do anything foolish.

*   *   *

Finally, one day, to his surprise, Desai saw his parents approaching to deliver his lunch instead of his little sister. He knew that they had to have something of utmost importance to say in order for them to come together, leaving their work behind. His mother would seldom venture far from home, so seeing her coming really surprised him. Upon their arrival, he dismounted from the old ox and turned him out to graze. The three of them sat under a shade tree and had an extra special lunch as Punit talked about the time when he was a young boy doing the same duties that Desai now performed.

While eating lunch, Punit congratulated Desai on the fine job he was doing with the herd. After a bit of small talk, Punit explained that the parents of Desai's bride had come to visit. The time had come for

Desai to claim his childhood bride. There would be another wedding at Punit's house. Soba explained that it would be nice to have another woman in the house to help with the various duties since Beti was now married and gone. They continued on about the pundit picking the proper time and agreeing on some minor details about the bride's family needs.

Desai was probably a little embarrassed about the discussion, but all he could think about was that he would be able to touch his angel, whose feet kissed the earth with her every gentle and graceful step. He would no longer have to stand by the road to gaze at her beauty; she would be there every day and every night by his side. He was so excited that he had a hard time controlling himself.

After some discussion, Punit put his hand on Desai's shoulder and said that he had some bad news. Punit said that he was sorry, for the bride was not the one that he expected. Disappointed, Desai looked at his mother with curious eyes, asking like, "Is she …?" The "Is she?" questions went on for a while as Desai tried to figure out who was his bride. He kept naming off all the girls in the area only to be told that they were not the one. It got really tense as he asked the last desperate question: "She's not the ugly giggler? Is she? *Is* she?"

Then silence fell. The only sounds were the rustle of the trees and an occasional moo from a cow. The human silence was finally broken by Punit's apology and his wife's sobs. There was nothing else to explain. Faith and tradition had dealt the young man a losing hand. His tradition dictated that he must obey. His parents had promised him to that girl when they were babies. There was no other choice. The parents' promise was a promise, and that promise was a debt only to be paid with the young man's future.

Desai slowly stood up and turned away with a look of utter disappointment. His watery eyes now saw a blurred image of the tall, sexy goddess while his ringing ears heard the shrieks and giggles of the one to be his wife. Then he turned around, looked at his mother, and asked, "Of all the girls in the world, why her?" To which only a mother's arm could offer consolation. She walked over, reached up to her tall son, embraced his broad shoulders, and stroked his long hair. Together, they cried, like a mother with a sick baby. There they stood on the bank of the canal among the grazing cattle. They felt the warmth of the sun and the cooling of the gentle breeze. An occasional fish made ripples in the water, and the cattle meandered about. It was a difficult moment for them. It was reality.

Punit could not stand that sight. His stern wife was not the crying type, and neither was his son. But there they were in tight embrace, allowing their tears to flow like the River Ganges. At that moment, he caught himself turning away to dry his own tears and to rid himself of the sniffles. It was of no use trying; his tears were gushing like water through a broken dam, wild and uncontrollable. He wished that they had not done such an unforgivable deed to their precious son. But what was done was done and could not be changed according to the family tradition.

There was nothing else to say. The bad news was delivered, and tomorrow would be another day. Soba gathered up the dishes, folded the sheet, and placed everything into her homemade bamboo basket. She told her husband to stay with the boy, and she cried her way down the ditch bank, along the dusty cattle trail, and into her little house. Her young daughter could not understand the tears. She had never seen her mother cry before.

Punit stayed with his son for the rest of that day. He talked about many things, especially about being a husband. He assured Desai that he would learn to love his wife. He explained that love would grow, and they would have a happy family as time passed. He gave several examples of others in Desai's position and how well things turned out. He also gave many examples of couples who were pleased with their respective match and grew unhappy as the years passed. Desai did not hear a word his father spoke. Anger and confusion were his companions at that moment. That evening, they drove the cattle home together. Nothing was said. They did their chores, ate supper, and quietly went to bed.

The next morning, Desai did not wait by the roadside, but from inside the cattle pen, he heard the shrieks and giggles of the one he least desired. She was stomping down the dusty road to the community well. As she passed, Desai tried to see something good about her, but her ungraceful, bobbing body; unruly hair; and cantankerous howls made it difficult to see any potential beauty in such a creature. All the other girls in the group had some grace and appeal except that one. Besides, it was hard to see beauty in the one he so despised. His anger forced him to speed up his chores. From a window, his parents saw his grief and understood his pain, for which there was no antidote other than time. Punit told his wife that such illness would heal from within, and time was the only medicine. But he, too, felt the pain of the unlucky lad.

Soon Desai was back on the banks of the canal herding the cattle. The difference now was that he did not have the same dreams and motivation. He could not look at his home site and could no longer visualize his perceived heaven. He saw the site as hell and lost all motivation to fork up his future garden. He felt sick to his stomach and sat under various trees as the world turned with its preprogramed speed that gently revealed the western horizons.

On rainy days, he sat patiently as thunder and lightning passed unnoticed. In a semi trance, he walked to the building site and gathered up the lumber that was supposed to be used for building his home. He made a large heap and burned it all to ashes. With burning eyes, he heard the dwindling sound of the crackling logs as his hunched body slowly gravitated back to the cattle herd.

One day, he was lying facedown crying when he heard a familiar voice. It was Beti with a lunch basket. Again, they sat under one of their favorite trees on a cotton sheet and tried to eat lunch. The difference that day was that neither of them ate. It was a sad and tearful luncheon as she complained about her abusive mother-in-law, and he protested about not wanting to marry that girl. It was comfort for both of them to just sit there and remember the fun times they had had just a few years ago. It was a classic case of misery loving company. She told him that she would always be there for him and that was all she had to offer. She explained that he must claim that girl as his wife and try to make a life together. She also told Desai that she was going to be a mother, and for that, she was thankful.

Then she gathered up her stuff, put it in the basket, and sniffled her way home to face her tyrannical mother-in-law. She did not play the skip-rock game. She did not joyfully kick pebbles, and she did not throw a rock into the water and watch as the ripples kissed the reeds. She grabbed her pregnant belly as she sobbed, and the little bamboo basket crashed to the ground. The contents mingled in the uneven grass. She noticed not, nor did she care.

That evening, as Desai drove the cattle home, his mother stood along the dusty trail, probably to get a good look at him. His red eyes and sad look were all she needed to see for those were confirmation of his continued misery. She simply stood there. The only movement was her cotton frock blowing in the wind like a sheet draped over a female statue as the herd of cattle walked by toward the gate and into the pen, expecting freshly cut grass.

As the days passed, Desai's behavior was almost as bad as a zombie's. He did not eat much, and his lethargic movement was a complete reversal of that of the agile, athletic boy who once lived there. Depression soon consumed him, and insomnia coupled with anger was his constant companion. He managed to convince himself that he could not tolerate that girl for his lifelong companion. The mere thought of taking her in his arms was, to him, incomprehensible and repulsive. *That will never happen*, he told himself, and he considered suicide. He also considered kidnapping his goddess and escaping to a faraway place. At least those were options.

CHAPTER 2

The Crime and Escape

As the weeks passed, Desai's behavior did not improve. He would lay awake almost all-night listening to silence and planning how to elope with his favorite girl. Eventually, he would doze only to be interrupted by the rooster's crowing. He slept periodically during his daily chores. Occasionally, the herd scattered and wandered. But with some effort, he managed to gather them together. One day, riding along the ditch bank, he fell asleep on the back of the old ox. The animals continued their usual pace and soon found themselves in a luscious green field of rice paddies. The farmer who lived some distance away from the Punit farm noticed the herd in his field and rushed out to investigate. He grabbed a stick and waded through the puddle only to find a sleeping herdsman and his cattle in his field. The crop was in a mess, demonstrating that the animals had been grazing there for some time. Angry, the farmer grabbed the slouching Desai by his long hair and dragged him off the back of the old ox.

Desai fell facedown into the mud. It was literally a rude awakening. He struggled up, wiping the mud out of his nose, mouth, and eyes. He hardly spoke when the cussing farmer hit him with the walking stick. Again, Desai fell into the mud. He tried desperately to apologize and, on his back, offered compensation for damages done to the crop. But the abusive, angry farmer hit him once more with his stick. Then the farmer started a series of beatings. To avoid injury, Desai covered his head with his hands and knelt facedown, taking the strikes on his back. The frustrated farmer suddenly dropped the stick and jumped on Desai's back, pushing his face into the muddy water. That started a wrestling match.

The strong farmer finally got ahold of Desai's long hair and was suffocating him by pushing his head into the clay slurry. He was a rather large man and was exerting all his weight on Desai's back. With all his might, the equally strong Desai hurled his opponent off his back. Trying to catch his breath, he saw the farmer again charging at him. At that moment, Desai saw the walking stick. He grabbed it and with a prodigious groan, he struck the farmer with all his might. His strike hit the man on the head, and Desai staggered away to find clean water to wash the mud off his face. He laid the stick down, and while washing, he saw the bleeding farmer coming toward him again.

Desperation and survival instincts fused with fear and fatigue, Desai grabbed the stick, which was planted next to him. He picked it up, and again, with all his might, groaning prodigiously, he struck his opponent once more on the head. The farmer fell as Desai once again struggled to clean the mud out of his eyes. His long hair matted with mud and rice paddy leaves gave him the appearance of a Rastafarian instead of a Hindu boy. For a few minutes in the blazing sun, he just stood there in shock, eager to comprehend what had happened. Then he saw the blood. The farmer in the mud had a hole in his skull. The red blood that oozed from the wound slowly mixed with brownish-gray slurry. Desai ran over and picked the man up. He asked him to wake up. It was of no use. The blood continued to ooze. The man was dead. He could have suffocated in the slurry while unconscious or bled to death, but either way, he was dead.

Desai felt warm all over. He was petrified, and he felt the sweat that dripped from his muddy body. He looked at his blood-covered hands and called himself a murderer. He stared at the corpse as the cattle continued their wandering in every direction, all except the old ox, who stood by him like a faithful dog. He made no attempt to gather the herd but ripped off the farmer's shirt and covered the hideous face. He knelt down and begged for his forgiveness. Then he looked to the sky and said a prayer. Finally, he apologized to the corpse and aimlessly walked away.

He went to the canal and washed the blood and mud off his clothes. He tried to scrape some of the mud out of his hair. Satisfied to be partially clean, he continued his walking. He walked and walked for several hours and into the night. Tired and confused, he leaned his body against a tree, stretched out his legs, and fell asleep.

He woke up with the rising sun, hungry, cold, confused, and disoriented. He continued his walking. He finally came to a small village consisting of a few small houses and children wandering about. He walked up to a house and asked for some food. The woman asked him to wait outside and soon returned with a handful of food wrapped in a large leaf. Then he continued walking, begging for food along the way.

Days later, he arrived at a small town and found a church where people were feeding the local beggars. He hurried over and joined the beggars. He ate a good meal for the first time in days. He then walked into the church and sat on the floor. As he was lost in tears, prayers, and confession, his entire body shook like a captive animal's. The residing pundit kept an eye on him. He noticed the boy's filthy condition and perceived pathetic state of mind and decided to approach him. He did so cautiously and tried to investigate his misfortune. It was of no use, for the boy was too confused to even speak. Not sure what else to do, the pundit gave him some clean clothes and some homemade soap and sent him to a pond located behind the church to wash up and change into the clean garments.

The church was a good place for him. Slowly, he started communicating with people who dwelled about the premises. The pundit told him that he could stay there and help with some odd jobs. In exchange, he was given food and a blanket. Occasionally, the pundit offered him sweetened tea in an effort to get him to chat so he could learn about what had happened to him. It took some time. Then one day, he shared some of his guilt with that "man of God" and asked how he could ever wash the blood off his hands. For lack of a better answer, the pundit told him that could be accomplished only if he bathed in the salty ocean for several days. So, the next day, with the pundit's blessing, he packed up his blanket, his change of clothes, and some food and set out on foot to find the ocean.

The pundit's help was priceless. He gave the lad an old handbag with a few things to ensure his survival. He told him that from strategic locations, public transportation traveled and that he should always travel in an easterly direction until he came to the large ocean. He must pray every morning for a higher power to guide him to his destination. Although he was not a wealthy man, he gave Desai a few coins to be used in extreme and desperate conditions. He also taught him a short prayer, telling him that anytime he felt lost, he should repeat the prayer and that powers unknown to mortals would help him to find his way. He warned him to avoid alcoholic beverages and to use his universal instincts when chaos engulfed his environment. Then he watched the young man with his packed handbag walk barefoot toward the rising sun. He seriously considered calling the authorities but decided instead to pray for him during his self-inflicted punishment.

It is not known how long it took or how he survived, but he found the ocean. Speculation is that he walked a lot, and on occasion, when the opportunity presented itself, he hopped on eastern-bound trains to Calcutta. That big city was overwhelming, but he was utterly amazed by the immense body of water and the huge waves that rolled and tumbled in the ocean. He never dreamed that the world had such vast quantities of water and that many people. He walked up and down the beach in confused and curious amazement. He found the ocean sounds to be fascinating. He saw hovering birds that were alien to him. Then he walked into the water and did as the pundit had instructed him to do. The blood, in his perception, began to wash off, and for the first time in weeks, he started to feel cleansed.

As he bathed, he felt a burning sensation on his feet. Later, when he sat on the beach, he looked at his burning feet and realized that they were bleeding. After miles of walking, sometimes on less-desirable paths, the cuts and bruises from various incidents raised havoc with his feet. The ocean's saltwater aggravated those wounds, so he got pieces of linen from the handbag and tied them on his sore feet. Then he repeated the prayer that the pundit had taught him.

It did not take him long to realize that people came there to pray and to feed the less fortunate souls who lingered along the beach. So he took up residence on the shores of the Bay of Bengal. He found the warm, salty water fascinating and would swim and play there for many hours. He gently walked along the shores in search of a group that offered prayers to God and food to the needy. He ate stuff that he could not comprehend. People spoke dialects and dressed in garments that were alien to him. But it was survival. At night, he buried himself partially in the warm sand and covered his body with his blanket. In the morning, he swam and prayed that he would find a group that would feed him that day. He was obsessed with washing all the blood away as the holy man at the church had instructed him to do.

Those Hindu worshipers at the beach used ghee as fuel during their rituals to maintain the flames of their holy fires. He walked along, picking up any ghee left behind. When he had an ample supply, he used it to soothe his injured feet. Then he tied his linen shoes on and slowly walked about. That process helped his feet to a fast recovery, and before long, he had no more need for ghee and abandoned the shredded rags that covered his injured feet.

That was his lifestyle for several months until one day he was approached by a group of men. One of them spoke to him. They were friendly men and offered him a tasty meal. He had no idea where he was so they explained that he was close to the city of Calcutta. The men called themselves arkathies. They were recruiters for a ship that took passengers across the ocean to a new land to work on sugar estates. They were recruiting passengers for a ship called the *Lena*.

Desai had no idea what those men were talking about and did not see the reason for their interest in him. Nevertheless, it was better than loneliness, so he followed them about. Occasionally, the men had food in cans, and they played strange games like cricket and football in the sand. They laughed a lot and genuinely seemed to enjoy themselves. For such laughter and joy, he traded his loneliness and followed the men whenever they appeared on the beach. When he questioned their periodic absence, he was told that they were busy getting enough passengers to fill the ship. They explained that the captain was impatient and wanted to leave the harbor within thirty days. That was why his "friends" had to hustle to secure enough people, especially women. They further explained that it was costly for ships to sit idle in the harbor.

It was the first time Desai had come face-to-face with a white man. That strange-looking creature accompanied the recruiters one day. He had had glimpses of white people before in Calcutta and along the beaches and on the train, but he had never seen one close up. At first, he was puzzled by the skin color of that individual, but the others assured him that he came from across the ocean and that he was a friend. He soon realized that companionship, like loneliness, had no color and decided that the man was probably okay. He accepted him as a friend and playmate, regardless of his unusual appearance and strange language. To him, that was one more piece to the puzzle in an environment crowded with diversity and copious amounts of water.

Then one day, after several meetings, the men suggested that Desai should meet with the captain of the *Lena*. They all went. At first, Desai was intimidated by such a large vessel, but the men encouraged him along to the captain's quarters. He was not surprised that the captain was a white man, just like his playmate on the beach. But he was puzzled about the whole process and tried to act bravely in an effort to minimize his concerns and astonishment. He gazed at the captain's desk and at all the books, papers, and instruments. His tall figure with long hair and now a full beard stood there and stared at the captain with his dark piercing eyes. The captain asked him to sit and have a cup of tea. He avoided the chair and sat on the floor, but the captain assured him that the chair was safe. On the chair, he drank a delicious cup of warm sweetened tea. The gentle rocking of the boat was somewhat frightening, and he held on to the tea cup with both hands to avoid spilling. The recruiters interpreted for the captain, and they convinced Desai that when the ship sailed, he could accompany them to a new land. In the meantime, they suggested to the captain that he should hire Desai to load supplies onto the ship. They knew that the ship's porter had quit and the captain needed a strong porter, so he hired Desai. The boy did not get paid, but he was given food and was allowed to sleep on the deck of the *Lena*.

Desai had many questions but could not communicate with the English-speaking personnel. So he learned a few English words. The shipmates took an interest in the handsome young lad and encouraged him to speak as much English as possible. In fact, the captain was impressed at how quickly and effectively he could communicate with them. But the thing that impressed the captain the most was his strength and determination. He carried heavy loads into and around the ship all day without taking much time for a break. He could carry three sacks of rice at once. He balanced one sack on his head and carried the other two under his arms. He kept himself busy all day and was especially happy when the recruiters came around. They played cricket on the beach close to where the *Lena* was anchored along a river some distance inland from the bay. A long dock extended from the shore to the ship. There was an abundance of food for him, and his appetite was impressive. He ate a lot and worked hard.

Nights were hard for him. His aching body was cocooned in his blanket as he lay on the floor of the *Lena*'s deck. He had visions of his family and their agony. He saw his mother's tears and his father's breaking heart. He saw the questioning eyes of his siblings, and he cried for them all at once. He knew that he could not go home. He was now considered a criminal and an embarrassment to his family. He realized that he should have accepted things, claimed his wife, and dealt with the consequences. Then he would have a vision of his goddess, and that was too much for him to deal with. He tried to focus on the captain's assurance that if he so desired, his lease in the colony would end after five years and he could return to India. It was a speck of hope, and such little comfort would relax his confusion and allow him adequate sleep one night at a time.

The ship's personnel did explain the indentured process to him. He knew that he should escape for a while and leave his sins behind.

That group of people on the ship, and his job as a porter helped him keep his sanity during the day, and his aching body helped him to sleep better at night. So day by day, he accepted the ship's personnel as his surrogate family. He sometimes inquired about the rest of the passengers but was given an incomprehensible generic answer. He decided to wait and see.

One day, the ship's personnel convinced him to shave. He did. The captain was very impressed with his handsome appearance and suggested that he should also get a haircut. To that, he strongly objected. He explained that a trim would be fine, but he could never cut off his long hair. He explained that a holy man once told him to keep his hair long and that would guarantee that he would possess great bodily strength and leadership capabilities. No one argued with that statement because he was a remarkably strong young man. So the staff trimmed his long hair and gave him some clean clothes, and within a short time, he was like a member of the staff. They adopted him.

Desai went through all the legal and medical processes required of an Indian indentured servant going to a British colony. He was told that he would be going to a place called British Guiana. There, he would be paid one shilling per day, and he would be expected to complete a task assigned to him by the overseer every day at the sugarcane plantation. They would sail on the *Lena* across the ocean and disembark at a port called Demerara. The Indian folks referred to that place as Demra. From there, he and the rest of the passengers would be escorted to a building from where he would be assigned to a sugar plantation as a field laborer. If he performed his daily functions to the plantation's specification, he was guaranteed a return trip to India after five years. With limited options at that time, Desai was set and ready to go on his journey to Demra. He was even somewhat excited to be given such an opportunity. So the documents were shown to him. A signature was required, but because of his illiteracy, his thumb was dipped into ink and the print was applied to the paper. That paper became the legal document that branded him as an indentured servant going to work in a sugar plantation in British

Guiana. He was checked by the ship's doctor, whose approval made it all legal.

Desai was one of the few individuals who were told the truth about the indentured process and what was expected of an indentured servant. Many of them were coursed with a pack of lies. Most were led to believe that there was a lot of money to be made by what was referred to as *cheney chaley*, which means "sugar sifting."

The day finally came for the *Lena* to sail. All the scared and confused indentured servants, along with copious amounts of supplies, were loaded onto the ship. Desai and the crew kept busy with the various details. With screaming passengers and shouting workers at the harbor, the industrial-sized ropes that secured the *Lena* were released from the harbor as the giant diesel engines roared. Then the *Lena* slowly pulled out of the harbor and sailed down the river and into the ocean, where it was gently tossed about on the waves and over the white caps. In mass confusion from the human cargo, the *Lena* rocked her way into the twilight. To Desai's surprise, a woman jumped overboard during the loading process and desperately tried to swim to safety.

The evening rays danced on the waves, and soon darkness found the little *Lena* inching her way into the majestic blackness of the ocean. The Indians, referred to as coolies, called the ocean Kala Panni, meaning black water. The hissing waves and the roaring engines filled the darkness only to be interrupted by the ever-present moaning and heaving of the seasick passengers.

Those passengers became increasingly seasick and scared. Most of them had never been on a boat before. The moaning and groaning, combined with the smell of vomit, was everywhere. Men, women, and children were all rolling about the filthy floor on the lower deck, plastered with vomit and excrement. The rocking *Lena* and her stinking cargo could be compared to a huge decomposing carcass that floated about into the darkness. Faint voices of regret were occasionally heard among the moans and groans as that first night slowly passed into eternity and the sardars tried to maintain law and order. They knew from experience that the seasickness and panic would become less intense as time passed, allowing the excited people to accept their fate and become more relaxed.

At last, there was light on the scattered clouds on the eastern horizon. Dawn was upon them. That large red globe of light inched its way out of the water with spectacular dances that brought hope to the eyes of that stinking mass of confusion. They were on their second day, making their way to the port of Demerara at the colony of British Guiana in South America.

People on those ships died along the way, and the *Lena* was no exception. There were occasional crimes and murders. The dead, from whatever cause, were wrapped in a sheet and tossed overboard. Tension existed, especially between the Hindus and Muslims. Some ships were lost at sea, and the entire crew vanished with their ship when it descended to the bottom of the ocean. Occasionally, someone jumped overboard, committing suicide. There were constant conflicts between the ship's personnel and the passengers. There was sexual and physical abuse on board. Such behaviors were upsetting to Desai, and he tried to lodge complaints with the ship's personnel. But he was told that such occurrences were rare and people were lying. Indeed, some of those were typical occurrences on the various ships that transported indentured Indian servants to various ports in the world to work the various plantations. Desai saw the injustice and bullying but could do little to prevent them. The captain refused to discuss the issues with him and said that the ship's personnel had to maintain law and order on board.

Desai, in contrast, felt very privileged to be favored by the captain. He was given special treatment, and he sometimes ate with the ship's crew above deck. He was assigned cleanup duties and hard labor, which he performed without complaining. Occasionally, the captain invited him into his quarters to check on his English. He did well learning the basics of the language. After about three months, he was communicating in English at least well enough that the captain could have a short conversation with him. However, when the captain asked why he left India, he became sad and reclusive, pretending not to understand the question. It bothered the captain as to why that intelligent young man had left India all alone for a miserable life as an indentured servant on a British sugar estate located on the opposite side of the globe. Without an answer, he directed the *Lena* toward her destination, toward the harbor to unload the human cargo of indentured servants.

As the *Lena* approached the Demerara harbor, the crew was busy getting the indentured ready for inspection by representatives of the plantations. At about that time, the captain asked Desai to join him for a cup of tea. He explained to Desai what to expect when he arrived at the plantation. He got a pad of paper, wrote some English words, and stamped it with his personal seal. As he folded the paper, he looked at Desai and told him to give that paper to the estate manager. He explained that it was a letter of recommendation that could help him secure a decent position at the plantation. Captains were encouraged to identify passengers with unique skills because there was a need for potential supervisory personnel at the various estates. Then the captain pulled out a wide cloth belt and gave it to the young man. Desai was puzzled as to what the belt was all about, and the captain explained that it was a money belt. The belt had secret compartments sewn in. The captain explained that a lot of crime existed at the colony. He told Desai to keep the belt tied around his waist and to keep his money (coins) stashed away in the belt's compartments.

It surprised Desai when he opened the compartments; there was already some money in them. The captain smiled at the lad's confused look. He explained to him that throughout the journey, he did not receive any compensation for his hard work. The money in the belt was his salary for all the hard work he did over the past several months. The captain further took the time to explain the currency value and how it was used in exchange for goods and services. The captain also explained value and what things were worth. He did explain one final thing, and that was how the indentured process worked and why some people would never satisfy their contracts and therefore never be able to return to India. The easiest way to speed up the process, the captain explained, was to buy themselves out of their contracts. Buying out from the contract was a process in place. It was for people who wanted to cut ties with the plantation before their bound period ended. That required money. The money belt was a start in securing the young man's early freedom and his independent future to do whatever he chose to do, including returning to India.

There were no words for such parting. The two men stood up facing each other—one a captain of a British ship, the other, a young, somewhat scared, but mostly excited indentured servant boy. They looked each other in the eye and shook hands. Desai secured his money belt, and the captain wished him all the best. He showed Desai how to tie the belt under his shirt, and they smiled. In broken English, Desai thanked the captain for all that he had done to help him. If the words were not proper, the body language was genuine. The captain understood the lad's sincerity. Filled with hope, he slowly turned around and walked out of the captain's office, saying the silent prayer that the pundit had taught him.

The tin tag with his identification number dangled on the string that hung around his neck. They were escorted to the immigration building in Georgetown.

*   *   *

Desai, after going through the immigration process, was assigned to the Port Mourant Estate in the county of Berbice. He was in awe when he observed the living conditions. There were many races, but most were descendants of African and East Indian people. Some of the people seemed alien to him, but at that stage, nothing surprised him anymore. Gangs and cliques existed everywhere, and Desai found himself in the company of a man named Jaman and his so-called friends, who called him Juman.

He was assigned to a logie (immigrant housing) with two other single men for his living quarters. It was a sorry excuse for a home, and the neighborhood stank worse than a pigsty. But as an indentured servant, he had few choices. That would be his new home for the immediate future. Those conditions did not totally surprise him because the captain of the *Lena* did explain to him some of the horrors that he was about to embark upon.

That was how Desai came to Guyana, South America. The year was about 1898, and Desai was about eighteen years old.

CHAPTER 3

Radha's Family

There was a grand celebration. It was held in the so-called mansion of a local landlord referred to as Zamindar. He was not a true zamindar, but because of his status in the area and the wealth he had acquired, people in that geographic area simply called him Zamindar, or Zamy for short. Many of those people were directly or indirectly employed by him and his diverse business operations. The year was about 1845. Rich, sophisticated guests were arriving at Zamy's residence in beautifully decorated horse-drawn chariots. Servants dressed in white apparel and red turbans greeted and assisted the guests in their traditional courteous and respectful manner, using the namaste greeting. The horses and chariots were carefully directed to the stable area, while the drivers were given their respective parking spots and horse grooming areas, where the animals were fed and watered. Then they were put into grassy bedded stalls to rest. While the outside activities were attended to, the official guests were assisted by resident domestic servants and respectfully escorted into a large hall.

It was described as a grand ballroom. The floor was draped with hand-woven rugs, and from the ceiling flickered images of countless lights that sprang out from silver and brass chandeliers. Sculptures were scattered about in uniform order for the mingling guests to admire. That ceiling was supported by decorative marble pillars. Zamy and his staff had spent many hours decorating that hall, and the results were quite impressive.

Eventually, the guests, consisting of diverse people, were escorted and respectfully assigned to the rugs on the floor, where they sat and propped themselves upon and leaned onto pillows of varying sizes all cased in colorful silk. The Indian men wore exotic traditional Indian garments, while the women were carefully wrapped in expensive saris of various sorts and colors. It was a moment for some of those women to display their scarce and expensive jewelry. Gold, diamonds, pearls, rubies, sapphires, and other exotic gems were on display. It was quite obvious that the status of those women was determined by the quality and abundance of their jewelry and by the position held by their respective husbands in society. Their long black hair was all tied with silken ribbons in every fashion imaginable, and on their foreheads, they wore perfectly circular tikkas.

There were a few who did not dress in traditional Indian garments. Some were not even of Indian descent. Those were people from England living in the area during that period and were most likely affiliated with the British East India Company. The British heavily favored people like Zamy because his support was of utmost importance to them. In return, Zamy was given low-interest financing and additional land and power for his unconditional loyalty to the queen of England, Queen Victoria. To show their support, the English families attended some of those events. They were dressed in British attire, and many spoke the Hindi language. By socializing with people like Zamy, they quickly learned local customs, culture, and traditions that had existed in India for thousands of years. That night was time for all to celebrate with Zamy and to have some fun.

It was truly a gala event. A gathering of that magnitude was only sponsored for auspicious occasions, and it was considered an honor to be invited to such an exclusive event. It was a mid-1840s Indian who's-who gathering, more accurately described as a hybrid between affluent society and snob hill. But every "who" wanted to be invited and be part of such a group. It was an opportunity to hobnob and to keep up with the gossip of that prestigious and relatively rich and famous society.

Zamy was an impressive man. He was also well educated and spoke fluent English. He had a tall, slim build, dark hair speckled with gray strands, and a moustache. His hair and moustache were carefully groomed. He and his wife, Shabina (or Bina for short) meandered around the crowd, meeting, greeting, and thanking their guests for attending the function and for participating in their joyous celebration. He spoke the language that corresponded to the listening guest. The men talked mostly about business issues relating to farming and trade, while most of the women discussed other social subjects, stood in strategic positions to display their most precious pieces of jewelry, and in some cases, expected compliments. Bina, however, understood her role as hostess and gracefully walked along with Zamy while keeping an eye on their servants who were offering refreshments to the attendees. She was an attractive and graceful woman, daughter of a prominent Brahmin family. She was well educated, and like Zamy, she spoke the different languages. She and Zamy were partners in their business endeavors.

As the group settled, Zamy and Bina migrated to the slightly elevated stage at the front of the hall. The band and drum roll on stage announced to the audience that it was time to sit and pay attention. The main events were about to commence. The audience obeyed and retired to their respective assigned seating areas as Zamy began to speak.

He first offered a short prayer in Hindi and thanked God for a bountiful harvest. Then he said a prayer in English that concluded with "Amen." He said that the monsoons were not severe that year, and his crops were magnificent. His livestock were healthy, and they reaped a good profit from his various endeavors. The other landlords in the audience echoed their approval. The Englishmen nodded with approval. Next was the big announcement. His beautiful daughter had graduated from a prestigious dancing school and would be getting married the following day. The gathering, with friends, business associates, and family, was a celebration. She was asked to perform an Indian classical dance to display what she had learned at the dancing school. The following day, her husband would come and officially take her for his wife. But that was her night to shine and to make Daddy proud of raising such a gorgeous lady with superb dancing ability.

The show began with the tapping of drums and the rattling of bells, followed by music from the band. Then at the right moment, there were rattling steps on the stage as a beautiful young lady appeared. She shook her hands and feet to synchronize the rattle of her jewelry in harmony with the sounds of the band. She was starting the performance of an East Indian classical dance. Her long black hair, skillfully breaded down her back, circled her head in a horizontal position as she danced around in circles with flawless grace. The audience was in awe as she bobbed and wiggled in perfect harmony with the sounds of the musicians. She was a beautiful and privileged young lady and was always the pride and joy of her father. That was her finest moment.

The dance was exquisite, and the audience cheered her on by waving their hands and displaying nods of approval. Because of her charm and graceful manner, the frequent English visitors called her Lady, and as time passed, she was generally referred to as Lady. She was fascinated and honored by the name and would introduce herself as Lady.

At the end of her performance, the guests came up to congratulate her on a stunning performance and on her marriage the next day. She acknowledged their thanks and approval, accepted their wedding presents, and was escorted by her mother back to her chambers. The group shuffled about as the band played quiet, soft music. They socialized, relishing the snacks and beverages while discussing, among other things, the current political issues about the status of the British occupation of India.

As the celebration was ending, the servants assisted the chariot drivers with harnessing the horses. The animals were led out of the barn. They were carefully brushed to remove any dirt or pieces of grass stuck to their bodies. Then they were hitched to their respective wagons. The drivers stood by the heads of their horses while the occupants were assisted on board. That process completed, the cacophony of parting farewells, drivers directing their animals, and the stomping of hundreds of shod hooves slowly came to a calm as the menagerie departed down the hill and onto the roadway.

As tradition dictated and as planned, Lady was married the following day and moved to her husband's family mansion. Because she was accustomed to being pampered, it did not take very long to adapt to the new environment.

Her new housemaids and personal servants ensured that her every need was met and that she understood the rules and customs of her new family. She was perfectly happy to let her husband assist with the family business while she enjoyed the luxury and comfort of her quarters.

Her marriage was a happy one. She read various fashion books and had a personal seamstress to ensure that her evening dresses were sewed to perfection. She knew nothing about cooking or cleaning. She had no concept about financial issues. Every place she went, she had a personal chariot driver to take her. She was quite happy in the new environment and periodically visited her parents and other siblings. Her older sisters and sisters-in-law were always ready and willing to advise her on proper methods of being a good wife and the need for proper nutrition when she became pregnant. Her mother took a keen interest in her new responsibilities and offered good motherly advice.

The weeks turned into months, and soon, she was pregnant. Her husband was elated with the good news and looked forward to a healthy baby boy. Every day, he pampered her with fresh flowers, good nutrition, and a lot of tender love and care. They had learned to love each other, and the pregnancy pulled them together like a magnet. From whatever was available during that time and in that place, she most likely received the best medical attention and even more attention from the female domestic servants, who were her constant companions and friends. Her mother-in-law became her best friend. She was a lovely woman and became quite excited about becoming a grandmother for the first time.

Then the baby came. It was a disappointment to her husband that it was a girl, but at least he now had bragging rights, having attained the status of fatherhood. He was assured by his wife that there would be many children. She promised to bear many sons for him who could grow up to inherit and run the family business. His only comment was that at least the girl child was healthy and the maids would ensure that she was well attended to. Lady was happy to be a mother and not at all unhappy that the baby was a girl. Her mother-in-law shared her enthusiasm. They called in the pundit to bless the baby. After consulting his astrological books and the zodiacs, he named the baby girl Radha.

As the weeks passed, the family started to notice something unusual about the baby. Her skin complexion was getting progressively darker. That was troubling because both parents had lighter-colored skin. A light complexion was a desired characteristic among those wealthy Indians. People with dark complexions, especially girls, were not given the same respect. In fact, they were teased and occasionally excluded from social functions. Most of all, men of any status would refuse to accept a wife of such perceived lower standard in that culture. For that reason, family members on both sides quietly discussed their concern. Zamy was the only family member who did not show much concern about the baby's complexion.

Zamy explained to his daughter that having such a child was not unusual. His father was a person of such skin color. But because of the family's wealth, they recruited a wife for him who was very light skinned. He assured his daughter that they would love the baby unconditionally, because Radha would need all the support that she could get. He promised to spend as many resources as it would take to ensure that she secured a kind and handsome husband, preferably one with the desired skin complexion. It was his way to deal with the situation. He was of the opinion that money, wealth, and social status was the answer to all the world's problems. If it meant buying a suitable husband for his granddaughter, then that was what he would do.

By the time Radha was two, it was obvious that she would grow up to be a person of dark complexion. Even her grandfather, Zamy, was surprised at how dark she had become. Her father ignored her altogether, partly because she was a girl, but mostly because of her dark skin. He had become very involved in the family business, and he used that excuse to leave the child-care duties to the mother and to the various domestic servants. Besides, his optimism was again high when he learned that his wife was once again pregnant. He was getting a chance to prove that he possessed better genetic capability than what he considered their first mistake.

It would be an understatement to say that he was beyond elation when the second child had arrived. He was a handsome baby boy, who was heavily laced with the accepted skin color. He was everything his father had wished for and more, for as the boy grew, it was quite obvious that he was an intelligent lad. He was always properly attired, and most evenings, his father spent quality time playing with him and escorting him around in an almost bragging manner, saying that he had fathered an almost perfect specimen.

Radha did not spend much time with her father, but her grandfather Zamy filled that void in her life. She and her mother frequently visited him, and Radha spent extended periods of time at Grandpa's house. She called him Nana, for that was the Hindi word for maternal grandfather. Hence, she and Nana spent a lot of time together, leaving her brother to the full attention of their father. It was a good situation for Zamy too. Now that all his daughters were married and moved on and his sons were old enough to handle most of his business, he was semiretired, only serving as advisor to the family business. He had a lot of time to give attention to a little girl. Of course, she enjoyed such attention and such affluence that her skin color became insignificant. If she was ever teased by any of the cousins, Nana was right there to discipline the teasers and to rescue and pamper his little Radha.

Zamy and Radha spent most of their time with the horses. He had acquired some excellent Arabian horses and spent many hours studying their pedigree and how to adequately match the mares' breeding to selected stallions in an effort to improve his herd. It was always exciting when the foals arrived. Radha would follow her nervous Nana around the maternity pen, waiting for those magical moments when the new foals were born. He celebrated when such births showed desirable characteristics.

The next several days were spent monitoring the foals' progress. Zamy stayed busy studying their characteristics while Radha enjoyed watching them galloping around the pens, investigating their new world. Such an environment was almost heaven for Radha. She could not wait for those frequent visits to Nana's mansion. Being there, playing with the horses, and having Nana for companionship was exactly what she wanted. Climbing on the fences and running about the fields had turned her into a tomboy instead of a girl of her family's stature. Bina, called Nani for maternal grandmother, was very concerned about a girl of her status behaving like a common peasant boy in the fields. But her protests bounced off Zamy's selective hearing as they continued their horsing around. They were pals and played together as time went by year by year.

Some ten years had passed since the grand celebration. Radha was nine, and her brother was seven. By now Lady had a third child. The boy was two and was a carbon copy of his older brother. Their father was so pleased with his two sons that he totally ignored Radha. To him, it was a genetic blunder. Due to such exclusion, she seldom stayed at home. Now she was even more aggressively running and jumping around the horse stables, and that was where she spent most of her leisure time. She refused to be tutored by the local teacher, and she refused to dress like a girl. Such behavior drove Nani absolutely crazy. Her biggest concern was the gossip among the society ladies. She had a dark-skinned granddaughter who dressed inappropriately, wore no jewelry, was illiterate, behaved like a tomboy, and lacked all the social graces compulsory for a girl in their society.

Her protests could no longer be ignored. She insisted that the girl be sent to some type of boarding school where she would be forced to learn at least the basic skills of reading, writing, and elementary mathematics. Such schools, according to her, had strict rules and were designed to handle difficult girls like Radha. Her husband and daughter knew that she was right about those issues and agreed to investigate further. Bina took it upon herself to investigate such institutions. During their travels, while Zamy was conducting occasional business matters or mostly horse trading, she visited schools with strict discipline for somewhat wayward girls.

Radha's mother still danced occasionally. She had hired professional musicians who came to her residence to play the music while she performed her dance for her husband and children. She tried, on numerous occasions, to get Radha to join her, but her clumsiness was obvious. Occasionally when she fell, her brothers would laugh at her lack of grace. Dancing was not her forte. She argued that she could climb over the fence, catch a horse, and ride bareback better than most and that she did not have to dance to prove anything. They had to look for some alternatives. Radha had tantrums every time the subject of going to school was addressed. She only wanted to be in the stables playing with the horses.

Zamy and Bina devised a plan to get her involved at some school. They suggested that Radha tour the city where she could casually visit the various schools selected by Bina. The hope was that she might see something that would pique her interest, something that she might be willing to pursue as a career other than horses. They discussed the options with Lady and her husband and started planning for such a trip. Within a fortnight, the tour was scheduled. Radha was told that it would be a family vacation.

Radha's father refused to go along, on account of his business commitments. But everybody knew the main reason for the objection. Zamy and Bina agreed to accompany Radha and her mother on the journey. It took several days with a horse-drawn chariot to complete such a trip. But Zamy had contacts along the way and was familiar with the various inns. He, Bina, and their daughter had made that trip many times when she attended dancing school.

Arrangements were made, and the trip details were finalized. Radha would be accompanied by Nana, Nani, Lady, and her seven-year-old brother. Taking the baby brother was up for discussion.

It was standard practice for a servant to be dispatched a fortnight before their trip in order to make the necessary reservations and to notify the various friends and business associates along the way. That was normal procedure when Zamy traveled, so they dispatched someone earlier to relay the itinerary. Although there were fewer business reasons to travel now, he and his wife used their time for vacationing, to visit friends, and to stroll through the various shops and bazaars looking for exotic clothes, rugs, and of course, jewelry for Bina and their daughters. But Zamy was obsessed and determined to find that next special stallion that could further improve his equine genetics. He also used the occasions to market his foals.

Excitement grew as time for the trip approached. Unfortunately, the day before departure, Zamy fell ill. His doctor diagnosed a respiratory infection and prescribed some medication and plenty of rest. The trip was out of the question for him. His wife did not want to leave him in such a condition and suggested that they postpone the trip until he felt better. Radha was happy with that because she saw no purpose in touring the city in search of clothes and jewelry. She wanted the event to end and to get back to the stables. The only excitement for her during such trips was the opportunity to visit the city and shops where there were various candy stores that sold her favorite treats.

Lady was filled with disappointment. She really wanted Radha to go and visit the various sights and to possibly enroll her in a school of some sort. It was time to get the girl out of the stable and into a school that would teach her the basics. Through his coughing and wheezing, Zamy suggested that the trip be rescheduled, but his daughter had other ideas. After several hours of contemplation, she saw the planned occasion as an opportunity to have some personal freedom and to bond with her children if her father and husband were not present.

After much discussion, a decision was made. She would go with the two older children. Her husband insisted that the little boy stayed home with him and the servants would care for him. He protested that his wife and children should not travel by themselves. The discussion turned into an argument, and he departed rather angry, taking his two-year-old son with him.

Almost immediately after he left, the chariot was selected. Lady, being somewhat embarrassed about her husband's rude behavior, was now more determined to make the trip with the two children. They would leave on schedule the following day. The selected driver had made that trip several times for the family. He had been a loyal employee of Zamy's family for many years, and she trusted him to take them on that journey. He assured the family that he would guard and protect Lady and her two children and ensure their safe return on schedule. They all agreed that he was the best driver to escort the woman and children. He was an impressive-looking man who was almost intimidating to most. To Zamy, he was more of a bodyguard than just a mere driver. His loyalty to that family seemed unquestionable.

Morning greeted the driver harnessing two white Arabian horses to a luxury chariot. He carefully checked all the leather straps ensuring that all the reins were properly adjusted and the buckles securely fastened. He checked the brakes on the wheels and all the spokes ensuring that they were in good operating condition. He knew the various service techniques necessary to keep the luxury equine mobile in ideal operating condition and how to perform any necessary repairs. He always carried a spare wheel with necessary tools in the event of any wheel issues along the way. As he worked, the coughing and wheezing Zamy did a final inspection. He kept warning the driver about hanging around unsafe places, especially gambling spots. Throughout that process, servants were busy loading luggage and other necessary supplies that were required for such a trip. That was all routine for them as they had done such chores many times before.

Radha's father soon returned. He was in a better mood. Realizing that the trip was still on schedule, he offered some last-minute instructions to them. He was rather amazed at how well Bina had cleaned up Radha. Apart from the fancy hairstyle and the pretty dress and matching shoes, Radha wore several pieces of expensive jewelry. He noticed that in spite of her dark complexion, she was becoming a pretty little girl. He complimented her for looking so fine. Her mother was also very well-dressed and wore several pieces of jewelry. But he was especially pleased with his son. The boy was a handsome lad and even more so that day, all dressed up for the big trip to the city.

They did the usual parting ritual, and soon the clip-clop of eight hooves pulled the wagon down the brick driveway toward the main road. Zamy tried to yell something to them but only succeeded in aggravating his cough. They waved to one another until the wagon pulled around the orchard and vanished down the hill. The echoes of the driver's commands and the thundering hooves informed Zamy that they were well on their way down the main road, and he wished that he was going along. His wife suggested that they go inside where he could rest. They did.

The three passengers were enjoying the ride. It was a beautiful morning. The sun was getting higher and higher over the horizon, and soon it was time for the horses to make their first stop. It was at the home of a family friend who was expecting them. They warmly greeted the travelers and expressed their disappointment at the grandparents not being there. Following the greetings and a brief discussion, they were escorted into the house while servants helped the driver with the equine duties. They ate and rested for some time in order to allow the horses to be properly fed and groomed and to allow them to get a well-deserved resting break.

At the scheduled time, they were on the road again. The kids talked about the food and desserts, and the driver sang while the horses moved along with variable speed that matched the terrain. There was not a lot to see. What they saw were trees, hills, valleys, farmland, field laborers, orchards, meadows, and an occasional wagon passing them going in the opposite direction. It was becoming a monotonous ride for the children, and to avoid the "Are we there yet?" routine, Lady kept them entertained with stories about incidents she had encountered on her various trips over the years with her parents.

As the children listened to their mother's stories, the horses clipped and clopped along while the driver continued his singing. The driver knew exactly how to pace the horses to ensure their arrivals were on schedule. He had made that trip with that team of horses many times before. During those trips, he had made numerous acquaintances over the years. He enjoyed gambling. During most trips, while Zamy was busy with business transactions, the driver entertained himself at the various gambling sites. On a few occasions, Zamy had to pay his gambling losses in order to get him out of trouble. For that reason, on that particular trip, he was warned not to participate in such obsessive stupidity. Zamy was emphatic about that. He warned the driver that he was responsible for the safety of Lady and her children and was expected to take his responsibility seriously. He thought about the warning as he continued his singing. He sang quite well with a deep voice. Suddenly, the singing stopped, and he started talking to the horses as they ascended a zigzag path to the top of a hill. At that point, he pulled the horses to a halt and explained that their next stop was a short distance down that hill. Then he proceeded. His skills and experience worked the brakes and the reins with flawless maneuvers, and the chariot descended the hill without a jerk. He was a good driver. But at the back of his mind, between the singing and the driving, his thoughts were focused on the various establishments along the way where he planned to do some harmless gambling.

As scheduled, the horses pulled into a narrow driveway and parked in front of an inn. The driver did the routine of getting the innkeeper and his staff to help the guests while he took the horses toward the stables. Radha wanted to go with him, but the driver warned that thieves might be in the area ready to snatch some of that expensive jewelry. He warned her to go straight to her room with her mother and not to wander about in such a strange environment looking at horses. Mother repeated the driver's warning to the children and reminded them that it was even more unsafe since they were not traveling with a male companion from their family. The only such person was the driver, so they must be very careful not to be robbed by a loitering thug. That was enough to scare the children. After supper, they were escorted to their suite, where they stayed and slept comfortably until the following morning.

They traveled for a few days and visited many sites from markets to schools. They stayed at luxury establishments and ate at some of the finest dining establishments. They even visited the dancing school that Lady had attended. The children ate candy and snacks. But the majority of the time, their mother spent buying expensive clothes and jewelry. It was a wonderful vacation and a time for her to do some bonding with the children. That was an unusual opportunity for all of them, and they took full advantage of and enjoyed such precious moments. They did visit a few schools for girls, and Radha thought that the uniforms made the students look silly. She quietly thought that those girls were imprisoned and needed to get out and do fun things, like riding horses. Hence school visiting became a secondary preference. They were having fun enjoying their leisurely vacation and lost track of the main reason for the trip.

Within a week, they were getting ready to start the return journey. Lady wanted to give the children one final treat. She knew of a park where numerous plants and flowers were grown. She had frequently visited that park when she was a child and decided to treat the children with a short visit there. The driver was informed, and the children were told of the unscheduled stop. It meant a short delay, but they figured that it would be time well spent though they would be a little late arriving at that evening's destination. It seemed like a simple and harmless thing to do.

The driver, as instructed, steered the horses on an exit road and toward the park located a short distance off the main road. Upon arrival, he suggested that it would be unsafe to leave the carriage unattended and volunteered to park under a shade tree and wait while the children played and explored the sights. He suggested that they remove all their jewelry and leave their money and valuables with him for safekeeping. Realizing that the trusted driver was making good sense, they left all their money and jewelry with him and hurried down the pedestrian lane admiring the various flowers and other plants and the multitude of birds that congregated in the vicinity. Numerous butterflies fluttered from flower to flower, competing with the buzzing hummingbirds and bees for droplets of nectar. It seemed like a magical place as the children ran from one attraction to another, pointing in utter amazement. It was the best part of their trip. The children ran and giggled and threw stones in the ponds, creating tiny ripples among the lotus flowers. Radha loved the outdoors, and the botanical garden was a dreamland to her eyes. They wandered far into the park, where they sat on stones admiring the beauty of the environment.

It was an unusually quiet day at the park. There were only a few visitors, and they were leaving as the family treasured the quiet. As they sat there, Lady told the children that she had never seen that paradise without visitors, and they decided to stay longer than planned to admire the joy of nature.

Then it happened! The calm became windy. Some dark clouds appeared suddenly like amoebic quilts that rapidly merged into a dark heavenly canvas, and within a short time, there were the sparks of lightning and the cracking of thunder. The howling of winds increased in intensity. They started running toward the parked chariot. The torrential downpour of rain became blinding. It happened so quickly that the family was caught by surprise. They could not find the driver or the horses and carriage because in the panic, they had walked in the wrong direction. The monsoon-like storm was upon them, and they had difficulty navigating their way in search of their safety. In the midst of the chaos and panic, Radha found a large hollowed-out tree, and the three of them partially huddled in there, trying to avoid the dangers of the storm. Mother, after screaming for her driver, assured the children that the rain would soon cease and the driver would come to their rescue. So they huddled together, cold and scared, shivering and waiting for help in the partially hollowed tree trunk.

Mother Nature did not pity affluence, for it was an equal-opportunity storm. As the hours slowly passed, the storm increased in intensity. The winds howled louder and louder, and the lighting flashed creating an almost continuous rumbling of thunder, which, coupled with the howling wind, produced frightening sounds. Small branches blew off trees and danced around in the swirling wind. They created an almost ghostly appearance in the sparking lightning. It had turned to night, and there was no sight of their driver.

In the darkness, they stayed huddled in their tight quarters as the tempest continued its wrath. Hunger crept in, and they knew that it meant big trouble. The driver did not come to their rescue. The minutes turned to hours, and the night passed slowly. They took turns crying and dozing as time moved on at its normal pace. Time did not favor affluence either. Tearful prayers did not bring relief. There was nothing to do but wait and hope that the storm would pass and they could hurry along to the next hotel, where there would be a warm bath, an abundance of food, and warm blankets awaiting their arrival.

Time maintained its perfect schedule. It was morning, and the storm continued. Mother decided that it was time to go out and find the driver. They crawled out of their wooden hole and stumbled among the broken branches, frantically looking for help. They called and called, but nobody answered except the pattering large raindrops, the howling wind, and the occasional now familiar cracks of loud thunder. Fear turned into panic as they scrambled about the garden like insects engulfed by a Venus flytrap. They stumbled and fell in the mud. Their clothes were getting shredded, they had lost their expensive shoes in the mud, and they were starting to lose their voices. There was nobody around.

Tired, hungry, scared, lost, and confused, they found themselves sitting at the entrance of the park waiting for something or someone. Lady was angry at herself for suggesting such an unscheduled stop. But anger was soon replaced by hope as the storm subsided. The downpour was now a misty drizzle, and the winds had calmed. The parting clouds revealed that the sun was almost overhead, telling the children that it was lunchtime. But there would be no lunch. Barefooted, they stumbled toward the main road. There, they sat together in utter denial, waiting to wake up from their respective horrible nightmares. They were now too tired to cry. It was as if the world had abandoned them as sacrifices to an evil botanical garden. They found themselves flirting with insanity.

Then there was the faint sound of horses' hooves suctioning the waterlogged ground. They assumed it was the driver looking for them. It was a driver, but not their driver. It was a strange man in an old wagon being pulled by a struggling, boney sorrel horse. The animal plodded along through the streams and ripples of the confused waters that were trying to obey the laws of gravity. The family sat there and watched as the old wagon slowly approached, carving shallow ruts in the soft mud and the wet slurry closing the gaps. The wagon pulled up next to them as the man driving the sorrel pulled back on the reins with a hard jerk. He shouted a loud command for the horse to whoa.

The man was not pleasant to look at. He was dressed in wet rags, and on one cheek, he wore a large scar. No mother would dare risk her family with the likes of that, but this mother was out of options. She stood up and pleaded with the man for some assistance. She explained their situation and that the children should have food and water and dry clothes. They needed transportation to the nearest inn.

Scarface gladly obliged. He told them to climb in and said that he knew of just the place for them. She looked at the children and hesitated. Something about the man seemed suspicious. His appearance and manners wrote dishonesty across his forehead. She was about to decline his suggestion when her son started to cry. Such tears encouraged her bravery, and with trembling legs and shaking fingers, they climbed aboard the back of the half-broken old wagon with holes in the floor.

They were barely seated when the man poked a sharp stick into the back of the skinny horse, and they went bumping along the muddy trail that meandered through some woods. The family had no idea where they were or where they were going, but under such circumstances, in their frail condition, they tolerated the bruises and endured the trip. It broke their hearts to see how cruel and inhumane his behavior toward the horse was. He poked and beat the animal constantly as the poor beast struggled to pull the load through the muddy lane. There was no shortage of desperation during that trip. Unfortunately, empathy did not relieve any suffering. Some relief only came when they rolled into higher ground and unto a better road that was not laden with as much mire. It minimized the horse's struggle but not the abuse. Scarface continued his cussing and beating, and the animal continued with submissive behavior.

It was toward midafternoon when Scarface drove his wagon through some gates. The attendant who opened the gates informed him where to go. It seemed different from any of the inns they were familiar with. It was a dismal-looking place, almost abandoned, except for the security guard who paced about the grounds. He wore some dirty police uniform and carried a gun. As the wagon approached the old, dark building, the security followed. The squeaking sounds announced that the gates were being closed behind them. The wagon rolled toward a large door, and the armed security guard told the passengers to disembark. He escorted them through the door and into a waiting area.

A woman arrived at the scene. She only spoke to the security man. They whispered together for a short while, and the armed man departed through the door. It was quite obvious that it was no hotel. There was no exotic carpeting on the floor. The walls were not painted, and cobwebs plastered parts of the ceiling. Occasionally, a rodent scampered by, trying to avoid the foraging cockroaches.

Apart from the unusual sights, it was a warm and dry place. The woman offered them each a bowl of warm soup and told them to drink it slowly. Then she poured water for them from an old clay pot. They had no cups. The water was poured into their hands, and they slurped it down. She then brought out some oversized robes and buckets of cold water. She drew a cotton sheet along a curtain rod hanging close to the ceiling. It created a little private corner. She ordered them to use the water and bathe behind the cotton sheet. They obeyed and draped themselves with the large robes provided. Then she took them down a narrow hallway, through a door, and into a small room. Upon her departure, she ensured that the door was securely locked from the outside; the family heard her footsteps as she walked away. The wooden floor creaked with her every step.

The room had one small window with iron bars similar to jail cells. On the floor was a large cot on which was stacked blankets and pillows. It smelled of mice. An occasional cockroach scurried along the floor. In the corner was an old white chamber pot with a single red handle that was supposed to be their toilet. They checked the door. It was locked.

Through the window, they saw the armed security man pacing about the yard, waiting for something to happen. That was confirmation that they were imprisoned.

The door suddenly opened. It was the woman who met them when they arrived. She had a basket of food and told them to eat. They did not question. They were now warm and extremely hungry so they devoured the food and washed it down with the water from the familiar clay pot. The woman waited as they ravished every morsel and drank every drop of water. She did not speak much. She gathered her food basket together and ensured that the door was again securely closed and locked. They could again hear her footsteps creaking down the narrow wooden hallway.

With warm bodies and full stomachs, they started questioning their future. They also needed to perform bathroom duties but had no privacy. So they sat there huddled under the blankets and tried to be brave about the whole situation. They avoided looking at one another. The mother felt sorry for the children, and the children pitied their mother. They had never seen her bruised and battered before. They were no longer in their luxury environment. They were prisoners without a crime, totally confused, waiting for someone of authority to come and straighten out the whole misunderstanding that had placed them in such an uncompromising situation.

The shadows in the little window told them that it would be dark soon. There was no sign of the guard outside. Radha decided to fight with the door. It was hopeless. The door was tightly secured and locked from the outside. She pounded, yelled, and screamed, but such actions only added tears to her frustration and caused the others to cry along.

As the panic ended, they found themselves again huddled under the pile of blankets. It had turned to night. They had no light. The cockroaches continued their foraging. But the darkness solved one problem. It created privacy, and they used the opportunity to relieve themselves into the single red-handled chamber pot. Even the darkness had its purpose, and humiliation was dwarfed by desperation. They stayed under the warm blankets, praying, and wondered if even God had abandoned them. They continued repeating mantras, one after another, until slumber graced their eyelids and evoked their subconscious. They slept and dreamed of whatever, as time maintained its perfect schedule. Each passing hour greeted them deep in sleep until light reappeared through the little window. Reality had once again made its presence.

They heard footsteps up and down the creaking hallway. There were occasional screams probably from other imprisoned people. But their door stayed locked. Radha looked out the barred little window and saw the security pacing about the yard in the same manner as he had done the previous day. He still wore the dirty police uniform. She also saw two wagons with horses hitched to them. Once she saw the security man walk toward the building and march a small group of people into the wagons, which pulled out through the gates.

They heard reality unlocking their door. Like captive animals, they stared at the opening door with petrified looks. The suspense was overwhelming. Swarms of butterflies invaded their stomachs, and their bodies shook with intimidation. They were scared. The element of surprise was upon them as the door creaked wide open. It was Scarface. He was the hybrid between hope and uncertainty. His gesture suggested that they follow him. He did not speak.

Radha's mother decided to plead their case. She explained to the man that they must go to a better place. She tried to explain her social status and offered to bribe the man. She might have succeeded except that she had nothing of value available to negotiate such a deal. She asked him to take them to their home, where he would be highly compensated. She rambled on in desperation about her family's wealth and social standard. Through her drooling mouth, sniffling nose, and tearing eyes, she crawled toward the man. She held on to his leg and begged and pleaded for his compassion.

Scarface finally spoke. He accused her of being the biggest liar he had ever met. He explained that wealthy people do not travel alone. He described wealthy people wearing expensive jewelry wherever they went. A desperate woman wearing rags and no shoes claiming to be the daughter of a landlord was the most ridiculous story he had ever heard. He described her as a beggar with two hungry children trying desperately to escape. He growled that they were fed and clothed by the establishment and must honor the rules of that establishment. They needed to follow him at his command. He concluded by saying that there would be no negotiations.

He turned around toward the door and again gestured to them that he expected to be followed. Lady held on to his leg. As he started to walk, he dragged her along with her desperation. The children followed. Into the creaking hallway, they walked as the woman continued to be dragged. The man demanded that she should stand up and walk. She refused. Then with all his might he kicked out, and the woman was slammed into the wall. He was angry. She hunched over, cradling her midsection. That infuriated Radha. She had never seen her mother abused in such a manner. She walked over and told Scarface to back off. She picked up her mother and tried to comfort her. It became reality that they must obey or pay the consequences. She motioned to the man to walk on. He did with a growl, and they followed with Lady still partially hunched over and wincing.

They found themselves in the familiar room where the curtain rod hung from the ceiling. There were buckets of water and food available. They were told to eat and bathe. Scarface suggested that they hurry for they had a long journey and they must utilize as much daylight as possible. He slammed the door shut and left the family to perform their duties as ordered. They realized that under the circumstances, reality would be unkind. Obedience was the short-term solution. They could not fight the devil's case in hell and expect to be victorious. Reality was probably telling them that there was little difference between poverty and hell. It was an environment they were experiencing for the first time, and they found no comfort there. But survival instincts must have awakened within them, and they chose to embrace obedience. They bathed and ate and waited for the next round to start. They had all stopped their crying but still avoided looking at one another's faces.

As promised, Scarface honored punctuality. His now familiar gesture meant that they must follow him. They obeyed. Outside, the guard held his gun and stood to attention. They were led to the same spot where they had disembarked the previous day. The only difference was that Scarface had a newer wagon and a well-fed horse. They understood what he wanted. They climbed into the wagon and sat on the wooden seat. Scarface climbed into the driver's seat. He put his supply bags and his gun next to him and took hold of the reins. Then, with a flick of his wrists, the reins swatted the horse, and with a growl, off they went. Out through the gate, they went, and they continued onto the main road to a destination unknown.

It was a bright and sunny day. The tempest that had betrayed them had now abandoned them. The only evidence that such a violent storm had recently swept by was the swift little streams and broken tree branches that littered the landscape. Occasionally, the horse was abusively encouraged as it struggled to pull the load through the low-lying areas where stagnant waters congregated at the direction of gravity. On numerous occasions, they all disembarked while Scarface led the horse across deeper waters. Of course, they all got wet and dirty again as a result of walking through ponds and puddles. Reality was their constant companion, and obedience prevented further abuse. They continued the perilous journey to a destination unknown.

CHAPTER 4

Riches to Rags

The perilous journey continued, but the roads were improving as the miserable miles were left behind. The scared and confused family consisted of Lady, Radha, and her brother, Kesha, short for Mukesh. They were being taken by force to another unknown destination by a man whom they obviously could not trust. Scarface became rather kind to them during the interim part of the journey. He gave them food and blankets and tried to keep them comfortable as they could be in the bumping wagon that plodded along a somewhat muddy dirt road. The lack of wheel tracks in the wet soil made it clear that the road was not well traveled.

Occasionally, the wagon had to cross shallow waterways. Although such streams were rather shallow, the muddy banks were relatively steep and slippery. The outward reaching grasses that lined the banks were laced with mud and debris deposited by the continuously receding water. The slimy mass was pointing in the direction of the water current, which was slowly receding and creating amoeboid-shaped eddies with unguided and uncoordinated dances along the flowing waters. During such crossings, Scarface would lead the horse by a short rope tied to a slightly rusted metal bit. The willing animal would scramble and groan agonizingly to pull the cart up the slippery inclines but understood that not performing such duty would result in severe punishment. So, the animal pulled with all its might, knowing that there would be other waters to cross. The passengers had to wade across the rippling streams that dissected the road. On numerous occasions, they would slip and fall only to be helped up by the standing ones. When they all fell, well, they got wet and dirty together. It did no good to complain, for they had come to the realization that their situation was in the hands of another and that they were not going to a luxury hotel but to another destination unknown. At that point, unknown was better for them than imagining the unthinkable.

The one good thing about getting drenched was that they did not have to excuse themselves for bathroom breaks. Wet was wet, regardless of the source of moisture. They must have realized that such embracement was a social thing. During survival mode, their natural duties were parts of natural functions. Peeing on their clothes was of no serious consequences during those difficult times. Fear and exhaustion minimized their individual embarrassing trauma.

It was time for someone to take charge, and Radha's tomboyish status emerged. She recognized the suffering of her frail mother and her pampered brother and instinctively knew that she had to be strong for them. It was major responsibility for an almost ten-year-old girl. Under such extreme conditions, she had to be brave. Her relatively strong body, groomed by years of climbing trees, jumping over fences, and chasing after colts and fillies in the pastures, had developed muscles strong enough to cope somewhat better with the current physical exertion. She could at least help her younger brother, groomed for business and politics, to cross the muddy streams and climb the slippery embankments without repeated falling. On occasion, she helped her mother, whose affluent upbringing meant she could have never imagined such a disaster. Radha started to think about an escape plan. Getting caught could result in severe punishment, but the mental and physical punishments they had been encountering and tolerating for the past twenty-four hours were also quite severe.

She quietly whispered the idea to Lady, who whispered back that she was also thinking about trying something, but what? She told Lady that when the driver suggested the next stop to water the horse, they would pretend to go into the bushes for bowel relief duties. During that time, she would gather up a rock and hide it under her dress. When they resumed their travel, she would wait for the right moment and hit the man on his head, and while he was out, they would steal the wagon and gallop away. They shared the optimism with Kesha and sat quietly, awaiting their moment for the ambush.

It was the middle of the afternoon. The blazing sun showed no mercy. Occasional scavenging birds sailed high above on rising air currents, looking down for food. Even the wild creatures were napping under trees to avoid the sun's rays.

Then Radha said, "Sir, we need to go into the woods. Do you have to attend to the horse?"

"Okay," said the driver and pulled the horse to a stop.

They hurried out, and the driver proceeded to give the horse a drink. Radha gathered her fist-sized rock, and as she approached the wagon, she started to limp, using the palmed rock to massage her upper leg under her dress. After they had resumed their seats, he swatted the horse with the reins, and off they went with Scarface humming an unfamiliar tune. But due to his raspy voice, it was more of an annoying grunt than humming.

At Lady's signal, Radha quietly crept forward, and with trembling hands that squeezed the rock, she hit Scarface in the back of his head. Lucky for him, she hit too low. He was stunned and stumbled off the wagon. He bounced off the wheel and unto the ground. Radha, wasting no time, scrambled forward and grabbed the reins. She was trying to get the horse into a gallop, but only succeeded in getting the animal into a trot. The stunned, disoriented driver got up and, with wobbling legs, started to chase after them. He looked more like a drunk than a hurt man, but he was gaining ground with every desperate leap. The horse maintained a steady pace of trotting along. There was screaming and panicking, but the horse refused to gallop. Scarface caught up to the moving wagon and with a wild and desperate swat, grabbed Kesha's foot and dragged him off the back of the wagon. The horse was then pulled to a sudden stop.

With a bump on the back of his head, he gathered some rope from his sack and tied the boy on the front seat next to where he sat. Then from his sack, he pulled out a handgun and fired it. Looking back at them, he warned that the next time they attempted something stupid, they would be shot one at a time, starting with the boy. Then he pointed the gun at Kesha's head, standing over him as the extreme heat coupled with his rage caused him to sweat profusely. After a few minutes, he slowly sat next to the boy, put the gun away, and drank several gulps of warm water from a bottle.

Then he told them that he couldn't blame them for trying to escape and that he did not hold any grudges. He further explained that he would just shoot people who were uncooperative but agreed to give them a second chance if they promised to behave. They all agreed to behave and went along their journey as if nothing had happened.

As they continued wading occasionally across small streams, Scarface, with gun in hand, encouraged them to hurry because, according to him, it was better to travel during the daylight hours. He gave them more food and extra blankets to sit on. The bread was stale, and the blankets stank, but those necessities were filling, and the cushions softened the ride. Radha asked the driver why he provided those items. Scarface took a deep breath, massaged the bump on his upper neck, and explained that he had an investment in her family. Keeping them healthy and alive was more profitable than the alternatives. She could not understand such logic and chose to ignore his answer. Her greater concern was the western horizon. Twilight was creeping upward as the clouds displayed a fiery appearance, as if hell itself was on its way upward to greet them. Bats began their evening rituals, and soon it was getting darker and darker. They could hear the faint hooting of owls some distance away. Birds fluttered about in search of roosting spots as the skies became filled with countless bats darting about with organized sonar precision and consuming copious amounts of flying insects along their aerial paths.

Slowly, the wagon turned off the main drag, and the bouncing wheels disturbed the daydreaming passengers and the scurrying rodents along the way. The hellish horizon had vanished only to be replaced with darkness and an occasional twinkle from some nearby galaxy. The night insects made their buzzing presence. The owls' hooting drew nearer and nearer. It was their scary welcome to the approaching intruders on wheels. The family could barely see the outline of the scattered trees, and they felt the stings of creatures that were unknown to them.

The wagon came to a halt. Scarface untied the boy. He told them to stay on board. They did and wrapped themselves in the smelly dry blankets to keep away the slightly descending chill on their damp clothes, but mainly to minimize the stings from buzzing insects. There was a light. It was coming from the fire that the driver had started. It lit up a small cave that, in the darkness, seemed like an indentation on a side hill. It was more of a dugout than a cave. They heard the clanging of metal pots. After a while, they were invited to share the fire and to watch as Scarface placed an old kettle on a piece of wire hanging over the heat. He went to the nearby ditch and brought back water in the pail that the horse drank from. He poured some of the ditch water into the pot. It was getting colder. The warm fire and the light brought some calm and comfort to their weary souls as they watched the man add a few morsels of whatever into the boiling water. They had watery soup and stale bread, which at that moment might have rivaled the taste of the food prepared by the gourmet chef in a luxury restaurant. They had plenty to eat and then huddled together in their smelly blankets, listening to the driver gruntingly hum a now familiar tune as he leaned against the dirt wall by the entrance. He was twirling his gun with one finger. The flames eventually became a mere flicker, and the smoke that engulfed their space irritated their eyes. The multitude of stars made their appearances in the perpetual darkness. The new moon cradled the remnants of the faint old moon as the owls continued their hooting. The family coughed occasionally, said their respective silent prayers, and one by one, drifted into slumber.

It was a horrible night—a captured family trying to sleep in a hole by the roadside where their captor became their protector. His snoring was their constant reminder that all was not well. They prayed for a miracle. But as scheduled, morning came hand in hand with reality. The nightmare did not go away with the hooting. The sun replaced the stars, and twittering birds emerged from their roosts, flying from tree to tree in complete freedom. Soon, the morning sun evaporated the droplets of dew as Scarface served them bitter tea in crude-looking tin cups. He made the tea from the same water he had secured from the ditch. They had no sugar. But the warm tea and stale crackers filled the voids in their stomachs. As he tied up Kesha, the women were ordered to get their bathroom duties done. Then he took the boy with him to the woods, and they did their bathroom duties. Then he ordered them to get into the wagon as the willing horse awaited the signal to march forward. It was finishing the few blades of grass that it was served for breakfast. Radha petted its nose and massaged its body as the others climbed into the now familiar wagon. Scarface, twirling his gun, ordered her to use his pails and offer the animal some water. She carried the water. The animal drank it all. Scarface, with a big lump on the back of his head, smiled at her obedience.

*   *   *

There are very few further details about that journey. Many of the stories told have been buried with listeners of the past. The vague remnants that had been told and retold have survived the generations. The fact is that those affluent people were captured and hauled around in a bumpy horse cart driven by a man with a scar on his face. It could not have been a pleasant journey. Their circumstances were pitiful. But nothing can change what happened. Further facts about the journey are limited.

*   *   *

Finally, Scarface drove them to an isolated bank of a river, most likely the Ganges or one of its tributaries. They camped there in isolation until a boat arrived. There he collected his fees and turned the family over to the boatmen. Then he drove away.

They arrived at Port Unknown, to a place like Garden Reach around Calcutta. More than likely, they were in the Kidderpur area along the Hooghly River. Here, they were escorted into a large compound with some two hundred people, mostly men. Some of the few women who roamed about behind the closed gates did not appear ladylike. Other women sat reclusively in isolated groups and appeared distressed. There were constant arguments among the men and occasional pushing and shoving were not uncommon. There were few children. There was no apparent system. But there were police walking about with wooden clubs ready to discipline those who displayed unacceptable behavior, especially to the women. There were buildings that looked like prisons. Those were the prison depots that held the waiting passengers in confinement until it was time for departure to final destinations, beyond Kala Panni and into foreign lands to sift sugar, so they were told.

Every day, the gates opened, and new people arrived with wondering eyes and blank facial expressions. On occasion, a small group of women would arrive, but some of their behaviors were peculiar as judged by Radha's family. There was enough quality food to eat, and the "authorities" encouraged the occupants to eat as much as they wanted. They were told that the journey was going to be a long one and that they would need their strength to survive such a trip. Radha almost chuckled at that for she figured that they had already survived a series of horrible journeys. But her chuckles were nonexistent. *How much worse could it get?* she wondered silently. And another group came through the gates.

As the days passed, the family began to communicate with some of the people, especially the groups of abject women. They had to seek out those with dialects that were familiar to them. It was there that they understood where they were going. Many of the people there had volunteered to go to Demra to work on the plantations sifting sugar, as they were told. They had signed up with the arkathies for the five-year term for various reasons. Those folks were escaping India because of poverty, crime, marriage problems, caste concerns, prostitution, political issues, and a host of other desperate reasons. The family learned from some of the women that they were paid extra because the ship could not sail until some 30 or 40 percent of the passengers were female. It was the law, and the quota varied from time to time.

The police staff stayed on the compound for the duration of the detention period. They had their private quarters and worked on shifts. Those men were recruited and well paid. They were very loyal to the process. There were armed guards around the outer perimeters. They were ordered to shoot any suspicious person who tried to violate the unwritten rules. The resident police were no exceptions to severe discipline. So, when Lady tried to bribe some of them with promised money, they did not entertain the idea. She was emphatically told to shut up and behave. Those men had heard unimaginable tales from people trying to escape. Even if they believed the stories, the risk was too great. They chose to stay confined for the period and accept the lucrative wages. None would risk violating the system's rules.

There were some good people in the detention group. Many were husbands and wives seeking their fortune elsewhere. As the family became acquainted and visited with some of those family types, they were told bits and pieces of the indentured process and why some of them had chosen to leave their homeland. One couple told them that everyone must pass a physical exam in order to make their journey. The old, feeble, sick, and those with other undesirable characteristics were rejected. Demra only wanted younger, strong, and hardworking folks and women for obvious reasons. In addition to the medical exam, performed by the ship's doctor, they were told that they would be questioned by the immigration man.

Meeting with medical personnel for physical examination was the best news Lady had heard for several days. She told the children that they would explain to the doctor about the mistake and get a message sent to their family, who would promptly get there in record time to rescue them. Such comforting thoughts must have brought relief and hope, and they continued about the premises getting to know the various unfortunate souls who had to flee India for whatever reason. From time to time, they encountered other females who told stories about being kidnapped from their village wells and other places where women visited with some frequency. An arkathy was always on the lookout for a young woman to kidnap because the authorities must ensure that the quota of females was met. Not meeting the quota meant that the ship could not leave the harbor. Some of the women were prostitutes looking for money and possibly a fresh start elsewhere. Those women were welcome subjects, especially prior to departure. Some single men teamed up with them, and they pretended to be husband and wife to each other. Such a union simplified the immigration process and brought companionship and security, which minimized attacks on the women by lonely, desperate men looking for sex. Such situations generally resulted in rape. Because of such horrible stories, many of the single women adopted and bonded with single men as husbands in relationships that lasted throughout the journey and beyond.

The day finally came for the family to meet with the doctor. Lady told the other few kidnapped women that they must insist on being released and that when her family's money arrived, she would ensure that their releases were guaranteed. They boldly marched to the doctor's office and started the protest. The doctor smiled and told them to sit and wait their turn for the examination. Lady protested, and security was called in. They quietly sat and waited. The mother was called into the doctor's office. He ordered her to remove some clothing for the medical exam. Unaccustomed to such an order, she was reluctant to shed her clothes, which caused the doctor to become irate. She removed her clothes. As the doctor inspected, she continued her protest. The doctor finally listened and told her that he had no authority to send messengers to some remote area. Her sobs, tears, bribes, and screams were more than the doctor could handle. He told her that the only way they could be spared the journey was a protest prior to departure. He explained that before boarding the ship, there would be some questions. One of the questions was if the people were leaving of their own free will. If the answer was "no," the subject may be released. Now she knew what to do. She quickly dressed and sent Radha in to see the doctor.

After the examinations, they hurried back to tell the other kidnapped women what they needed to do to ensure their release. What they did not know was that during that period of time, prior to 1864, the immigration man would be asking the questions of the whole group, not individuals.

By the time of departure, there were some three hundred passengers. The ship's quota had been reached. They were given clothes and a certificate, and tin tags were placed over their heads and hung from their necks. The tag had an identification number. It was a fine day as the group was marched toward the ship. It was there that the questions were to be asked. As soon as the crowd gathered, a group of arkathies gathered and pushed the kidnapped ones toward the back, segregating them. It did not help to protest in such mass confusion, where police with wooden clubs were yelling and rowdies were jostling about. The family never heard the question. When they quietly asked that particular question about leaving of their own free will, all the planted personnel in the crowd yelled, "Yes!" at the top of their lungs. They knew their jobs well, and an innocent mother and a few sorry souls had no idea what had just happened. They were escorted to the dock and, to a certain degree, forced into the ship. Some tried to escape, but the authorities performed their duties well by flogging the uncooperative ones and putting them back in line. They were on their way to British Guiana. There were screams and sobs as two women jumped overboard, desperately trying to escape. It was their choice, and Radha watched as they perished from exhaustion.

In her panic, Lady searched for her "friends." At least the kidnapped ones could stick together. They did. The small group found a corner and huddled together in the lower level, each complaining about her misfortune and the uncertainty of her future. Many of them instantly became seasick. They had no idea how long of a journey it would be.

They recognized that they were sent below and that the hatches were closed. There were initially segregated into four groups. One group consisted of married couples, one group for families, one group for single women, and one group for single men.

Those earlier sailing ships, unlike the *Lena*, took longer for the journey compared to the diesel-powered steamships. It was a long and trying journey as the sails were hoisted. It was the strength of a few desperate women whose determination and prayers helped to minimize the monotony and comforted the occasional illness. They told about the families that they had left behind and how they wanted to send messages to them. Those messages never got sent. It was distressingly painful when someone died on the ship. Some of the passengers did die, adding to the grief and mourning. But the bobbing vessel continued its slow journey westward toward the colony as an occasional corpse, wrapped in cotton, was dumped into the salty ocean water. One of the indentured men kept notes on the daily activities. He tabulated and documented the deceased.

It was especially dangerous for the women. They were potential victims of sexual abuse from various sources, especially from the ship's personnel. A few committed suicides by jumping overboard to drown their shame with their struggling bodies as death consumed them. Such incidences were acceptable practices for the perpetrators, who repeatedly committed such acts time and time again and justified their actions with excuses about being at sea for extended periods of time. Other atrocities and shameful acts occasionally occurred as the ship continued its rocking motion, and seasickness was minimized. Ships weathered storms and crashing waves during rough seas. But they continued month by month in a westward direction, around the Cape of Good Hope and toward South America.

Radha's family eventually arrived in British Guyana and disembarked at the port of Demerara. After the usual immigration rituals, they said tearful goodbyes to their shipmate friends, and like marked cattle, they departed with tin tags dangling from their necks. They were assigned to the Ruimveldt Estate, where they were contractually bound as indentured servants.

CHAPTER 5

The Brahmin

There was a Brahmin family in northern India in the area some distance between Kanpur and Lucknow. The year was about 1850. According to the Hindu caste system, the Brahmins were the elites. They were the educated pundits, and many of those families, for centuries, had enjoyed life on the upper tiers of the Indian social structure. That family lived very well, and one generation after another, they tried to elevate their social status with wealth, education, and other convenient and opportunistic means.

Although they did not like the recent imperial occupation of India, some of them were smart enough to tolerate that political process. After all, their ancestors had seen dynasties come and go. History had taught them that, other than internal conflicts, their land had survived invasions, occupations, and dynasties from other civilizations for thousands of years. The occupation by the British, in their opinion, was just one more intrusion that would soon end, and the intruders would be evicted after the demise of the British East India Company, which was established in 1600. Then once again, they, the Brahmins, would gain control of their homeland. They further saw the current occupation as a system that would help drive the Muslims out, so they were told by some, allowing Hinduism to once again continue as the dominant religion.

However, during that period, many Indians, including a few Brahmins, did not share such a vision of the perceived British benefits to India. Such opinions and beliefs led to a series of disagreements and conflicts on both establishments with the losses sustained on both sides.

One of the sons from the family being discussed was fourteen years old. Because of his family's standing and his good academic achievements at local schools, he was sent to a prestigious ashram to continue his education. The boy was uniquely talented, and his father continually bragged about the genius that he had sired. Not only was he talented in academics, but he was also a good athlete with excellent speed and good balance. He proved to be a great student of the martial arts and a top student in mathematics, science, and astronomy. His father had every right to brag. He was a wonder boy. His name was Vishnu.

Vishnu grew up and became increasingly suspicious of the British motives in India. The British East India Company was gaining further control of his country. He recognized that the system gave too much authority and power to those intruders, and that the British East India Company was usurping power at an alarming rate. He started complaining that the intruders had armies with sophisticated guns and that they controlled the surrounding waters with their ships. He recognized that that system was squeezing the Indian economy and shipping the profits and precious stones away from India. He could see that those intruders were robbing his motherland and collecting high fees and outrageous taxes from the working people to boot.

When he returned from the ashram, he began to investigate the activities of that organization. He speculated that they controlled the opioid production and sold the drugs to the Chinese. In return, the British could afford to buy the Chinese silk. Unfortunately, many Indians became addicted to the opioids and suffered to support their habit, so they worked on the production farms, which subsidized their addictions. High taxes were levied on the small farmers. If those farmers died without paying the taxes owed, their lands were confiscated. The zamindars were the tax collectors, and they helped to promote the ruthless system because they were part of it. Vishnu's tenacity increasingly discovered the various surreptitious avenues that the British company used to exploit India and the people.

He further discovered that the army consisted of numerous Indian soldiers, called sepoys, who were confined to lower ranks. The British military, with ongoing nepotistic practices, conveniently promoted their kind to the higher ranks, ignoring very qualified Indians because they did not see the Indians as their equal. The more he investigated, the more corruption he found, and it always seemed to put Indians at a disadvantage. He knew several British subjects, both civilians and soldiers. His parents periodically had some of them at their home for social occasions. When he complained to his father about the unjust system, he was told that they were doing fine, and his family felt secure having such people of authority as acquaintances and to a certain degree as friends. He was not enthused by his father's response, but he agreed that their standard of living was relatively high, and he enjoyed his family status. He appreciated the beautiful mansion with plenty of marble and silk. They had a state-of-the-art transportation system, and they enjoyed a variety of good food on a daily basis.

Although that wonder boy got married as a teenager and was expected to live the life of a true Brahmin, he started having secret meetings with others who shared his views. His father eventually found out and was very disappointed at such behavior. He emphatically tried to discourage such rebellious way of thinking. He knew that the British would show no mercy on the young man when they found out that he disagreed with their various practices. But the warnings and entreaties from his father did not stop Vishnu. He became more and more aggressive in denouncing the British occupation and quietly started recruiting other young men to join the cause. They became a small group and had periodic meeting to vent their anger at the establishment. But in time, that group disbanded, and Vishnu met and joined a larger group of rebels whose mission was to evict the intruders before they could destroy the Indian structure that had existed for thousands of years.

The situation became worse prior to the 1857 Sepoy Revolution. He was young, angry, and determined to do something about it. There were many others who shared his views, and within a short time, they banded together and became the outlaws and rebels that terrorized the colonial people. Vishnu did not participate in the attacks. He kept a low profile and operated by messages on a regular basis.

What really infuriated him was the introduction of the Enfield rifles. The paper cartridges that held the ammunition used with those rifles were laced with a combination of cow and pig fat. That coating kept the paper dry, but prior to use, the soldiers had to bite off one end of the cartridge to release the contents. That was a major concern to the Hindu and Muslim soldiers. The Hindus did not eat beef for religious reasons, and the Muslims did not eat pork because they considered it unclean. The soldiers were severely punished for refusing to properly open the cartridges. One punishment was discharge from the military and being put into hard labor camps for several years. In addition, they were demoted to a lower caste.

Vishnu heard the story about a Brahmin soldier named Mangal Panday. That soldier refused the British command to use the rifle and the cartridges containing the ammunition. The commanding officer was infuriated, and they got into a physical fight. Panday was subsequently arrested and hanged along with one of his supporters. That started a whole new movement, as many soldiers refused to use that weapon.

Vishnu had been using his skills and social status to be somewhat of a double agent. He became a gambler and studied the rules of the gambling games that the British played. He managed to convince the local English personnel in the area to allow him to join in their regular games. He had the money, and the players understood his worth, so it was not a difficult task to convince them to have him participate. Initially, they easily took his money. He had to learn the details. His wife was annoyed because he came to bed smelling of alcohol. The more he lost, the more he drank. But after some weeks of losing, he figured out the rules and slowly started to win. But the drinking continued.

Not only did he win during those occasional gambling series, but he also overheard conversations about the opponent's plans and strategies. His winnings infuriated some of the British players, and they continued to increase the stakes. The young Brahmin knew exactly when to lose and waited his moment to pounce on the large purses. The games continued because the British "masters" could not accept the fact that an Indian boy could beat them at their own games. He won a lot of money. He used the money to help finance the rebels, and he relayed the news he overheard to his group leaders. To him, this was the best of all worlds. He was able to have the enemy finance attacks on themselves. To him, he was supporting a noble cause. But after Panday was executed, it became very personal to him. Hanging a Brahmin for refusing to put cow fat into his mouth was disgusting, and that infuriated him.

The gambler was very careful and ensured that he was never seen associating with the rebel group members. His job was to help finance the operations. During the daylight hours, he could be seen with his beautiful young wife at public places like the markets and eating establishments. They were an enviable couple, and they walked about with such refined dignity. But at night, he drank and gambled with the Englishmen. Messengers continued to convey money and secrets to the gang at a remote hiding place. He did not know the location of such hideouts, nor did he know the leaders. In time, his clan had joined with other small groups and became a force that concerned the British. Vishnu stayed away from all personal associations with them. The only headquarter contact he maintained was a man called Nana. Quite possibly, he was associated with Nana Sahib's group.

His lifestyle not only angered his father, but it also cost the British personnel a lot of money. His wife detested his evening absences and his habitual night drunkenness. She protested, and he and his father quarreled, but he continued his rebel ways for several months. During his association with the gamblers, he studied their behavior and speech patterns, and he rehearsed his English grammar and pronunciation. His goal was to master the English language, and as time went by, he succeeded in doing just that. He started dressing like the British. He wore a suit and tie, polished his shoes, and carried an umbrella. His skin complexion was unusually light for an Indian, and the umbrella was the key to avoiding any tanning from the sun's rays. To an ignorant observer, he could be mistaken for at least a half-white Englishman. People who did not know him perhaps assumed that he was part Indian and part white. Such children were not unusual during that period, especially with the lonely Englishmen partnering with East Indian women. To avoid his father's wrath and his wife's complaining, he started traveling about.

Vishnu visited places like Residency Park in Lucknow and key places in Kanpur. To avoid suspicion, he moved from place to place and conveniently found himself in places where the British congregated. Because of his speech and charisma, he found himself in the company of some Englishmen. He partied and gambled with them. He drank plenty, but during the gambling sessions, his drinking was limited. He was very careful to study the players' body language and kept a close watch for potential cheaters. Because of his large purse, he allowed the others to win, and some nights, he lost large sums of money. But he was patient. He waited for the right moments when the stakes were unusually high, and then he put his strategies into gear and collected large sums of English money. Most of the time, he operated from his home area, and on schedule, the familiar messenger met him at a previously arranged location and did the money and information transfer. Most of that money went to support his cause and to buy ammunition. There was no accounting, and Nana did not question anything. He graciously accepted donations from people like Vishnu and stole and ambushed supplies from the British when the opportunity presented itself. He was ruthless and despised the colonial occupation of his country.

Vishnu was enjoying the lucrative process. He became good at the games by using his mathematical skills to calculate the odds. He ate well and drank English ale. He continued to have no direct contact with the rebels except for the occasional messenger. Any news he heard about the British operations, he relayed to Nana, who directed any necessary action to counter the British. More and more, the rebel group grew, and they terrorized the English settlements with speedy attacks to steal their supplies and ammunition and quickly retreated.

However, after Panday's execution, things got very ugly. That led to the 1857 Sepoy Revolution. The rebels went on the attack and started a widespread massacre in several cities, including Lucknow and Kanpur. They turned into an angry mob and, in many locations, brutally killed several British subjects. Men, women, and children were slaughtered. The British retaliated, and lives were lost on both sides. Nana Sahib once offered to help the desperate English families by escorting them into a boat. Then he had the boats burned and watched as the flames consumed the helpless. Only a few survived by jumping overboard and swimming to shore. Many could not make it to shore, and the river consumed them. Many years of perceived imperial suppression was awakened, resulting in horror.

Eventually, the angry Queen Victoria sent some thirty thousand troops. They joined the Indian soldiers who were loyal to the British, and together, they managed to defeat the Indian rebels. Their leaders were captured, escaped, or went into hiding.

After several months, Vishnu's headquarters personnel, who were still in hiding, sent him a secret message. The authorities were getting suspicious of his alleged association with the rebel groups. It appeared that the secret messenger blew his cover and told the authorities that he was involved with the rebels. He was being monitored to verify the accuracy of such an accusation. The warning from the rebel group was to quit all activities associated with them and to keep a low profile. He was told not to have any contact with them during that interim period. He was told what to do in the event he felt that his life was in danger.

He obeyed the order, but because of boredom and habit, he continued the drinking and gambling. The only difference was that now he kept his winnings. Nothing changed at home. The verbal abuse at the home front intensified. His father knew that he was under surveillance and lectured him about the consequences of his actions. His wife ignored him. She spent most of her time locked up in their bedroom in a state of depression. They seldom took leisurely strolls, especially to the markets. She used to enjoy those outings with him. His mother was very concerned and did what she did best; she fed him and ensured that the servants took care of his laundry.

As the weeks passed, he realized that he was in big trouble. The authorities had proof that he was affiliated with the rebels. His arrest was guaranteed. Any such criminals were beheaded or banished. Minor offenders were banished to remote places like the Andaman Islands. Major offenders were executed. If the subject was Muslim, he was forced to eat pork prior to decapitation. In the case of the Hindus, beef was the choice of meat prior to execution. Muslim and Hindu heads alike were hung on trees and used as visual examples to deter any potential recruits who were sympathetic to the rebels' cause. Vishnu had seen heads of his clansmen hanging from trees. He could not wait for the soldiers to come and arrest him. It was time for his exit from that neighborhood.

It was a difficult decision. He had lived in luxury in his father's house. He had a beautiful wife specially selected for someone of his stature. He enjoyed dressing up and partying with his gambling associates. He especially enjoyed winning the Englishmen's money at the gambling tables. He had to give up all those luxuries, for what? He stayed up most of the night as his depressed wife slept next to him. There were many questions but few answers. His only choice was a quick escape or risking the death penalty. So, he used the secret messaging system to notify the rebel headquarters personnel about his exit plan.

The next morning, pretending to act normal, he had his mother make his favorite breakfast. He spent the morning with his depressed wife, who did not speak to him. He tried conversing with his father, but that soon escalated into an argument. That evening, he went gambling. It was a good night for him. He won a lot and sang his drunken way home to the disgust of the neighbors and the embarrassment of his family. He was now regarded as the neighborhood drunk. His angry father greeted him at the door with the usual bitterness. It was suggested that he should leave the house and stop embarrassing the family. He ignored the abuse and walked into his bedroom where his angry and depressed wife slept. He stood there for some time until he heard his father stomping his way to bed. Then he took some of his money and laid it on the furniture next to his wife's head. He reached over, wiped the tikka from her forehead, and quietly walked out. He gathered up all the money that he had hidden. It was well past midnight as he walked down the stairs, squeezing the tears from his eyes. His pockets were full of money, his head was full of grief, and his eyes were full of tears, but his heart was empty. His wandering legs kept staggering along in the darkness, one step with whiskey and the other with uncertainty. He slept by the roadside long enough to rest and continued his walking until morning.

He bought food from vendors by the roadside. He rested and ate on a bench at some roadside park. There, he watched the children playing and their parents keeping them entertained. In the midst of all those laughing children, he felt very lonely. He hired rickshaws to pedal him toward the far side of town. It was evening when he arrived close to a secret camp where suspects like him were told to hide during times of trouble. He knew the process. It was all preplanned. It was customary for rebels like him to hide in the woods close by a river and wait there until someone from the organization found them. He had some food and water that he rationed himself during the lonely waiting process. He found a comfortable tree to lean against. There, he folded his legs in yoga form and meditated, trying to visualize his future.

The days were long, and the nights were dark, but his discipline kept him focused. He had an occasional snack of dried processed chickpeas and washed the grit away with a swallow from his water pouch. Then he continued the silent humming and reciting of his favorite mantras. At night, he quickly bathed in the darkness and swam in the river. He kept watch for an approaching vessel in the river. He passed the time by humming mantras and counting stars. His astronomy training at the ashram surfaced. On clear nights, the stars became his companions, and he spoke to them between his mantras. He had every faith that a rescue party would soon arrive.

On the fifth night, he ambushed a young man carrying a lantern. They spoke in codes, and the message was for him to follow. He did.

They put out the lantern and stumbled out of the woods and into a small vessel. Two men paddled him all night downriver. It was the Gomati River. Hiding the boat in the weeds, they walked with the rising sun to a village of shops and markets. Very few people were stirring during that dawn hour. They walked past several retail establishments that were not yet open for the day's business. They entered into what appeared to be an apparel store. Nothing was said, but he nodded at the few apparent janitorial men who greeted him, and they sent his escorts away. In the silence, they offered him warm tea with a roti and some fried vegetables. After that, he was led down some stairs, through what seemed like a tunnel, and into a small room. The men nodded goodbyes, closed the door, and departed. He slept for many hours. It was a poorly lit basement room, but his tired body was relieved to have a warm, dry bed with torn blankets and sheets. He slept there all day, and toward evening, the janitorial party returned with clean clothes and showed him where the latrine was and where to bathe. Together, they ate a large supper and chatted for a bit, and upon their departure, he bolted the door and went back to bed. He slept all night.

Morning arrived on schedule. He was awakened by loud tapping on the door. He greeted a man who had a bag of food and a pot of sweetened tea. He drank the hot sweetened tea. The man sat next to him and finally spoke. They talked about him and what was happening. The man thanked him for all his contributions to their common cause and assured him that it was just a matter of time before the insurgents would be ousted from India, and Vishnu would be recognized for his patriotism, bravery, and heroism. He was informed that there would be another massive attack on the British when the time was right and that would finally chase the British out of India.

He was then informed that the morning after he left, his father's house was raided. The authorities ransacked the entire premises while his family was held at gunpoint. He nodded, saying that he had expected that would be the case. The good news was that after several hours of interrogation, they let the family go. He asked about his mother and was told that she was hysterical to find out that her son was accused of being involved in such radical and unacceptable behavior. She kept denying the whole accusation, as she truly had no idea of her son's involvement with a rebel group. His depressed wife and disappointed father said very little, claiming that he was out some place drinking and gambling. His father told the authorities that he had evicted the boy from his house for being a public nuisance and embarrassment to his caste. His wife showed them the money he left and the erased tikka from her forehead.

He was told that his identity would be temporarily changed and that he must relocate to some distant area. It was too risky for him to be caught by the British for now he also knew of the group's local headquarters and hideout area. He had also seen the faces of the local leadership group. They spoke most of that day about the operation and what else could have been done. He had done all that he could do, and it was time for a temporary self-exile. They both again agreed that the British would soon be driven out of India and that all of them would be reunited with their respective homes and families. Staying alive and out of sight was the priority at the moment.

That night, the man gave Vishnu some cheap cotton clothes, a pillowcase full of stuff, and some liquor. He told Vishnu that his new name would be Pyroo. His caste was that of an untouchable, and he would be referred to as a *chamar*. An untouchable named Pyroo had recently died, and the authorities in his camp had disposed of the corpse and given his identity to the Brahmin. Instantly, he was demoted from the highest caste as a Brahmin to a chamar. He understood the process. He ate another full meal, trimmed up his beard, and left late that night, wandering about as any common chamar would in his cheap cotton dhoti and a shirt to match. No more fancy suits and ties. No more umbrella. No need to protect his skin color. He was now a homeless and wandering chamar with money.

He kept his money in the pillowcase, which dangled on a drawstring from his neck. After some wandering, he secured the donated liquor. He drank alone from the bottle by the wayside, gazing at some familiar stars. He had to figure out where to go when morning arrived. Partially drunk, he fell asleep by the roadside talking to the stars. His wandering about continued by day, and he drank himself to sleep every night. His constant companions at night were the stars, which he recognized from the astronomy lessons at the ashram. He spoke, and they twinkled as the contents of the bottle vanished and left the one-time wonder boy sleeping by the roadside as a despicable, homeless, lowly chamar. People avoided him.

Pyroo eventually arrived at Calcutta one day. No one knows how he got there or how long it took him. Being from the Lucknow area, he must have traveled by boat down the Gomati River and eventually down the Ganges. Calcutta was a long way from home, and he made no attempt to make contact with anyone in his home area. He still drank cheap liquor and ate whatever he procured from the occasional food vendors. He bathed at night in the rivers and occasionally washed his clothes. He kept his pillowcase within reach at all times. From time to time, he had to defend his belongings, but that was an easy task for someone skilled in the martial arts.

The weeks passed, and dressed in a dhoti, he continued to explore the city of Calcutta. He had nothing to do, so he walked. He had a full beard, and his hair was quite unruly. Day after day, with the pillowcase dangling from his neck, he walked about in his shabby clothes, looking at the sights and admiring the city. The one thing he did not like was sleeping in the streets, so he decided to find a home. He traveled to the poor side of town and rented a small flat. He still walked about the city, but many of the daylight hours, he spent reading. He read whatever he could get his hands on, especially any documents that had a story about his hometown or his rebel group. He had to be careful not to read any English publications in public. It would arise major suspicions if a street chamar was reading such prints. But he collected them from whatever sources he could and read them in his humble home. He was fully convinced that the days of British occupation were numbered, and soon he would no longer be exiled and could return home.

Then one day, he read a publication about several rebels being captured and executed. The article named the rebels and also commented that Nana Sahib had escaped and supposedly gone to Nepal. That reality convinced him that his group no longer existed. It shocked him to read the news, but it was reality. He was on his own until another uprising occurred and chased the intruders away. Then, he would find his way home and settle down with his pretty wife in that mansion of marble that his ancestors had built.

With time, Pyroo started making friends in his new neighborhood. As far as they were concerned, he was a drifter who had arrived in Calcutta trying to find a job. He kept asking if anyone knew where he could find employment. He went from one establishment to another in search of odd jobs. But because of his new caste, people refused to hire him. Then one day, a neighbor took him to meet his boss. It was at a hotel. His neighbor worked there attending to horses. Many guests came in expensive chariots drawn by special horses. It was the hotel's responsibility to ensure that the horses were well fed, groomed, and stabled while the guests enjoyed their stay in luxury.

After a series of interviews and discussions with the hotel personnel, Pyroo was hired to help with the horses and with general duties fit for his new caste. He mostly cleaned the horse stalls. It was hard work, and the pay was minimal, but it occupied his time. At night, he entertained himself with an old habit. He gambled with some men in the neighborhood, betting whatever they could afford. He enjoyed gambling and taught the men games that they had never heard about before he arrived. He enjoyed the games and the company. When asked about his past, his response was always the same. He claimed to have lost his family in some disaster and claimed to be a lonely chamar drifting from place to place in survival mode.

It was during one of those gambling sessions that a strange phenomenon occurred. Two bandits tried to rob the gambling party. One appeared to have a large concealed gun. The robbers were focused on the few coins on the table and asked the group to stand with their hands on their heads. The flickering lantern and the barking dog were the only distractions at that moment. They were then ordered to empty their pockets and to put all their coins on the table. They obeyed. One by one, the men placed their few coins on the table and stepped back with hands back on their heads.

Then it was Pyroo's turn to put his money on the table. He slowly walked toward the table, keeping a close eye on the man with the concealed gun. As he pretended to fumble around for his contribution, the gunman pushed him and yelled at him to hurry up. He did. He hurried to the man's arms. In an instant, the man was tossed to the ground, and before his associate could understand what was happening, he, too, was being tossed about. The two were soon running away, bumping into each other and stumbling over themselves. Pyroo chased after them, seizing what was supposed to be a gun. It turned out to be a piece of wood carved into the shape of a gun. Pyroo grabbed the piece and chased the two away, swatting them on their backsides as the gamblers laughed louder than the barks of the neighborhood dogs. They resumed their games with occasional bursts of laughter about the two stumbling robbers being spanked with a wooden toy gun. Pyroo did not laugh much. He didn't finish the game. He went to bed.

The following night, as the group gathered, there were many questions. They did not participate in the usual gambling sessions. They were more curious about where Pyroo learned to fight the way he did. They were starting to believe that their Pyroo was more than he had revealed to them. So they kept asking him about his past, about where he learned such strange games, and about how he could fight like a champion.

In a semistoic manner, Pyroo tried to explain that it was a burst of adrenalin during the panic that caused him to react with such bravery. He tried to convince the men that he had to survive on the streets for a long time, and during that period, he had to learn self-defense. But somehow the men did not believe him. He was too "cultured" to be a street dweller. He further tried to explain to the men that those few coins were all he had to feed himself and pay his rent and that he could not let the robbers steal all of his possessions. It was his story, and he stuck to it.

After a few days, the group resumed their evening activities of gathering and talking about their respective day's activities. It was after one of those gatherings that a group member asked Pyroo for a serious discussion. He was a young man, and they both lived at the same rental building. As the group collected their coins and put away the crude, homemade chairs, the two stayed and continued discussing trivial things. Then the question was asked of Pyroo. The man wanted to know if Pyroo would be interested in a professional fight. It appeared that the young man had connections with a local wrestling group, and he wanted Pyroo to go for an audition. He explained that it was not the major league wrestling but a venture sponsored by local people for entertainment. They both looked at each other, smiled, and went to bed.

In his lonely quarters, Pyroo sat on his bed. He did not drink that night. Solitude was his companion, and the silence was deafening. It was dark, still, and quiet, and he could hear his heart beating. Faster and faster, the thumping of his heart raced on. It had been a long time since he had stayed sober, faced reality, and examined his future. He was starting to accept the fact that he might never go home again, at least not in the immediate future. With good intentions, he had made some bad choices, and the consequences had banished him to dwell with the lowest caste and forced him to live in the slums and shovel horse manure for a few measly coins. He had no purpose in life. Every day, he went to work shoveling horse manure and serving pompous people with utmost humility. The embarrassment was stifling, but his choices were limited. To be discovered meant death to him and humiliation to his respected family. He mourned for the happiness of his mother, who loved him so much. He missed the gentle touches of his lovely wife. He reflected on his teenage years in the institution that catered to privileged people. But he had no regrets for being part of the rebel group. He did not want his beloved country to be occupied, ruled, and plundered by some inconsiderate foreigners whose sole purpose had become to exploit the resources of his homeland. He did his patriotic duty and was proud of that. He paused and heard the barking of the neighborhood dogs. It was getting toward morning as he heard the greetings of activities by early risers.

He had to find a purpose in life, something to focus on that would channel his thoughts away from the bottle. He took inventory of his current status and recognized a twenty-something-year-old man with a poor diet and too much alcohol. That was too much to face. He felt the urge to drink. There must be bottles close by. His trembling hands and aching heart wanted to escape, and the bottle spelled relief. His heart continued to race as his old personality surfaced. He understood the power of meditation and recognized that was the one string he could play on and the one friend who could console him. He did not drink. Instead, he began a slow breathing exercise. His racing heart was replaced by tears on his cheek as full doses of reality consumed him and led him into Slumberland. Into the morning he slept without a drink for the first time in many months.

Pyroo did not respond to his friend's request about the wrestling audition. Physically he was not conditioned for such an activity. Proper nutrition and training were prerequisites for such undertaking. But the idea of becoming a small-time wrestler fascinated him. At night, he sat in loneliness, spoke to the stars, and replaced the bottle with meditation. After work, he browsed the markets, buying supplies that he knew to be health enhancing. He ate right, did the proper exercises, and used the body-to-mind connection that he deemed necessary to improve his physical and mental strength. They still gathered every evening to discuss the daily activities, but the group recognized that he was in a state of metamorphosis. They saw a new man and wondered what was happening. He looked healthy and appeared to be much more confident. One day, he went to the barber and got a haircut and shave.

He was transformed. Even his friends could not believe how different he appeared. No one made a big deal about it, but they were individually convinced that he was someone of a social status much different than the one he was portraying to them.

After work, he did his shopping. Then he engaged into various exercise programs. He went out running. He found tree branches that were suitable for pull-ups, he did push-ups, and he stretched and twisted his body in various ways similar to what he learned at the ashram. On his days off, he went to the river and swam for long periods of time. He continued eating nutritious meals. His conditioning process lasted for a few months, and once again, he felt strong and purposeful.

When the moment was right, he approached the wrestling contact. They discussed the possibility of him becoming involved in the sport. But they both agreed that the authorities would not allow a chamar in the ring. His friend encouraged him to reveal his true identity and face the consequences. But Pyroo did not encourage that. He told the man that he was a chamar and that was how it would have to be. They considered trying to legally change his caste, but every chamar in India would try that if it were possible. That was not an option.

The only thing they did was start loitering around the arena during the various events in an effort to meet with one of the officials. Pyroo's friend knew who they were, but he was just a hired hand in the crowd. Everyone seemed busy. Pyroo realized that during the interim period, he could observe from the spectators' bench and learn the rules and how the referees did their scoring. He wore hat and baggy clothes so that no one would pay attention to him as he sat away from the crowds. He watched the fighters and learned their various tricks. When he got home, he mentally replayed the fights and envisioned how he would have handled the various moves that the participants and the referees made during the fights.

Pyroo had to trust someone, and his friend seemed like an honest person. He was an enthusiastic young man about twenty years old, and Pyroo was curious about his life and his past. So one evening, he made the man swear to secrecy about him not being a chamar. He did not reveal too much but explained that he needed his identity protected and that he would only communicate in English to any potential fight promoters. That language confused his friend, but he was not surprised. He knew that there was something unique about his so-called chamar friend.

The young man was then questioned about his past and why he was living in such poverty. He told Pyroo that his family were farmers. He wanted to become a tailor so he joined a company as an apprentice and learned how to cut and sew clothes. His family could not afford the high land taxes imposed by the current system. Not able to cope with the stress, his father committed suicide. His mother had died some three years before from malnutrition and stress. His sisters were married and moved away. His two brothers took up drinking and fought constantly. The local zamindar confiscated their land in lieu of taxes owed and evicted them. He was the youngest and decided to move away from such a toxic environment and to fend for himself elsewhere. At eighteen, with little money and very little education, he climbed on a wagon then another wagon and another and finally found himself in Calcutta. He did odd jobs, stole food, and lived on the streets until he secured a job at the hotel grooming horses. In addition, he did janitorial jobs for the wrestling association. When time permitted, he spent time with the local tailor to learn from him with the intention of owning his own shop someday.

Pyroo was sorry to hear about the unfortunate life that young man was living but was impressed about his plans for the future. He also noticed that although life had not been kind to the young man so far, he had a vision of his future and had a good attitude toward life. After they had both shared their stories, Pyroo was even more determined to pursue the wrestling potential.

His patience and observations paid off. One day, his friend managed to approach one of the fight promoters and had a serious discussion about a mystery fighter who could beat any of the wrestlers in Calcutta. His friend told the manager that this fighter would not reveal his identity, and he would choose to be in disguise, probably wear a mask over his head and face in order to conceal his identity. The manager was told that the mystery man would only be in Calcutta for a short time, and if the promoters were interested, an audition could be arranged. The only stipulation was that nobody would be allowed to see his face. In addition, all communications would have to be in

English, for that was the only language the mystery man spoke. All negotiations would have to be discussed in English.

The conversation abruptly ended when the manager was called away by one of his partners to meet with someone at the planning committee. Pyroo's friend was elated at his ability to create such an ingenious story, which he had rehearsed well. He hurried about, found Pyroo, and shared the great story that he told. Pyroo had to agree that it was rather clever, and now that they had the attention of the wrestling management, it was just a matter of time before their curiosity consumed them and they secured the mystery man before any other group signed a short-term monopoly with him. The seed was planted and watered. It was just a matter of time before something happened. In the meantime, they continued their daily labor and sat about at nights gambling and telling stories of their respective days' events. Pyroo quit drinking and intensified his physical training.

After work one day, Pyroo went shopping. He had to buy a new suit, shoes, and mask. He traveled to markets, shops, and tailors that did not do any business close to his living domain. He convinced the tailor that he needed a mask for some type of costume party. The one thing was that it had to have knots that would be almost impossible to remove. The only visible parts would have to be his eyes, mouth, and nostrils. He also had the tailor sew some tight-fitting pants with wide suspenders to keep them in place.

One piece at a time, he brought his garments home and hid them in his apartment. At night, he would put on the garments and rehearse the athletic dance he had created. He practiced his English in a deep and mysterious voice with a profound British accent. He was getting ready for the big day. He was planning and rehearsing to be an English fighter in disguise. He no longer craved alcohol as much as he once did. Instead, he had a purpose and a mission that consumed his time. He appreciated those exciting times.

He kept the whole thing a secret. Even his friend who accompanied him to the various wrestling events knew almost nothing of his preparation. Like all secrets, Pyroo knew that telling even his best friend could be risky. What they both knew was that there was talk of an English-speaking mystery fighter in the area who would soon make his debut in their arena. The challengers were many. Each one of them was planning how best to remove the mask and reveal the mystery man to the public. It became the most anticipated fight, and yet nobody knew who the participants were or when it would be.

The day came when Pyroo had to meet with the fight promoters. His elated friend breathlessly delivered the message. They scheduled the meeting at a secluded hotel away from the arena. Pyroo had a chance to wear his new suit and polished shoes and the colorful mask. He also wore some thin gloves in order to hide his callused and pigmented hands. He changed clothes in a wooded area close to the meeting place and hid the shabby garments. He was quite warm covered in all those new garments, but he managed to control his breathing and stay focused. After all, he had been waiting for that day for several weeks, and now that the moment had arrived, there would be one chance to get this right and earn some money.

They arrived at the hotel rather early. His friend joined him later and was in awe when he saw Pyroo's attire. He sat on the bench next to Pyroo, and together, they waited. As the meeting time approached, they ensured that the outfit was properly adjusted and that the mask was properly fitted so that Pyroo could see, breath, and talk properly. Then there was a knock at the door, and the visitors entered.

The meeting commenced with Pyroo representing himself and the promoters offering their terms. The proposal was simple. As an audition, Pyroo would fight the number-three fighter. If he won, he would challenge the number-two man and ultimately could fight for the local championship. Pyroo was stunned at the somewhat large amount of money they offered just to be in the ring with the number three, but he expressed his concerns about the amount not being adequate. He counteroffered, and a compromise was reached. The bout would be in two weeks. If Pyroo could beat his opponent, he would get two-thirds of the total purse. If he lost, then he would only get one-third. Either win or lose, it meant a relatively large amount of money compared to the measly wages he earned at his job. So he decided to quit the job and focus on training for the next two weeks.

The only concern from Pyroo's standpoint was his friend. He knew that someone would track him down and offer a bribe in exchange for information about the mystery man. Although he trusted his friend, he could not risk anything. Someone could ambush him and use force to extract information from him, for those men were ruthless fighters. There was too much to lose, and he just could not risk the possibility of exposure. So he did the only logical thing. He sent the man away on a paid vacation for several days far away from their domain. He bought him new clothes and shoes. He got a haircut and trimmed his beard and moustache. He told his friend not to worry about his job and not to have any contact with the wrestling association. The man understood the danger from all angles and instantly agreed to take Pyroo's money and leave town all dressed up, not to return until the day before the fight.

The chamar personality was banished during the interim period and was replaced with a mature Brahmin. Now he was not only well-schooled in various academic disciplines, but he had also graduated from the university of street dwellings. He really believed in himself and knew that competing with those fighters would not be a major issue. Whatever training methods he used were confined to his small apartment and in the woods. He ate indoors, trained there, and slept there most of the time. He only went out to get food, and during the evening hours, he sat with his friends and neighbors and participated in small gambling games.

As scheduled, his friend, dressed in new clothes, arrived the evening before the event. They stayed at the hotel and talked. The friend talked about his trip, and Pyroo talked about his preparation. Pyroo explained that he went back to the old neighborhood and, in the evenings, gambled with the group. That was better than leaving the group wondering about their absence. He explained to the men that his friend went on a trip to visit relatives. The story was that there was a death in his extended family, and he was in line for some inheritance.

The day of the anticipated audition had arrived. They went to their arena quarters early enough to avoid the crowds. As the hours passed, they heard the hoopla and chants from the arriving spectators. The formalities and introductions customary for such events were performed, and it was time for the fight to commence. Pyroo's challenger was no stranger to those events. He was a good fighter, and the crowd liked him. He got into the ring first, bragging to his fans about his plan to unmask the mystery man. The fans cheered, whistled, tossed their hats about, and screamed encouraging chants to the man in the ring, whom they had come to love so much. It was supposed to be a small crowd, for it was just an audition. But the word about the mystery fighter drew a much larger crowd than expected.

Then came the mystery man. He was greeted with pitiful boos and shouts of disapproval. The referee introduced the challengers, and the event was about to begin. Pyroo was asked if he wanted to address the spectators, and he shook his head, indicating that he did not.

The bell informed the fighters that it was time to fight! Nervousness, fear, anger, and a host of emotions propelled Pyroo from his corner with lightning speed. He circled the ring. They had brief encounters but not much action until the bell sent them to their respective corners. The second round was more of the same. On the third round, Pyroo was severely attacked as the crowd screamed their approval to their favorite man. They wanted him to finish the mystery man and unmask him. Pyroo retaliated in kind, and before the crowd realized what was happening, the fight was over. Pyroo won in the third round.

He stood in the ring long enough to ensure that his opponent was fine. After Pyroo verified that he was okay, they shook hands and migrated back to their respective corners. The crowd was stunned. They had never seen such speed and agility coupled with force and accuracy. There was utter silence as the defeated fighter made his exit from the ring. He slowly walked past his beloved fans, who sat there in total disbelief. Pyroo did not say much either. The few words he uttered were in English, and he used a deep voice, portraying his adopted British heritage. He found his friend, and together they meandered back to his quarters, where he was paid the two-thirds share with cash and was told that the next fight with the number-two ranked fighter would be in one month at the same arena. They agreed to meet the following day to discuss the terms.

With all the formalities out of the way the next day, Pyroo and his friend had a whole month to do nothing except get ready for the next fight. They decided to leave town for a while and do some traveling. Not wanting to leave town together, they met at a remote location where they boarded public trandportation and went off. It was a nice vacation, and they both enjoyed themselves, eating well and sleeping in nice hotels. They did not share rooms because Pyroo needed his privacy for his daily training.

Within a couple of days of the fight, they were back in Calcutta. They rented a rather large suite at the hotel and waited there for the scheduled event. They stayed close together because Pyroo was always concerned about his friend betraying him and revealing his identity. They ate and slept in the hotel suite and conducted meetings with the wrestling association in their quarters. The promoters told him that wrestling fans were elated about the upcoming event. There were bets and speculations, and discussions were happening in all kinds of places, from restaurants to barber shops. There were hypes, lies, and arguments about his tactics on the streets with some fans putting up posters of the mystery man. Fans had a lot to look forward to as they started to make predictions on the fight's outcome. Many of them were hoping that he would win that second fight in order to witness a bout between the mystery man and the current champion.

The moment had arrived. There were chants for and against the mystery man. The applause and boos were blended together into one loud noise as Pyroo sized up his new opponent. He was a tall man with long, dark hair tied into a ponytail. He had piercing eyes. He stood in his corner and stared at Pyroo as if he wanted to physiologically intimidate him. But Pyroo knew that trick and returned the favor, staring him down through his tightly fitting mask. Pyroo must have realized that that fighter was intelligent and much stronger than he was. That fight would require focus and concentration. In order to win, he had to fight smarter than that man in the opposite corner.

The noise was deafening, but neither fighter heard a sound. The seconds ticked by in slow motion as the fighters focused on their strategies. They waited for the anticipated bell, and instantly the loud clang erupted with fans screaming and yelling, their eyes glued on the circling fighters. Like two bulls in a pasture, neither wanted to make the first move. They circled and circled, staring at each other with eagle eyes in the initial battle of nerves and intimidations. It must have been quite a sight as the two clashed together like two bulls locking horns, pushing and shoving in brute force. Pyroo had many years of training in the martial arts, and that was the moment he exercised some of his most aggressive actions. It was no longer psychology and intimidation. It was now strength versus technique. In the fourth round, Pyroo felt that he had the edge. He realized that he was in control as his opponent started to back away in an effort to avoid him. The bell ended that round. In the fifth round, Pyroo showed more speed and agility. He delivered punches with precise hits that staggered his opponent. And just in a flash, his challenger was on the ground, defeated. Pyroo won again, and the crowd went wild and crazy. He had suddenly won their trust, and they were now his fans. He walked around and bowed and waved to the spectators as he walked past them toward his quarters with his friend at his side.

Behind closed doors, they waited for the promoters to come and deliver the cash. They came, delivered the money, and scheduled the next meeting. It was a relatively large sum of money. They stuffed it all in a sack and hurried out. Pyroo needed to remove his mask and garments, for his sweat was burning his eyes, and he itched from the perspiration that oozed from every part of his body. It was obvious that he was slightly hurt, for he limped along, trying to keep up with his partner.

Down the lane, they walked and continued into the hotel suite. Pyroo cleaned up, and they ordered supper. Slightly limping, he began to laugh. The laughter continued, and his partner joined in because Pyroo seemed fine. They tossed the sack of money about, trying to guess how much was in there. The laughter continued through supper and as they counted the money. They were surprised. It really was a larger sum of money than they had expected. They continued the laughter, which turned into smiles, and the night consumed their occasional celebrations. They slept well in their respective rooms only to wake up and laugh during breakfast. They were like two kids in a candy store and did not want the shopping to cease. Things were too good to be true. But they had the money to prove that it was real. It was no dream or illusion. The smiles and laughter continued all day long.

That night, in old cotton dhoti and shirts, the two visited their old neighborhood and gambled with their usual group of friends. They explained that the friend had inherited the money, and the two of them were traveling about in search of some business opportunities like operating a tailor shop. Nothing else was discussed as they gambled with the few coins and went to bed.

The men felt great walking about the old neighborhood where Pyroo could be Pyroo. He once again felt like Vishnu. He did not need a mask and strange garments to disguise his identity. And within a few days, they returned to the hotel to meet with the fight promoters to discuss the championship bout. They were told that it was the most anticipated fight that anyone in the organization could remember: the champ versus the mystery man. The terms were the same as the previous fights, where the winner got two-thirds of the profits, and the loser had to settle for one-third. The promoters told Pyroo that losing that fight would pay as much as winning the first. They kept on telling him about the losing side of the event. To that, Pyroo objected. He told the promoters in loud English words that he was going there to win that fight and planned to leave with the larger share of the purse. They looked at Pyroo and smiled and then continued with the discussion on the losing side of the subject. That infuriated Pyroo, who hurried through the meeting and escorted the visiting party out the door.

They had to wait almost two months for the next fight. So, the two packed up their luggage, secured their cash, and in traditional Indian clothes, went about to see other parts of India. Where they went and what they did would continue to be unknown. Pyroo was well read, and he knew about such sights. They probably ventured about and into some of those historical and spiritual sites. He grew a beard and moustache and wore a hat just in case he crossed paths with someone who could recognize him from his childhood neighborhood, from the rebel group, from the ashram, or from anywhere else. He just had to be cautious. Again, they ate well, stayed at relatively expensive hotels, traveled in style, and lived a luxurious life as most young people with money would do when on vacation. India is a large country. In those days, the country of Pakistan did not exist. It was all India, and the two had time and money to seek and explore.

Their vacation had finally come to an end. It was time to get ready for the championship fight. They had to get back and get ready. One week before the event, they were back at their hotel.

The procedure was becoming routine. The only difference was that the mystery man made new clothes that were created from the finest garments sold in the area. His friend explained that Pyroo needed new garments for the fight. The mask had to be fitted so that the perspiration would not cause irritation and blur his vision. He explained to Pyroo that he had tailoring skills; they needed to acquire a sewing machine, and he would make the necessary garments and a unique mask. They did. Together, they ensured that the new headpiece would keep the sweat off his eyes and the rest would aid in less itching during perspiration. As Pyroo practiced, his partner cut and sewed. The garments, after several modifications, were quite colorful, and the comfortable fit enabled Pyroo to be much more flexible than he was in the previous ones. He was very pleased with his new outfit.

With confidence, they marched toward the arena early enough to avoid the crowds. They stopped along the way and hid some old cotton garments. Then, they swiftly walked to the arena. There, they adjusted the new fighting garments and made small talk to minimize boredom. Pyroo believed that he could beat the champion, so he kept focusing on the various techniques in silent periodic meditation.

It was showtime. Pyroo entered the arena in his new colorful garments. He casually paraded about, showing off the new attire, and awaited the arrival of the champion. The crowd was screaming at the top of their lungs again, and Pyroo loved the attention. The arena was packed with no standing room available. But the cheering and chanting came to a sudden halt as the champion made his entrance. He looked and behaved like a champion. He had been the reigning champ for over a year in that neighborhood. He had been challenged many times but was still undefeated. He did not seem too concerned about his challenger. His goal that night was to unmask the mystery man and humiliate him in his usual ways. He was a mean and merciless fighter who intended to maintain his place at the top. He was a very proud man, tall and muscular with a receding hairline and wore a perpetual frown on his face.

Pyroo had done his homework on that fighter. He knew that that champion was again stronger than he was, but he knew that he was smarter and faster. He would have to rely on his speed and his intelligence if he was going to beat the champ. He also knew that he was in excellent physical shape and had the stamina to wear down the champ by dodging about and frustrating him. That became his primary strategy.

They did not make eye contact in the arena. Pyroo kept waving to the spectators, and the champ sat quietly in his corner. Clang went the bell, and the fight was on. The champ instantly went on the offense, trying to get a few early hits on Pyroo. All he wanted to do was to stun him and remove the mask. But Pyroo kept dancing around, avoiding all the attacks that the champ could deliver. Every time the champ failed to connect a hit on Pyroo, the fans laughed. It was what Pyroo was hoping to see. The champ was frustrated and wasted large amounts of energy being on the attack constantly. Pyroo saw that he was getting tired and frustrated, so he kept teasing and taunting him, to which the fans laughed louder still. Then Pyroo became very serious. He went on the attack with his lightning speed, beating the champ with punches like small doses of thunderbolts. The man took the beating and kept on fighting. It came down to the

seventh and final round, and they both knew that the time had come
to finish the other. It was brutal. Finally, Pyroo, with all his might
and precise focus, delivered and landed a solid hit on his opponent's
forehead. And down he went. The champ fell as Pyroo retreated to his
corner. The man tried desperately but could not get up. The referee
made the call, and that call made Pyroo the new champion.

They went through the usual process and gained the large purse.
Pyroo's friend came into their quarters all excited. He explained
that some of the champ's henchmen were planning to ambush them.
They were also informed that some British soldiers were asking
questions about the mystery man, for they had no record of any
British fighters in the neighborhood. So, the two of them escaped
through a back window with the sack of money and disappeared
into the darkness. Pyroo removed his mask. Together they hid in the
woods that night. The next day, Pyroo's friend retrieved the rags and
hats for Pyroo and himself from their nearby stash. They escaped to
the old neighborhood with a sackful of money and a bag containing
Pyroo's fighting garments. They traveled in separate rickshaws.

Pyroo was hurt and stayed in his little apartment as his partner
took care of him. He moaned and groaned constantly and sipped
on soup and water for several days. His partner told the group that
Pyroo had been ambushed in the city by a bunch of robbers, but
he had managed to fight off their attacks and chase them away. So
in the evening, he had a number of sympathetic visitors. It took
more than a week, but he was healing. He began limping about and
gently sat with the group and watched as they gambled. Then they
helped him up to his bed. It took some time, but he recovered fully
and started participating in the evening games again. He continued
his low profile, wondering what to do next. He considered several
options, but nothing excited him. He wanted to go home, but that was
not an option. He kept investigating about any rebel groups, but he
found none. He wanted to be far away where he could be free again
and to wait for India to be liberated from the British.

During one of the usual gambling sessions, one of the men said
that he had signed up to become an indentured servant in some

foreign land. It sounded like some island called Mauritius. That was news to Pyroo, for he had never heard about such things. The man went into details about the process of going to such a place to sift sugar for good wages and a guaranteed trip back to India within a few years with a lot of money. The excited man kept talking late into the night about this lucrative process and all the things he would do when he returned to India with a substantial sum of money. He would acquire a piece of land and then get married and start a business and a family. He would have a stable home and send his kids to school—and on and on, he went about his dreams of his future life.

The group had many questions for that man as to how he came into contact with such an organization. The man explained about his encounter with the arkathies. He was in the city markets when he was approached by a group of men who asked if he wanted to make some money. They explained the whole process to him. He explained that the ship would sail soon, and he must get things ready to meet with the recruiting men again. They would schedule his appointment with the doctor and get him in condition for the voyage. He told them that he did not have to worry about anything because his new friends had taken care of all the details. He claimed that he was very lucky to meet those men. They explained to him that the ship was almost full, and if he did not decide to make the journey within a few days, they would recruit others, especially women. He explained that the next day he would meet the men at the market and go with them to their headquarters where the doctor and other officials would ensure his passage to his new temporary home across the waters. There, he would be given food and shelter, and during the day, he would be sifting sugar for which he would be well compensated.

Pyroo did not say much. He did tell the man that he, too, had to go to the market the following day and would like to see if he could meet with those fine men. They agreed on a time to leave the next morning, and the man went to bed totally delighted. Pyroo and his friend stayed up that night and discussed what that process could mean. They agreed to go along and investigate the legitimacy of such a recruitment process. However, it would be imperative that they stay separated. Pyroo would travel with the new recruit, and his friend would be doing some shopping. They would be dressed in their traditional Indian garments.

They traveled as planned the next morning. Pyroo kept company with the man and his friend, who wore a big hat for disguise and stayed close by, the two pretending that they did not know one another. The market was a busy place as usual. Farmers, merchants, jewelers, spice traders, and a host of others were selling everything to anyone who showed any interest in whatever was being peddled. They pushed and jostled about until they spotted the recruiters. They greeted one another and sat down with hot cups of chai. The man being recruited was elated and told the group that he had all his personal things in his possession and was ready to go. Pyroo asked a series of questions and wished the man a safe journey. Pretending to be strangers, he and his friend returned home separately.

Within a few days, the two were on vacation again. They had time and more money than purpose, so they drifted from town to town and state to state. They visited the mountains and the ocean. Pyroo read scriptures and poetry to his friend, who was almost illiterate. They ate well and lodged at nice hotels. They did not stay very long in any particular location for fear of being recognized. They considered splitting up and going on their respective journeys. But they only had each other. Neither wanted to lose the other. It was friendship to the nth degree, and they cherished each other's company. But they were bored, and every day compounded the boredom. They both grew beards and wore hats that helped conceal their identity, but they were always concerned that someday, someone would recognize them, and that would be bad. The friend suspected that Pyroo was hiding from something, but he did not know what the details were.

One rainy day, the two friends were sitting in a restaurant sipping hot chai when Pyroo broke the silence. He told his friend what he had learned from the recruiters about the indentured process. He suggested that they should consider signing up for one of those voyages and see a different part of the world. He suggested that if things did not go well, that they could pay for a return trip and get back to India because they had money to do so. The discussion sparked excitement into the conversation, and the two decided to return to Calcutta, enlist as indentured servants, and travel to some distant land where people went to sift sugar. It was agreed, and they went to bed that night with some type of vision. They had purposes again.

Upon arrival in Calcutta, they found the recruiting headquarters and investigated the possibility of going overseas as indentured servants. They claimed to be orphaned street dwellers in search of a better life. Of course, it did not take very long to get them a meeting with the depot agent. They were informed that there was a vessel leaving shortly for British Guiana, and if they hurried the process, they could be sailing within days. They told the authorities to start the process and that they would be back within a day. They hurried to town, and his partner had a local tailor sew two money belts at his direction. Into the compartments, they stashed some of their cash. The belts were tied around their waist and secured with drawstrings that kept the cloth belts tied around their midsections. Then they returned to the depot to schedule the various details necessary for becoming indentured servants on some remote British plantation. They declared the extra cash to the authorities for safekeeping and got a receipt for the full amount. They did not declare the contents in the money belts. The clerk was surprised at the relatively large sum, but he did his job.

One fine day, Pyroo and his friend were among hundreds of recruits as the vessel departed the shores of the Hooghly River in the Kidderpur area and into the Bay of Bengal, which eventually merged into the Atlantic Ocean.

There were tears, vomiting, shrieks, and bullying as the hatches closed and confined Pyroo and the rest to the lower deck while the ship's personnel, including the doctor, stayed above. Instantly, Pyroo knew that it was a mistake to become part of that process, but there was no turning back. In the midst of the horror and the stench, he did the one thing that he could—he meditated. The days turned into weeks and the weeks into months, as the vessel bobbed along, stopping occasionally at some remote port for supplies and fresh water.

Because Pyroo and his friend had money, they bought favors from the ship's personnel. They could get extra helpings of good quality food, and the sardars allowed them adequate time on the deck. They got extra blankets and were allowed to sleep in selected areas away from the groups. The ship had the groups sectioned off: the men, the women, and couples. The women always stayed together in small groups even when they had to go get a drink of water. A woman walking about such ship alone was prime target of sexual abuse. The women knew that and stayed in clusters. There was always strength in numbers. People adopted each other as brothers and sisters. Any such group traveling together in a ship (*jahaj*) called themselves *jahajees*. Pyroo soon started referring to his friend as Jahaj.

Jahaj and Pyroo did not suffer as much on their journey. They befriended the ship's crew and paid them for small favors. But they were bored like the rest of the human cargo. It took months to make the journey from Calcutta to British Guiana. They played games and made music with some of the instruments brought on board. They sang and told stories, always eager to adopt one another to be a brother or sister in their new land. Some got married on the ship, and some were buried at sea. All standard practices.

One fine sunny and calm day, Pyroo and Jahaj were standing on the deck looking at the endless body of water. Then Jahaj looked at Pyroo and asked, "Pyroo, who are you?"

The question did not surprise Pyroo. In fact, he was surprised that Jahaj had never asked him sooner. Pyroo smiled, shook his head, and said, "Jahaj, it would be better if you did not know my past, but we have been together for a long time and have done some remarkable things. I know that my secret would be safe with you. I'll tell you, but you must promise with an oath in the presence of God, that you will tell nobody about this. I owe you this much."

And so, in the middle of the ocean in a gently rocking sailing ship, among ever-present whitecaps, Pyroo held Jahaj's hand and repeated an oath from the Ramayana (Hindu scripture) as his eyes watered. Jahaj was shocked, for he had never seen Pyroo cry before.

Then he said, "Pyroo, if you do not want to tell me, that's okay. I can see the emotion on your face and the pain in your eyes. You are my true and only brother now, and please do not feel obligated to tell me anything if it bothers you to do so. I do understand."

The friends sat on deck, hand in hand, as Pyroo told Jahaj about his past. Jahaj could only nod, for he had no idea of the rebel group and the underground movement to expel the British from India. It did not surprise him to hear that Pyroo was a Brahmin of such stature. He knew that Pyroo was special. As Pyroo spoke, Jahaj cried, and the time passed. The sun was soon setting in the distant ocean horizon. That red ball of fire appeared to have dipped its lower half, pretending to quench its thirst from that endless supply of water. Pyroo kept talking about his family, about his time at the ashram, about the Enfield rifle issues, and about his friends who were labeled as rebels, some beheaded in search of justice against an insurgence of foreign power in his homeland. And Jahaj recognized what a true son of India he was and was in awe at his patriotism. He sacrificed so much for India!

Morning found them sleeping on deck. They had missed supper the previous night, for neither had an appetite. The winds had picked up, and the ship rocked vigorously on the crashing waves that splashed water and mists about. No one on board got seasick anymore, but they tried to avoid getting wet. The sun did its routine climb into the arched sky as the winds calmed down, and soon there was land. They were getting close to their destination, and the ship's personnel were busy preparing for landing. It would be a matter of days as optimism united with confusion and danced with fear. Those and a host of emotions embodied the human cargo of indentured servants as the ship lumbered its slow journey toward the port of British Guiana, in the county of Demerara, and carried Pyroo and Jahaj to their new home. They withdrew their remaining cash from the ship's personnel. They were given coins called shillings and trusted the cashier that it was equal exchange. With their tin tags dangling from their necks, they went through the usual immigration process and received their assignments.

Pyroo was assigned to the Ruimveldt Estate and Jahaj was sent to a nearby plantation. It was the first time that those two had been separated ever since they became friends back in Calcutta. There was no reasoning with the plantation personnel. As indentured servants, recruits went to wherever they were assigned. They shook hands, divided the shillings, hugged, and departed to their respective plantations. Both had their money strapped around their midsections. They vowed to stay in touch with each other.

CHAPTER 6

Life Choices

In the 1800s, extended families in parts of India generally stayed together. This was especially true in some rural areas where small-scale agriculture was the primary source of income. Like in the Punit family, girls were generally sent to serve their respective in-laws, and the boys brought their newly acquired wives to live with and serve their parents' household. With every generation, the land that those families owned was divided among the worthy sons. For example, if a man owned ten acres on which he cultivated rice, he could make a good living. If that man had five sons, each inherited two acres. If the next generation averaged four sons, each of them would theoretically get half an acre. So, within a few generations, new occupations had to be realized for some of the respective descendants. To stay together, some families rented or purchased additional acres that could sustain such extended families.

The process, for the most part, worked well for those people until the British East India Company increased control of India. They adopted the politics of divide and rule. It was a lucrative system for the newcomers because there was always someone who was ready, willing, and able to potentially join with them in an effort to conquer the small farming communities. They were the zamindars who collected inflated taxes on the poor farmers. Those who could not eke out a living on their small parcels of land had to exercise their options. Some sold their shares to larger farmers, and some were evicted for not paying the recently imposed high taxes. Those British representatives worked independently, or they befriended some of those larger farmers and helped finance the land purchasing. One of the strategies was lending them low-interest money. Through such a process, some landowners suddenly grew their holdings and controlled large acreages. The profits ultimately went to the British company.

This story was told about one young Indian couple whose tragic lives were determined by such processes. His name was Kumar, and her name was Shanti.

In their geographic area, if someone decided not to sell his land, the authorities would increase the taxes to a point where such small farmers could not afford to pay them. When that happened, payment was considered delinquent, and the authorities confiscated the land and gave it to the local large farmer to cultivate. The tax delinquent person was given a reasonable period to secure enough money to pay the delinquent taxes plus a hefty penalty. If the money could not be raised, the delinquent party was forcedly evicted and put on the streets. If the landowner died owing taxes, his land was automatically given to the British representative under various terms that could ensure their success. Many of the displaced found employment working for the large farmers. But the small wages ensured that they could earn just enough to provide the basics for their families. Eventually, some of those larger farmers became local landlords. Men like Zamy, Radha's grandfather, profited from such schemes. Those landlords became rich and powerful as long as they danced to the British fiddle.

Kumar and Shanti were recently married, and she came to live in his parents' house. He had several older brothers, and they all had their wives and children living in or around the same household. Kumar was a young and energetic farm boy, and unlike Desai, he was lucky enough to marry one of the most beautiful and graceful girls in their village, and she loved him dearly. His mind, during that time, was no longer on field work, and because of the lack of privacy, he and

Shanti were always sneaking away to some remote areas to appreciate each other's company and to do whatever newlyweds do. It did not take them long to fall deeply in love. It seemed like a match premade in heaven, and they wanted to be with each other all the time.

The older sisters-in-law liked her too and treated her like a little sister. They all complained to her about their controlling mother-in-law. They were obedient and went about doing various duties like weeding the garden, carrying water, cooking, cleaning, and other domestic chores. Whatever mother-in-law said or assigned to them; they did not question. They did their duties and cared for the children. Kumar had also warned her about his mother's bossiness and explained that she would learn to live with the house rules.

His mother was quite concerned that the boy was not focusing on his daily chores of working in the cotton fields and that his wife was not helping with domestic duties. It was close to harvesttime, and Kumar was expected to help get the equipment ready. She repeatedly complained to her husband, who nodded and smiled. She became irate when Shanti spent time combing her long black hair and dressing up in beautiful saris. Occasionally, Shanti refused to wear her head cover and disrespectfully walked about allowing her hair to blow in the wind. His father could understand why their son was so preoccupied with that girl. She was tall and slim and had a million-dollar smile. She was polite and charming and used her social graces to charm all the men in the family, especially her father-in-law. He was pleased that his son was fortunate enough to have such a graceful creature for a wife, and he watched them being in love. He explained to his wife that they would soon learn to behave better and that they would start performing their respective duties in time. That did not happen, and day by day, the mother-in-law's dislike for that "lazy" girl increased exponentially. She hated Shanti.

The mother-in-law was a controlling woman, and her other daughters-in-law were somewhat afraid of her. Those women accepted their assigned duties and performed them to the best of their abilities. They did not want to, or could not, offend the matriarch. So, when the new bride arrived, she tried to dominate her too, expecting the standard submissive behavior. That did not happen. Her biggest fear was that Shanti's behavior would influence the other women in and around their household. That was a direct challenge to her position of power as the resident queen bee. She got even angrier when her husband refused to reprimand their son for such inexcusable behavior.

Shortly after the wedding, Kumar's father mysteriously died of a massive heart attack. It was a hot day, and he was working outside, getting harvest equipment ready. The children saw him fall and called for help. But when help arrived, he was dead.

After the cremation, their land was shared between Kumar and his brothers. His share was less than an acre. They were soon notified by the oldest brother that the house belonged to him, being the oldest son, and the rest would be paid proportionately for the years of service that they had provided to the family's farming operation. That meant that the young man was given a small amount of money plus his small parcel of land. They were told that they must find their own way within a reasonable time frame. There was no further reasoning. His mother finally had the chance to oust that girl from the premises. There was no negotiation. The decision was made. The oldest brother and wife would keep the home site and would care for the mother. The rest had to go in search of their own fortunes. So, with some personal belongings and the small sum paid to them by the older brother, it was time for them to move on.

Youth, arrogance, and inexperience advised the young couple to sell their share of the land and leave that neighborhood. They did exactly that and went off to join the thousands of homeless, some of whom had suffered similar fates.

Reality soon became their constant companion. It did not take them long to spend all the money that they had received from the sale of his share of land and his small inheritance. He could not find a job, and life on the street was dangerous, especially for his young and pretty wife. So like the prodigal son, they returned to their old neighborhood. Inasmuch as his mother was happy to see him, she had nothing to offer especially to her. His brother was angry that they had returned, for he could hardly afford to pay the high taxes and was at the verge of eviction. Some of his brothers had secured work with the local landlords, trying to put food on the table for their respective families.

He first walked to his father's grave and, on his knees, poured his grief out through tears and sniffles. Then hand in hand, he and his bride walked down the familiar trail to her father's house. The situation there was no better. His mother-in-law fed them, and then they were emphatically told not make a habit of showing up there for food. They were told that they must find work and a place to live. They could spend the night, but they had to move on the next day. They did, without breakfast.

What that young couple did during their interim survival period is not known, but during their search for employment and food, they were recruited by some strangers to go to some foreign land and make a lot of money sifting sugar. They were promised food in the transitional waiting period and a place to stay until the ship was ready to sail. With hungry bellies and no place to go, the promise of food and shelter was the best offer that they had received in a long time. They agreed to follow the recruiters on a long journey. They were fed several good meals and were given nice clothes to wear. And when the travel was over, to the depot, they were taken.

It was a good find for the recruiters. They were probably paid a bonus for finding a young woman who was so willing to go. The year was about 1877. During that period, the laws continued to make it mandatory for the ships to have a minimum percentage of female recruits. Although the system was still corrupt, now there were enough audits to ensure that there was no blatant abuse of the process compared to earlier voyages like the one that Radha and her family took. By that time, there were enough sympathetic individuals and organizations that investigated the system and made sure that such quotas of women were legally and ethically met. At least that was what was reported. Getting a female like Shanti was a real find, and the depot agent must have been very happy to have them.

They found comfort at the depot. Among the crowd, there were other young couples who were also in waiting for departure. Some of them had suffered similar fates as the newlyweds did. They had food, water, and newly developed friendships; and as the days passed, the group started to entertain themselves by playing games, acting, singing, and being comedians. So, in the midst of that misery, there were some temporary joys. They must have figured that reality was not far away. They could see things that did not seem quite right. The authorities and police were always on guard, and they showed no mercy if anyone did not abide by their made-up rules. Such reprimands to offenders did scare them and encouraged them to be on their best behaviors. Shanti was especially concerned because the men, at all levels, stared at her as she moved about. Somewhat scared, she always stayed close to her husband and other couples.

For volunteers like that young couple, the process was simple. They were willing to go to wherever, and they cooperated fully with the depot authorities. They were given physical exams by the doctors on hand and met with the immigration personnel. They were happy to leave poverty in India in search of a better life and were willing to go to the end of the world to seek out their fortunes. They wanted a whole new life. They were told of the travel plans. They were to go across the water, which was referred to as *kala panni*, or black water, serve their contracted years bound to a sugar estate, and return to India wealthy. They were fully convinced that upon their return, they would return to their village. With the money they acquired overseas, they would buy a significant amount of land and help both their families to escape poverty. They would become a family again with money to afford the finer things in life. So, they were told by the recruiters.

Then one morning, it was time to depart. They were going to a colony called British Guiana. That place could have been anyplace. They were both illiterate and ignorant of landmasses on the globe. They watched and listened as some celebrated while others protested. It was, as usual, utter confusion as the police and immigration personnel occasionally used physical force to control the crowds. The ship sat silently in the harbor as the recruits, with their tin tag identification numbers dangling from their necks, shuffled forward.

With each small step, they bustled forward in organized confusion. It was shocking when they saw the authorities using clubs and hitting anyone who refused to embark on the ship. But obeying orders meant no disciplinary action.

The people were eventually escorted into the ship. It was a terrifying moment for some because they had never been on a boat before. As it was customary, the human cargo was sent down to the lower level, where they were separated into categories. Then the hatches were closed as the ship slowly drifted from the harbor, more than likely from the Kidderpur area. The rocking motion started in the Bay of Bengal as the waves increased in intensity, resulting in varying degrees of seasickness from the human cargo. That ship was on its long journey to a port in British Guiana, once again bringing several hundred Indian indentured servants to work on sugar plantations. Those people had no idea that they were going to the opposite side of the globe. They were told that they were going to Demerara, and like other Indians, they called the place Demra.

The sails were adjusted, and the vessel headed westward. It was frightening as the sun began to set and their quarters became darker and darker. They were traveling in the direction of the African coast. Lumbering and bobbing, the small vessel had endured that journey several times before. Same ship, different passengers. The experienced crew must have seen the usual behavior from the passengers as they evaluated the female recruits and planned their usual tricks for gaining sexual favors from selected ones. To that new group of people, it was shocking to witness when someone died or committed suicide by jumping overboard. There was the usual tension between the Muslim and Hindu passengers. But those minor details were nothing compared to what was waiting for them in Demerara.

The young couple were model passengers. Apart from the initial seasickness, they were enthusiastic about the journey. It was always very sad for Shanti when one of the passengers died, for she was a sympathetic and trusting person. The rough seas, the depressed atmosphere, the occasional ocean burials, the poor diet, and the long journey into and across kala panni lowered their enthusiasm, but they endured the hardships and the distress associated with their voyage. They managed the journey quite well overall and maintained some enthusiasm with the hope and expectation of finding a better life and growing wealthy.

The somewhat innocent Shanti soon found out the motives of the ship's crew. Day by day, they secretly contemplated on who would be the lucky man to gain her favor. They ignored the fact that she had a husband. From experience, they preyed upon and attacked women, especially at nights. They pretended to be her friend and tried to lure her away from her husband. They promised her snacks like biscuits and sugar and other delicacies available to them. Then they would try to get her alone in some remote parts of the ship. The ship's doctor tried especially hard because he had his private area. Nothing worked for them. When they made inappropriate advances, she screamed and yelled and ran to her husband. Then one night, as she and some other women were returning from a nature call, they were attacked be two men. The men hid in a dark corner and waited for them the go past. In an instant, the trained men grabbed them. With handkerchiefs, they covered their mouths and dragged them toward a storage room. The other woman was quite strong and managed to pull the mouth covering away. She bit the man's hand as hard as she could, screaming desperately. The injured man ran away, and the women started beating on the one who held Shanti. Because of the commotion that erupted among the women, both hustled away. By the time the saddar and others arrived, those men were out of sight. They lodged their complaints, but no corrective actions were taken. She was learning a very hard lesson.

Kumar had warned her several times about the intent of those men, but she loved the candy and other snacks, for she was always hungry. At first, she thought that they were nice people sharing their good-tasting snacks with her, but things got very disgusting as she recognized the men's desperation and lack of honor, dignity, and decency. He again and again told her to stay close to him, and after the incident that night, he became very irate and yelled at her. With the commotion and his yelling, she took the fetal position and cried.

He had never seen her in that state before. He quietly walked over and wrapped his arms around her. Effortlessly, her arms were squeezing his body, and for several minutes, the two lovers consoled each other with their arms and their tears. He told her that he was sorry, and she promised to be more careful.

The next morning, the two hooligans went about their business as if nothing had happened. It was obvious that one of them had an injured hand, as it was wrapped in cotton. For the rest of the journey, Kumar and Shanti stayed close to each other. He told her that their only crime was poverty, and they intended to correct that when they returned to India with lots of money earned by sifting sugar. As they spoke, the ship continued its westward direction. For many weeks, the passengers anxiously watched and waited for their port of destination.

And then one day, they arrived at the colony called British Guiana and disembarked at the so-called port of Demra. They were deloused, cleaned up, and went through the standard and customary immigration process. Shanti and Kumar were sent to work at the Ruimveldt Estate.

Their logie was a sorry excuse for living quarters. There were foul odors, bad sanitation, drunken neighbors, abusive overseers and drivers, excess work, poor food, and exhaustion. Those were things common to all the immigrants. Some tried to escape, but they were always captured and severely punished. Some were whipped. It did not take very long for the estate men in positions of power to notice the new, young beauty who had arrived. To them, she was estate property to be used and abused at their discretion. To them, she was chattel. And soon, those men with "authority" began contemplating their usual shenanigans and planning how to get into bed with the young female arrival.

The planters were powerful, and they controlled just about everything. Many of the drivers and overseers were of the same mentality as those who worked and abused the Negro slaves. Now the newly arriving poor Indian women found it impossible to fight with such evil and expect to win. Many cooperated with the abuse simply because it became obvious that retaliating only resulted in brutal rapes followed by physical and verbal abuse in the cane fields. When the indentured servants arrived from different parts of the globe replacing the slaves, the men in power must have assumed that nothing had changed regarding their advances to the new arriving women.

The new girl quickly found out what their ulterior motives were. It was just as bad as and even worse than on the ship because of the vast landmass and many fields sheltered by tall sugarcane plants. After rejecting their advances, Shanti was treated very badly and was assigned very difficult tasks on a daily basis. The taunts from the overseers on horseback and drivers were intolerable. Their verbal abuses, coupled with hard field labor in the cane plantations, drove her into mental anguish and physical exhaustion. She became depressed. Tears did not solve anything, and her helpless husband had very little to offer except his loving arms and tired shoulders for her to cry on. Such sentiments were common to all the women but were especially tough on the attractive ones. So when time permitted, some of those women banded together in a sisterly support group and consoled one another with the hope that the time would pass and that they would be liberated from such hardship and be allowed to live a free life again. It was a classic case again of misery loving company.

There were still some Negro women around who told them about their own hardships during the days of slavery. They had some language barriers, but with limited words and body signals, they managed to get the messages conveyed to one another. The immigrant women and men had to learn basic English at a rapid pace. Although the new arrivals were not liked by the Negro population, a few of those liberated slave women and their descendants, mostly house servants, took pity on some of the new female indentured arrivals and carefully did what they could to comfort them. They all shared their miseries, and one day at a time, the young couple managed to survive the misery that was bestowed upon them. She contemplated giving in to those men who so desperately wanted her. She was told that letting those men have their way with her would help her with lighter field duties. Many of those women also had to wrestle with such emotional conflicts. Lower their bloomers or be punished!

By refusing the male advances, she was given very difficult tasks on a daily basis by one mean and demanding overseer. That man assigned the work schedule. He saw her as the current challenge and bragged that, in time, he would break her. She was given a cutlass and was ordered to weed the edges of the irrigation canals. She had to cut the water grasses that grew outward from the dams and spread into the waterways. Such waterlogged pieces were quite heavy, but no help was given. She had never learned how to swim. Alligators lived in those canals. She was petrified when one of those reptiles emerged from the waters. Hazard or no hazard, she had to finish her task for the day. She ate her lunch in wet clothes. Then in the evening, she walked home in her clothes, dripping and leaving a trail behind. She walked with her cutlass and lunch pail in hand and hurried home to help gather wood and get supper ready before darkness arrived.

She and her husband had to get out of bed before dawn to get the day's meals ready. Then she had to get her assignment from that tyrannical overseer. She was always exhausted. Her long black hair no longer got combed, and there was no new sari to dress with. She simply plodded along in her wet, dirty rags. Her husband was quite helpful, for his abuse by the overseer was only verbal, but he knew what that evil man was capable of. He worked extra hard in order to get back to the logie to gather the wood before she got there. They were still very much in love, and he tried extremely hard to bring comfort to her in that toxic environment.

Sometimes the overseer had her transport heavy fertilizer sacks. Sometimes he made her fetch bundles of cane on her head. Whatever difficult tasks existed; she was assigned to them. To the overseer, she was a challenge. He knew that, sooner or later, she would meet her breaking point, the same as his other victims, and let him have his way. She did not.

Two years after their arrival, she found out that she was pregnant. The bittersweet news did not change anything, for the next morning, duty called in the sugarcane fields. She once again marched down the now familiar trail, got her assignment, and continued the routine tasks. Day by day, the routine continued as her tummy grew. She found it hard to carry the heavy loads required of her, but the overseer had little sympathy. In fact, he was very angry to find out that she was pregnant. His solution was to work her harder, still hoping that she would miscarry. Most women, especially in her condition, were given lighter tasks like weeding on higher grounds, but the authorities used some of the "respectable" women as examples for being uncooperative to their demands. Such women were given harder tasks, and their work was judged harshly. Unsatisfactory work resulted in a dockage in pay, and because women generally earned less than men, their earnings were significantly less. Shanti kept on doing her assigned hard field labor.

One hot and humid day, she collapsed and was taken to the doctor's office. She explained to the doctor that she did not get much to eat that day on account that she was not well and did not cook that morning. She was hospitalized (in the so-called sick house) and given some basic nourishment, for they recognized that she was severely malnourished. It was in the hospital that she met a Portuguese woman. Her ancestors had emigrated from Madera as indentured servants. The woman took pity on that pregnant girl and started to help nourish her back to health.

Things went well for a short while, but as soon as she was perceived as being capable, she was ordered back to the field. Her new friend protested, but was unsuccessful. The overseer only laughed and informed her that the time in the hospital would only extend her time bound to the estate, because she must fulfill the full term of indentureship. They also informed her that because she sometimes did not finish her daily task work satisfactorily, her time at the estate could continue indefinitely. So day by day, she did her duties, trying to be careful not to affect the pregnancy.

It happened that one day her Portuguese friend, wondering about her, came for a visit. Seeing her in the field carrying a heavy sack of fertilizer, the woman became irate because that was against company rules. She marched over to the overseer and demanded that the pregnant girl be treated in a more humane manner. The arrogant overseer laughed and told her to go back where she came from and leave the field work and the assignments to him. She tried confronting him some more, but he aggressively spurred the horse and attempted to run her over. She narrowly escaped and marched back toward the hospital, mumbling profanity. The infuriated overseer saw Kumar and spurred his horse toward him. He narrowly escaped by diving into the irrigation canal and hid in the outward-reaching grass.

The irate Portuguese woman could not sleep that night. She knew about that overseer's reckless behavior and lack of respect for women. She had previously complained to management about such ruthless behavior, but disciplinary actions were never taken. The next morning, she filed another complaint and pleaded with management to take some action toward that pompous man. That afternoon, she came back with some other influential company personnel and showed them the abuse of that poor pregnant girl. It took some time for them to find the overseer, for when he saw the group marching toward him, he cowardly spurred his white horse and galloped away. When they finally caught up with him, he and his arrogance defended his decisions and told the group that he could decide who did what on any day. He was severely reprimanded by the visitors and warned that if he was caught abusing privileges and violating policies again, he would be demoted and transferred away from that establishment. That infuriated him, and later that day, he swore to his peers that he would handle things his way and show those lowly creatures what could happen to those who crossed him.

With the help of that woman, the pregnant girl was finally assigned to light duty work and was further given extra rations that would nourish her properly. Then one night in 1880, the midwife was called into the logie, and a healthy baby boy was delivered. They named him Lalla for short, seeing that his real name, given by the pundit, was Shamlal.

That couple had two children, the son, Lalla, and a daughter. They were still bound to the Ruimveldt estate when Kumar died. His body was found in a shallow creek. He was murdered. Speculation was that the jealous overseer figured that by removing Kumar, the desperate and lonely Shanti would have to come to him, and he would finally win the challenge. After all, in his opinion, he was just a lowly indentured servant whose life meant nothing. He wanted the man's wife, and that apparently would not happen as long as she had her husband. So, he decided to remove the obstacle. Another ship would bring his replacement from India.

There was no grave marker. Just another unmarked hole in the ground. Shanti watched as the shovels of dirt covered him. She placed wildflowers on the grave site, took her children by their hands, and walking toward the logie, blamed herself for his death. If she had cooperated with the overseer, that would not have happened. She convinced herself that his tragic death was a result of her stubbornness. And another ship brought his replacement from India. And the process continued one shipload after another.

She never recovered. She refused to go back to the cane fields. Her Portuguese friend continued visiting her and convinced the estate manager to give her basic supplies to feed the three of them. She became totally depressed and constantly told anyone who would listen that she had caused her husband's death. She sometimes did not cook, but Lalla was almost ten years old and was forced to assume responsibilities for the family. Neighbors helped, and the Portuguese woman visited often. Shanti did not eat much and was reduced to a mere skeleton covered by skin, with sunken eyes that cried a lot. She hallucinated and claimed that she was in the company of her husband. She quietly talked about Kumar and how much they loved each other. She told her children stories about India and the extreme situations that forced them to travel overseas in search of a better life. She stayed in bed for an extended period of time while the children brushed the flies off her face and cleaned up her messes. Insanity had consumed her.

She died one night in 1890, just her and her dignity, which she never compromised. The children found her the next morning on the floor. Another grave was dug, and the once beautiful girl now not quite thirty years old was lowered into a hole close to Kumar as the pundit performed his rituals. The sobbing children, with the help of the Portuguese woman, placed flowers on the mound that covered her as the crowd dissipated to face their own challenges. And another ship brought her replacement among the hundreds of excited newcomers to the Ruimveldt Plantation. That process continued without Kumar and Shanti.

They came from India, around the southern tip of Africa, toward the New World. Their assignments were to ensure the profitability of the sugar industry. Many died while still in their tender years. That young couple who died so tragically was one more statistic during those years of coolie indenture from India. But nobody maintained such statistics. They came to sift sugar and return home wealthy. Instead, misery consumed them.

The children were left at the Ruimveldt Plantation's orphanage. The Portuguese woman kept an eye on them. They suffered the usual treatment many orphans endured, but overall, they were treated well. Then one day, a man and his wife came looking for a boy to adopt. His name was Bhagwat Singh, and his wife's name was Gulabia Singh. They had no children. They had served their time on the sugar plantation and decided to remain in the colony. They traded their return passage for a plot of land in Berbice and became rice farmers. He was getting old and wanted a boy to help with his farming. Lalla was the chosen boy, but he refused to go because he would not leave his little sister behind. He was her protector. She was all that he had. They were inseparable. He made it clear that he could not and would not leave without her.

It was Bhagwat's wife, Gulabia, who sympathized with the pleading boy and spoke up. She could see the pain in the children's eyes. She understood their need to stay together. Her husband tried to explain that with their limited resources, they could not afford to have two children. After some long discussions, she convinced him that separating the children would be wrong. Eventually the couple agreed to adopt the two children. The Portuguese woman hugged them, and with tearful eyes, she departed. After the legal process and packing their few personal items, they took Lalla and his little sister to their farm. They lived in Number 64 Village on the Corentyne Coast. It was the first time the children had a home, and they were happy to be together.

It did not take the children long to adapt to their new home. Gulabia now had a daughter to pamper and raise. Lalla proved to be a workhorse. He soon discovered the Number 63 Beach, and whenever time permitted, he hurried toward the waters, where he swam with the waves and played on the sandy beach. He did not mind the hard farmwork because compared to the tragedies that he had witnessed at the plantation and the bullies at the orphanage, life with his new family was a joy. Like most adopted children, they found that their lives became rich and full, and they served the Singh family very well.

When he was a teenager, he went to visit the plantation where he was born. He went to the hospital inquiring and found the Portuguese woman who had helped his mother so much. He called her Auntie. She was delighted to see him, and after some special treats and a cold beverage, they went to visit his parents' grave site. They picked wildflowers and placed them on the graves. And though he was only sixteen, she told him about his parents' tragedies and his father's murder. Through her tears, she talked about his mother's dignity, which consumed them. He needed to know, she figured. She paused, dried her eyes, and walked back toward her quarters close to the hospital. He followed. They said their goodbyes, she hugged him, and they went their separate ways. He never saw her again. But he remembered her kindness. In years to come, he continued to refer to his auntie as the angel who comforted his mother during her darkest days.

When he returned to Number 64 Village, Mr. Singh took him to the justice of the peace and drafted a deed leaving his humble holdings to Lalla. He never left that home. It was his home for life.

CHAPTER 7

The Others

There were about 240,000 East Indian indentured servants shipped to British Guiana (now Guyana). Further information on the family tree documented two additional individuals who need mentioning.

One individual was a man named Kangal. He came from India to Guyana in 1879 on a ship called *North*. He was twenty years old and was five feet five inches tall. His father's name was Jewooth, and he had a brother named Juddo. He originated from a district (Zillah) listed as Jhazeepore and from a village called Kunda. The *North* sailed with Kangal from an address of 8 Garden Reach, Calcutta, and he was assigned to and settled at the sugar plantation in Port Mourant, British Guiana. He had a long scar down his lower back.

The other was a woman named Ramkulia. She was the twenty-five-year-old daughter of a man in India named Bohore, who lived in the village of Leoolahipore, located in Banaras. She was four feet, seven inches tall. She was accompanied by a daughter. This woman's immigration documents were issued on February 26, 1881, at 8 Garden Reach, Calcutta. She and her daughter departed Calcutta, India, on a ship called *New Castle* to the British colony of British Guiana. She was assigned to and settled at the Port Mourant Estate.

The woman Ramkulia was referred to by the name of Kalya, and she had an abusive husband in Banaras (Varanasi) in the Moghul Sarai area. He was a Muslim man who inherited substantial wealth from his family and did not have to work. He had several wives scatted in various neighborhoods. When convenient, he visited their respective places of residence. The women lived in small shacks, and the visiting man paid their meager living expenses and, in return, expected to be treated like their king. Opium and alcohol were his favorite things. When under the influence, he went to one of the women's quarters and expected to be fed, and they were expected to satisfy all his various needs.

In his constant state of intoxication, he did not even smile. He demanded his requests, and if they were not met in an instant, he became violent. The women understood his temperament, and upon his arrival, they stood to attention and delivered whatever his demands were. They were in constant fear of him and tolerated his abuse with no direct objections.

Kalya came from a very poor family. Not successful in securing a husband, she tried earning a living on the streets doing what she had to do. She was eighteen years old when she met the abusive man. He was rather kind to her and offered to "take" her. He promised her a place to live and food. He explained that he was usually traveling for the family business and needed a stable home when in town. It was the best offer she was ever given, and she agreed to move into the little shack that he provided. It was not much, but it was better than life on the streets. Because of his perceived kindness, she treated him with the utmost respect and fed him whatever his requests were on any day.

Within a short time, she was pregnant, and in 1874, she delivered a healthy baby girl. That baby became her pride and joy, and while the man was out, quite often, she fed the baby, sang, and rocked her to sleep. As the baby grew, they took long walks and drooled over the beautiful garments on display at the markets. One day, when the man visited, she asked him for some money to buy their daughter a dress. He frowned, muttered some unkind words, pushed her out of the way, and walked out. Later that day, he returned with some cotton, a pair of scissors, needles, and thread. He tossed everything on the floor and walked out. She managed to make a crude long garment that she wrapped around her daughter. There was no undergarment.

Every passing year brought increased amounts of abuse. He beat her sometimes for not having his meals ready on time. He slapped her, kicked her, dragged her about by her unruly hair, and did all sorts of mean things to her. Her daughter saw the violence and cried along with her mother, but they had no place to go. Eventually, she figured out that he had other women under his control. They all had his children, and he was an equal-opportunity abuser. It got to a point where she could not tolerate his increased consumption of drugs and alcohol. Her body constantly was in pain from the repeated beating. She figured that being on the streets again was an option. Her daughter was now five, and she encouraged Kalya to run away.

She tried to escape from the situation. But in that environment, a single woman with a child had very few options. Finding another husband was almost impossible for most women in her situation. But in Kalya's case, it would have been impossible. She was a skinny, short, unattractive woman with a pockmarked face. Most men probably would not look at her, much less marry her. So when the arkathies approached her to join the *New Castle* and go away to a place where she would get paid to sift sugar, she did not hesitate to join. She and her six-year-old daughter packed up a few personal items in a home-sewn cotton bag, and while the drunken husband slept, they made their escape. She was unaware that the *New Castle* was in desperate need to fill the stipulated quota of women for the voyage. To her, it was a new start for her and her daughter.

She explained their situation to the recruiting men and asked them to hurry up the process. If her so-called husband found out, he would object to the trip, and they would be severely punished for attempting such desertion. The men understood. They needed women to fill the ship's quota. So as she requested, they hurried the process. She and her daughter were given baths, clean clothes, and food. One of the men accompanied them on public transportation to the depot. They had never been on such a wagon before. It was like going on vacation. Most of all, they were free. They managed to escape from the abuser. They proudly walked into the depot, smiling and celebrating their newfound freedom.

They proudly went through the process required for all indentured servants. When asked about her husband, Kalya told the authorities that he was killed in an accident, and because she could not earn a living as a single mother in that area, she decided to take her daughter to a new place to sift sugar and earn money. That was what the recruiters told her to say, and she repeated their words. Then on February 26, 1881, mother and daughter boarded the *New Castle* and sailed away from India.

Apart from the usual seasickness, they survived the journey quite well. They were fed well at the depot and relished any food served on the *New Castle*. Compared to the miseries and partial starvation that they left behind; the trip was a welcomed relief. It was always difficult to see the ocean burials and occasional suicides, but they were accustomed to seeing people dying in their neighborhood. The six-year-old wandered about scavenging for food, and the sardars on board were impressed by her innocent enthusiasm and gave her plenty to eat. Kalya roamed about too. With her appearance, most men ignored her and focused on the more attractive women. Kalya, being the scrappy fighter, became the protecting sister to some of those women; and some of the men were intimidated by her aggressive behavior and her apparent meanness. People did not mess with her. So, at night when the group of women went for nature calls, Kalya was asked to accompany them. She became their bodyguard. Thus, she became popular on the ship and made many new friends. To a certain degree, she made the voyage somewhat joyful for the other passengers, and at nights with crude Indian instruments, she sang. She had a beautiful voice and was always encouraged to sing when boredom consumed her Jahajees.

They were at sea for some one hundred days. When the announcement was made that they were finally approaching their destination, Kalya held her daughter and prayed for the opportunity to have escaped from her tyrannical husband and safely reached her new home. It would be a new beginning for them, and through her prayers in her emotional state, her daughter saw her crying tears of joy. When she opened her eyes, she saw all her newly acquired girlfriends waiting to thank her. They thanked her for being there for them, to entertain them, and most of all, to protect them. Then they disembarked from the *New Castle* and were marched to the immigration quarters with their tin tags dangling from their necks. She hugged her new friends. They prayed for one another. They all looked about with astonished eyes and walked with uncoordinated sea legs. Then they were taken to their respective plantations to replace the sick and dead indentured servants.

Both mother and young daughter were assigned to work in the sugarcane fields at Port Mourant Estate. They lived in a logie with another single mother and two children. It was a fairly good life for them because they were used to hard work and could tolerate abuse. She soon planted a garden and collected her wages from the estate. A better diet of fresh fruits and vegetables, split peas and rice, and an occasional fish nourished her to better health. Soon she was gaining weight, and her face partially cleared up. She most likely would not have participated in a beauty contest, but her appearance improved significantly, and to her surprise, men started to notice her as being available. Of course, in that environment, with the acute shortage of East Indian women, the theory of supply and demand prevailed.

*   *   *

In the village of Kunda in Jhazeepore, India, lived the Jewooth family. The year was 1840. Jewooth left his family farm and moved to Kunda to work. With the British East India Company prospering, there was a demand for construction and transportation equipment. The young Jewooth found work building wagon wheels. The company he worked for specialized in making various types of horse-drawn wagons. They made crude wagons of all sorts. Some were for hauling heavy loads, and some were fancy chariots for transporting the British and the wealthy Indians. It did not matter to Jewooth who purchased the wagons. His team carved the logs and built the various components for the wheels. Jewooth mostly worked on the spokes and ensured that his product met the specifications for the corresponding wheels.

Within a year, he had saved enough money to return to the family farm and marry his childhood sweetheart. It was a grand, yet simple wedding. The pundit did the ceremony and the usual rituals that blessed the couple. With the formality over, the friends and neighbors celebrated. They played instruments, sang, and danced, and a lovely time was had by all. He stayed at the farm with his wife at his parents' house, and after one month, he and his wife went back to Kunda and rented a small apartment close to the business where he worked.

Every day after work, he carried home a bundle of rejected wood on his head. His wife patiently awaited his arrival. She greeted him with cold water from the clay goblet and watched him swallow every drop. Then she hugged him and carried some of the wood to their cooking station, built a fire, and cooked their supper. In the mornings, she built another fire before sunrise and made their breakfast. Then she packed his lunch and some snacks in a crude lunch pail. She filled a bottle with some sweetened tea, and with a string, it was hung around his neck. As he walked away to work, she watched him with lunch pail in hand and bottle dangling from his neck. It was a short walk, and she went about her housework and waiting for his evening return with his bundle of wood on his head, lunch pail in hand, and empty bottle dangling from his neck.

They had a good life. They built a nice home and raised five children, three girls and two boys. Occasionally, people would abandon their old wagons and replace them with a new one. Jewooth got two such broken-down wagons, and during the evening hours, he repaired them one piece at a time. Then he decorated the finished products with colorful paint. Later, with his savings, he purchased a team of horses and got into the transportation business. He hauled materials for a fee and earned a good income to raise his family.

His older son, Juddo, went along with his father during those hauling trips. He was very helpful with light duties and took care of the team of horses as his father handled the business. And as time went on, Jewooth retired and handed the business to his two sons. While the boys did the hauling, he stayed close to home, repairing and selling rebuilt wagons. His wife loved having him home, and during the day, when they wanted a break, they leisurely walked about the fruit trees that she had planted many years earlier. They enjoyed the fresh fruits together. Business was good for the boys. Customers came regularly with requests for hauling various materials and supplies.

Some years later, when Kangal (the younger son) was fifteen years old, Jewooth and his wife passed away. They both died the same year. His three sisters were married and had moved away. He and Juddo continued the hauling business. When he was seventeen, his brother married and brought his wife home. At first, Kangal was excited to have a woman in the house because she would cook for them and handle the home front while they were out hauling supplies for people. He called her Bhowji (meaning sister-in-law). But Kangal soon realized that he was an intrusion to the new couple's privacy. Bhowji did not want to cater to him, and he drifted farther and farther away from his older brother.

Things got complicated when Bhowji had a baby and did not have time to do anything for the young Kangal. He became a stranger in his father's house. Juddo tried to maintain some peace in the family, but his wife became more adamant about wanting to take care of her family and started to treat Kangal as an outcast. She continued complaining about his habits and disrespect for her. Juddo, being a fair man, offered Kangal money to buy his part of the business. At least his brother would have a sizable down payment for any future endeavors.

Kangal, frustrated with the tension at home, agreed to his inheritance and moved away to find employment elsewhere. With his experience, it did not take long to find work in the hauling business. He started driving and hauling for a man who had several teams and wagons and welcomed Kangal as an employee. He did the driving and hauling and occasionally saw his brother on the street with his team doing what they were trained to do. His plan was to save his money and someday buy his own horse and wagon and get into business for himself. From his savings and from his inheritance, he would buy a house and the team and manage his own business like his father did. As his horses plodded along, he dreamed about the future.

Kangal turned nineteen, and his plans were on schedule. His boss liked him and occasionally had him travel about and collect money owed to the company. He liked doing that job because it was easy work compared to lifting and carrying various supplies from and to the wagon. He could leisurely go about and collect money. He could stop at roadside stands and enjoy delicacies and tasty beverages.

During one of those money-collecting days, he went to a customer who owed his boss a large sum of money. The man made no attempt to make the scheduled payments, which became delinquent. Kangal had been there a few times only to be rejected and leave without the payments. The delinquent customer told him that he would soon collect money from his customers and pay his bill in full. One morning, Kangal again made the usual stop at that delinquent customers. He was told to come back later, and he would receive the full payment. Excited to hear such news, he went about doing other collections and browsed the market buying and eating various homemade candies. He returned later and waited for the money. The customer finally came and apologized for being late. He paid in full, and Kangal walked away with his money and money from other customers that he had collected during the day. He was carrying a fairly large sum. He noticed two men following him when he left the customer's premises, but it was a place of business where people entered and exited constantly. Kangal paid little attention to them and continued walking. It was late. He realized that the sun would set in about an hour. He was tempted to get food but decided to deliver the money before darkness arrived. He did not eat.

The two men kept following him. They were walking at a faster pace, and he could hear them talking. Eventually, he turned onto a quiet street toward his employer's business. There was nobody on that street except the two men who followed him. They grabbed him. One had a knife. There was a struggle. Kangal was stabbed in the back, and the robbers seized the money and ran away. Kangal was in pain. The blood covered the back of his shirt. His screaming attracted some local people, who carried him in a sheet to his boss.

He told his boss what had happened. They removed his shirt and cleaned up the wound. It was not very severe but bad enough. He stayed there for two days with stained bandages around his chest and abdomen. On the third day, his brother came and took him home. Juddo took care of him. Bhowji wanted nothing to do with him or his injury. She totally ignored him and his moaning. Juddo dressed his wounds, fed him, and picked fresh fruits from their mother's orchard; and they spent time together. He stayed there for about three months until his wounds were mostly healed.

He went back to work, but he was still in pain when lifting heavy loads. So, he quit his job, secured his savings, and asked his brother for his inheritance. Then he left the Kunda area in search of a better life. With his money from both sources, he moved about doing various jobs. But his back still hurt, and he lacked the drive and motivation that once pushed him along. Then one day, he encountered some arkathies. They told him the usual story about going overseas to sift sugar. He listened, nodded, and went about his routine.

He lived alone and did various odd jobs. But he found no satisfaction in just surviving. He missed the stable family life at his parents' house. He traveled about and visited his three sisters. They were happy to see him but had lives of their own and mothers-in-law to please. He could not impose upon them. After months of contemplating options about his future, he remembered the man who promised the trip to go and sift sugar for high wages. Such a thought intrigued him as he wondered about such possibilities. It seemed better than roaming the streets as a lonely bachelor. He would like to be married, but being somewhat shy, he did not know any women well enough to propose such a commitment. So, he went looking for the sugar man. He did not find that man, but after weeks of inquiring, he found another individual who was telling the same story and promising the same rewards. They spent many hours discussing the details, and he agreed to continue that discussion at a later date.

After a week, they had another meeting. Kangal was informed that a ship called the *North* would be sailing soon, and if he was willing to make the commitment to go, they needed to hurry up the process that would ensure him a spot on that ship. He agreed. One week later, Kangal was at the depot getting ready to travel to British Guiana. His wound was fully healed, but he wore a long scar down his back that stayed with him for the rest of his life. He did not inform his brother or his sisters. In his habitual quiet way, he sat in the depot awaiting the ship's departure.

One gray and cloudy morning in 1879, Kangal, with some money and plenty of enthusiasm, boarded the *North*. He walked with the other indentured servants onto the dock that was fastened to the *North*, and he stared at the water of the Hooghly River. He was leaving India and going to some unknown land beyond kala panni. He was twenty years old. He was basically illiterate but commonsensically very smart. He was quiet and reclusive, but he was a thinker. He conceptualized and understood things that textbooks cannot teach. His money allowed him to buy favors from the ship's personnel, enabling him to be treated better than most of the passengers on the *North*.

Months later, after disembarking at the port of Demerara, Kangal found himself at the Port Mourant Estate in the County of Berbice in British Guiana. He was assigned to a logie with three other single men. He was given a cutlass, and within a week, he was cutting cane in the tropical heat. He was experienced in being a loner. He learned quickly, did not complain, cooked and ate what was available, and explored the confines of the plantation. He became fascinated with the mules that pulled the punts.

Kangal noticed that the drivers of the mules that pulled the punts were not very coordinated with the animals, so he made suggestions to the overseer about teaching them better driving skills. He explained that as long as he could remember, his family drove animals pulling heavy loads. One day, when one of the drivers failed to report to work, the overseer asked Kangal to drive the idle team. That was great news to him, and after some minor adjustments and securing the proper commands, he started driving the mules that pulled the punts that delivered the cane to the factory. That afternoon, the overseer watched as Kangal put his skills to work, and the team seemed to pull the load with significantly less effort. Within a few days and under lots of observation, Kangal officially became a team driver, delivering cane to the factory. The workers cut the cane with their cutlasses and loaded the small bundles into the punts. The job was called cut and load. The workers were called cane cutters.

It was easy and fun work for Kangal. He sat on the seat and watched the cane cutters load the cane into the punt. He liked to swim, and while the loading happened, he swam in the irrigation canals along where the punts were pulled. Swimming in the tropical heat was very refreshing. So after his shift of driving, the mules were unhitched. He allowed them to graze for a while and then retired them for a long rest. He had plenty of time and was never tired. He refused to drink alcohol, so he generally requested a pass and walked about outside the fenced-in area. The overseer knew that he was a good man who enjoyed his job and did not worry about him trying to escape. So, he got passes whenever he wanted one.

During his evening walkabouts in the compound, he saw many people cultivating their gardens and picking vegetables for their supper. He always saw a skinny short woman with a little girl by her side. They had a weedy garden, and she always tried desperately to pull the weeds. She always seemed to be trying too hard, and her body language seemed typical of a frustrated individual. One evening, he decided to approach her. He did so cautiously. She saw him coming but assumed that he was one of those who wanted to gain favor for sex. She ignored him. He quietly walked over, pulled some weeds, and walked away. The little girl stared at him. She was eight years old and almost as tall as her mother. He said a parting greeting to her and left. She did not answer him.

The next day and the day after, Kangal went to the garden, pulled some weeds, and left. Nobody spoke. On the fourth day, Kangal got a pass and went out walking. The woman and her daughter kept watching out for him, but he did not show up. Another day went by, and the woman became curious about his absence. She asked some women about him and was told that he drove mules for the estate. At least she knew what he did.

A week later, Kangal returned to the woman's vegetable garden. He did not speak but resumed pulling her weeds. The little girl came over and asked why he was there. He told her that he hated weeds, and her mother had too many. The woman started to laugh. She came over and introduced herself as Kalya. He told her his name, and within a short time, they figured out that they came from the same part of India.

She invited him to supper and showed him the vegetables that she had harvested for that evening's meal. He accepted under one circumstance: that he did the cooking. He cooked as she and her daughter cleaned up, and together, they had a wonderful supper. Kangal departed, and Kalya was overjoyed. She had never had a man cook for her before. All the men in her life so far were mean and useless. She was getting ready for bed and thinking happy thoughts. Her daughter had never seen her smile so much, and Kalya displayed a surprising amount of gentleness as she tucked the child into bed.

They became friends. Kangal forked up a large garden plot, and together, they planted many vegetables. The spent all their spare time hoeing and tilling, and the neighbors noticed that they had an enviable garden with a variety of vegetables and a number of flower plants around the perimeter. Every evening, they cooked together, ate, and enjoyed each other's company.

One Sunday, when there was no work for them at the plantation, Kangal secured a pass for the three, and they went walking. He bought them snacks and sweet treats from street vendors. The little girl devoured all the goodies and skipped about like any eight-year-old should while on vacation. They ate so many things that supper was not necessary that evening. There were no pots or dishes to wash. So they sat under a shade tree and enjoyed the sunset. When the girl wandered some distance away, Kalya asked Kangal the burning question. She asked him why he never tried to kiss her. Kangal smiled and replied that he did not know how, on account that he had never kissed a woman before. She was shocked and surprised at his innocence and his honesty. She laughed and promised to teach him how to do that. They laughed, and she gently kissed him under that tree as the sun slowly sank into the western horizon. With smiling faces, they held hands and slowly walked into the twilight toward their logie.

They got married at the Port Mourant Estate. On their wedding night, during the celebrations, the crude instruments were tuned, and the music started. The elated Kalya sang a love song about her life companion and how blessed she was to have such a wonderful creature who chose to share his life with her. It was a beautiful song that was sung with the utmost sincerity. Kangal admired her angelic voice and enjoyed every word and the melody, and he realized that Kalya was an angel in disguise. They became a lovely couple, respected by all who knew them. They were model immigrant servants to the British plantation. They served the plantation well.

With his money and her savings, they petitioned the estate and bought out of their indentured contracts. They built a small house next to the estate and continued to work there for better wages. Kangal drove the mules, and Kalya did field duties while her daughter did light duty work for minimum wages. She did that until she became pregnant, and after her baby came, she quit working at the estate fields. She continued her gardening, and when there was a Hindu function, she was recruited to sing. People enjoyed listening to her charming voice and her ability to maintain a tune.

Their first child was a son. They named him Jaman, but he was better known as Juman. He was free from plantation work and soon wandered about, blending with other young men of other races, which soon resulted in a local gang. They had a total of four sons and three daughters, including the one that came from India with Kalya on the *New Castle*.

CHAPTER 8

Leaving the Plantations and Moving On

People like Kangal and Kalya and others like Pyroo and Radha, Kumar and Shanti, Lady, Kesha, and Desai had to finish their "bound" to their respective plantations. It was a tough life for most of those people, but some found creative ways to beat the system and enjoyed doing it. Tales were told of so and so who had a network of thieves. They stole from the estates and created a hidden distribution center in the forest interior or at some remote sites. The estate supervisors were usually part of the operation, and all shared in the profits realized from their various shenanigans. The system was that if someone wanted building materials—hardware, nails, or other supplies—that person would contact a middle man and give him the appropriate sum of money mutually agreed upon. The middle man would instruct the customer as to where and when his supplies would be available, and all parties, except the estate, came out as winners.

Justifying such stealing must have been easy. Because of the ill treatment by the estate personnel, the indentured people hated those establishments. Most of the stolen supplies were sold to folks who were no longer bound to the plantations. In that manner, it was difficult to trace the stolen products. Extreme care was taken, for the suppliers only dealt with customers they trusted fully. If a snitch was discovered, the consequences were brutal, and everyone was very much aware of the punishment inflicted on the perceived guilty party and his respective family members.

Pyroo was a whole different story. He was very intelligent; he spoke English and had a British accent that he had mastered in India several years earlier. He was an excellent fighter. But he kept all those things secret, and day by day, he performed his tasks at the sugar plantation and lived his life as a poor untouchable. He was passing time waiting for the political situation in India to improve. Then he and Jahaj would buy out of their contracts and return to India. That accomplished, Pyroo would be hailed as a national hero. Through the black-market process, he acquired some fancy English clothes, boots, and a hat. With his light complexion and British attire bundled with his language skills, he could again have looked, dressed, and spoken like an Englishman to an ignorant observer.

Soon after arriving at the Ruimveldt Estate, he met Lady and her family. He was very impressed with Radha's tenacity and work ethic. She worked very hard to finish her tasks and helped Lady with her work. She was almost twelve years old but worked harder and faster than most adults. Pyroo pitied Kesha. The boy was ten and had a difficult time performing the light duties assigned to him. So, on many days, Radha had to help him too. Occasionally, Pyroo helped Kesha with his assignments and taught him creative ways to perform those chores more efficiently. And as time passed, Pyroo became part of Lady's family.

He usually got his work done earlier than most and had enough time to help Kesha and to browse about. Because of his relationship with some key estate personnel, he frequently requested and was granted passes. His story was that, being a bachelor, he hated cooking for himself. He claimed to prefer food sold at the roadside stands.

After their assignments to the plantations, the two friends missed each other, so they met one Sunday and decided to use some of their money to buy Jahaj's freedom. They did that. As a free man, Jahaj walked about in search of a building to rent in the Ruimveldt area. He could not find what he was looking for so he and Pyroo bought a building in the outskirts of Georgetown using some of their remaining money. The building was modified to their specifications. Part was converted into living quarters for Jahaj. Part was used as a retail store. They used some of the money to acquire a few items for sale. Jahaj became the storekeeper. He also acquired a sewing machine, and during slow business hours, he fulfilled his lifelong dream and did tailoring duties.

Part of the building was sectioned off into a private space. That space was behind Jahaj's living quarters. The door to that section was structured to appear as part of the wall. Most casual observers would not have recognized that it was a doorway. Pyroo hid some personal items, including his British attire, there. Anything that had to be hidden was stored in that room. Only the two men knew about that room.

There was an overseer in Pyroo's group who was very mean and abusive to the people, and every one of the laborers was very frightened of him. He rode a horse and carried a whip, which he took pleasure in using periodically. That overseer made his biggest mistake one day. He was abusive to Radha and attempted to use his whip on her. She was not well that day and was rather lethargic. Pyroo observed the confrontation but said nothing. He had no personal issues with that man and did his usual submissive act. He generally kept his eyes focused on his task and did his assigned duty.

That night, he cleaned up, secured a pass, went to the store, and put on his English attire. He and Jahaj had supper in their private quarters and discussed what he intended to do. Jahaj smiled and quietly ate his supper. After dark, the English-appearing Pyroo boldly walked into the compound and paid a visit to the overseer at his residence. He also put on the face mask that he used during the wrestling sessions in Calcutta. The story is that he gave a sound thrashing to the little wimp and explained in a fine British accent that he would no longer abuse his power and that whenever he saw that Englishman, meaning Pyroo, there would be no questions but a sound thrashing would be appropriate. That incident cured many issues for the indentured population.

With time, Jahaj, with Pyroo's help, got into the black-market business. The estate thieves brought supplies to the store during the nights and were paid minimum amounts in cash. Before long, Jahaj had a system in place for selling various products. Legal things were displayed on the store shelves, and the stolen products were hidden in the private area. Anyone trying to disrupt the process was severely disciplined by the so-called Englishman wearing a face mask. Their unwritten rule was that you played by the rules or paid the consequences.

Their scheme became a lucrative operation. Pyroo kept a low profile, and Jahaj traded both the stolen merchandise and other supplies that were legally acquired. During the days, Pyroo did his estate duties. The frightened overseer never bothered them again, allowing the people more flexibility. He and Jahaj ate well and nourished themselves properly so that he could perform his daily tasks in record time and occasionally visit their hideaway to discuss business. He was always cautious not to be seen entering the store. As far as the buyers were concerned, Jahaj was the man. He was single, and like most young single men, he spent most of his spare time partying and sleeping with rental women. When the deliveries were to be made, Jahaj worked the system. Those two men were a great team in India and continued with the partnership in the colony of British Guiana. If at any time someone tried to disrupt the business in any way, Pyroo would put on his British attire and his British accent and gave the challenger an attitude adjustment. That word was out, and challenges became almost nonexistent.

By 1865, Lady was becoming quite frail. The tough estate life, the varying degrees of physical and sexual abuse, and memories of her luxurious life in India were taking their toll on her weary and broken body. Her shame was worse than her physical injuries. She was not strong enough to resist the powerful attacks from men using brute force on attractive women like her. Like many women at the plantation, she generally closed her eyes, lowered her bloomers in the middle of the sugarcane fields, and took the punishment. She was repeatedly abused by men at the plantation who had the power to commit such heinous acts because they could. Radha knew when such incidences occurred for in the evening, Lady was in a state of disgust and crying angry tears. She was a young girl, but she knew what occurred among the tall cane plants. She even witnessed a few incidents but casually walked away. She had no one to protect her or her mother. Not until Pyroo arrived. After the abuse stopped, day by day, Lady endured the shame and regretted her act and not protecting her children better. She was the victim but continued blaming herself for going to the park in India that brought catastrophe to her family.

One day, Lady approached Pyroo with a request: she wanted to return to India. She had saved her money and wanted to go home and reunite with her family. But first she wanted Pyroo to consider marrying Radha. Pyroo explained to her that at that time he had no intention of going back to India. But after several discussions, they agreed that the wedding would take place and that Radha would stay with Pyroo and her mother would return to India with her son. They agreed that when she got reunited with her family, she would notify them, and he and Radha could join them at some later date. Pyroo agreed to the terms because his desire to free India from the invaders was still a fire burning deep in his stomach.

It was a splendid wedding. The tall, well-built, and fully developed Radha became a fine young lady and made a beautiful bride. She was all dressed up in a borrowed sari. The Indians on the plantation as well as friends who had moved away were in attendance. The wedding announcements were posted at the store that Jahaj kept. They played their instruments, sang, partied, and celebrated the occasion. But the grand finale was what Radha requested from her mother as a wedding present. She wanted her mother to perform a classical Indian dance. So, all the local women lent her what jewelry they could, fitted her in a fine sari, and painted her with the appropriate markings. She again had bells around her ankles.

The musicians began to play. The various drumbeats were deafening. People cheered as Lady walked out and her bells chimed in harmony. She once more looked like Zamy's daughter. At that moment, the adrenalin must have surged to her head, and the burst of energy made her appear to float on the earthen stage. In an instant, she was back into her element of being the dancing girl that she once was. The crowd was in awe as she wiggled, twirled, and twisted like a puppet on countless strings in complete harmony to the sound of the crude instruments. She even made the instruments sound good. It was one of her finest moments as she laughed, clapped her hands, and danced away to the music and to the chiming bells strapped to her ankles. It ended with her twirling as her slim waist wiggled occasionally and her long, braided, now gray hair draped in fresh flowers protruded ninety degrees from her head, circling around, trailing her spinning head like the tail of a comet. Then the music stopped. She bowed and fell to the ground, totally exhausted, as the audience screamed and cheered, and Radha in her borrowed sari rushed to hug her mother with tears of joy. It was a splendid dance by a fine lady and a graceful captive daughter of India.

The return trip to India never happened. Weeks after the wedding, that fine lady became ill. Pyroo acquired a new mosquito netting and some good nourishment, but it was all too late. Her health continued to deteriorate. For months, she walked about the compound visiting neighbors and talking about getting better and making the trip. A year later, she was reduced to a mere skeleton and was fed by Radha in bed with a spoon. She was moved to the sick house, and Pyroo paid the nurses to ensure that she received the best care available. But some weeks later, she died one night in her sleep. She was thirty-nine years old. She endured emotional scars too many to count. Such pain, such shame imposed upon her innocence.

The same crowd that had recently cheered her dancing performance gathered at her funeral and buried her in an unmarked grave some place close to the Ruimveldt Estate. And just like that, she was gone. But her story was remembered by her daughter, Radha, who grieved her mother's passing and celebrated her love for dancing. She wished that regardless of what had happened to them, that Lady could have at least had the chance to see her family again, especially the son she left in India. And on several occasions, the people saw her and Kesha gathering flowers and kneeling at

Lady's grave site, where the dirt was sinking toward her body. They prayed that God would take her soul to India to have a peek at her son and ultimately go to heaven. They figured that she at least deserved that much.

Sometime after the funeral, Pyroo, Radha, and Kesha left the plantation. Jahaj stayed with his newfound life and ran the business, selling merchandise, some of which was stolen from the estate. But he became a shopkeeper or merchant in the Georgetown area, partially financed by funds that he and his partner had acquired over the years and mostly by selling merchandise at the store. He had the opportunity to live his dream of becoming a tailor. In fact, he opened a tailor shop and hired professional tailors and seamstresses to sew fancy clothes, which he sold to wealthy customers. He wore expensive clothes and dated beautiful women. He claimed that he was too busy to get married and did not want a woman to restrict his various activities. He was having fun living his dreams.

Pyroo, Radha, and Kesha moved to the Corentyne Coast to village number 64, known as Babylon. There they bought some land and cattle. Radha loved horses so much that Pyroo bought her two beautiful animals. He explained that the horses were the wedding gift that she never got at the plantation. They built a house and started life away from the sugar plantation, promising themselves that when the time was right, they would all return to India.

Jahaj kept the business going in Georgetown. Periodically, he sent money to his partner. The money was used to upgrade their home and purchase additional cattle. The pregnant mare they bought soon had a filly, and once again, Radha spent time playing with the horses. She did not ride much, but on special occasions, one of her horses, the stallion, competed at the local horse races. She was elated as the racehorses galloped and jockeys waved their whips about. She yelled and screamed as the steeds approached the finish line. On days when her stallion won, she celebrated, remembering activities at her Nana's farm. She loved the horses and kept them for many years. She also learned to love the cattle. They acquired and owned the largest herd in the village.

Of course, the return trip to India never happened. Soon after leaving the plantation, they started having children. They had a total of nine children: two boys and seven girls. The boys, Pancham and Bhagal, survived into adulthood, but of the seven girls, only one survived. That survivor would be Doormatie. Six daughters died from various illnesses; some lived only a few days.

The grief of losing his daughters and the years of other stress finally took their toll on Pyroo. He desperately wanted to make the journey to India, but with each passing year, his physical strength deteriorated, and eventually, the family knew that the end was close. Jahaj was informed, and he promptly came to see his dear friend. They stayed up late and talked about their exciting life together. Two days after he arrived, Pyroo died. He was fifty-eight years old. He was buried at the local cemetery in an unmarked grave. That wonder boy. Vishnu! That loyal patriot of India! That bright, witty soul, died dreaming of a Mahatma Gandhi who would someday be sent from heaven with a mission to rid his India of the British and let his beloved homeland be free and independent. Incidentally, the year that Pyroo died, a young lawyer named Mohandas Karamchand Gandhi was in South Africa fighting on behalf of the Indian indentured servants in that part of the world. The world later recognized that young lawyer as Mahatma Gandhi, who, in 1947, gained independence for India. But Pyroo did his part, and his efforts resulted in many good things for his native land and for several indentured servants in British Guiana. A good saying at his funeral could have been that he dedicated his life to helping others and asked for nothing in return. He believed in equality and justice for all. The Sepoy Revolution of 1857 is sometimes referred to as the First War of Independence. There could be some truth to that statement. Pyroo (Vishnu) sacrificed his personal happiness for that cause. His legacy lives on. This writing honors him.

Jahaj stayed with Radha and her family. He was tired of city life and the hassle of the trade he practiced. After selling the business, he had enough money to live on, and so he kept Radha's family company, enjoying home-cooked meals in a no-stress environment.

He eventually started talking about life in India and realized that Radha knew nothing about Pyroo's life in India. Pyroo did not tell her for reasons unknown. Day by day, he talked about the chamar who wandered into the town of Calcutta and how he beat up on the two so-called robbers at the gambling table. He talked about the rebels and the revolution, about Nana Sahib. He told her about the wrestling matches and the luxury hotels and the pockets full of money. Most of all, he talked about Pyroo's dream of returning home for many reasons. She listened and nodded, for she knew that Pyroo was a special Brahmin. She nodded again and said that her Nani (Zamy's wife) was also a Brahmin woman and that her descendants should be proud to be of such rich heritage.

As the months passed, they told stories, checked on the cows, and petted her horses. They became fond of each other as Jahaj continued telling all about the life he and Pyroo shared together. Their relationship grew, and one day, Jahaj proposed marriage to Radha. She accepted, and Radha had her second husband. They put some money together, bought more cattle, and enjoyed a good life together. Radha had her horses and spent time at the local race tracks watching her animals compete. Together, she and Jahaj had a son when Radha was forty-something years old. When the boy was still young, Jahaj became ill. He could not handle the field work, so Radha and her sons did the farming and tended the cattle. Jahaj spent most of his time in a hammock. He became obsessed with owning a rice mill and asked Radha to ensure that when their son was old enough, the boy had ownership of a rice mill. She promised. Day by day, she took care of his feeble body, desperately trying to nurse him back to health. But it was of no use. One day, in 1908, he too died. He was sixty-seven. He was buried in an unmarked grave close to Pyroo. Neither of them returned to India. They died and were buried in the colony.

She eventually realized that the years were pushing her into old age and that she had made a promise to build a rice mill for her youngest son. She hired the appropriate contractors and builders and supervised the construction of the rice mill. After completion, she gathered her children and explained that the three full brothers and sister would inherit all the property, but the half-brother would have exclusive rights to the mill. Then she went about her daily routine.

Her two sons from Pyroo were Pancham and Bhagal. They were both married. Pancham had children. He suddenly contracted some mysterious illness and died. Radha did not want to put the widow and the grandchildren on the street. So, she made the tough call. She expelled the younger bride, who had no children as yet, and had the younger son marry his sister-in-law.

Radha loved her cows. She let the two boys do the rice farming as she spent her time watching the cattle graze. She still admired the playfulness of the young horses. Her surviving daughter, Doormatie, did the cooking and other domestic chores. After Pancham died, her younger son, Bhagal, did the farming. Radha lived until 1928. She was seventy-eight years old. Her granddaughter talked about the tall, slightly bent, dark-complexed old woman she knew hobbling for miles every day with the help of a walking stick, checking on her cows and petting her horses. But soon, her legs could no longer support the daily trips, and her son assumed the responsibility of overseeing the herd. They let the horses roam about and fend for themselves. In her final months, Radha would sit in her hammock and tell stories about her life, about Zamy, about her father, and about Pyroo. Occasionally, one of her horses came to her hammock to greet her. She enjoyed that. Her grandchildren vividly remembered all the tales, perceived facts, and exaggerations. Radha told them about the kidnapping and the journey, the beautiful horses in her grandfather's stables, and all the joys of her childhood in a faraway land. Then one day, she, too, died and was buried close to Pyroo and Jahaj. None of them returned to India, and many stories were buried in those three unmarked graves and became lost and forgotten.

But some of the stories did survive. Her daughter told bits and pieces, but one granddaughter narrated them quite well. She told about being a little girl in the late 1920s, keeping her grandmother (Radha) company during her last months of life as the old woman sat in her hammock, swatting flies and repeating stories about her past and about the kidnapping and the tough life on the Ruimveldt Estate. She told about the abuse her mother took because she was beautiful and how she died in shame. She kept talking to her little granddaughter about returning to India when she felt better. She said she hoped to find her little brother, who stayed behind with their father. Those stories survived and are now immortalized in this writing.

CHAPTER 9

Desai and His Children

For years after his arrival, Desai lived in a logie at the Port Mourant Plantation located in the County of Berbice. His roommates were other single male indentured servants from India. He shared a room with two men at any one time because people's situations changed, creating new vacancies and occupancies. The occupants had no choice in selecting their roommates. They were assigned. If someone did not like the ones chosen to share his or her living quarters, that person could file a complaint with the authorities, but most of the time, the petitions were ignored.

Desai showed the captain's letter of recommendation to the authorities, but it initially did not help his situation much. He was assigned to field work. What neighbors admired about him was his work ethic. He worked hard on the shovel gang, and when not working, he kept himself clean. He usually finished his task early in the day, which allowed him some free time in the evenings. Fishing was his hobby, and most evenings, he was seen carrying his bamboo fishing pole and an empty pail. He would soon return with his pole and some fish in the pail. He fished at the estate irrigation canals that brought fresh water from the Canje River. He cleaned his catch, added some spices and hot pepper, and fried the fish in hot coconut oil. His evening meal generally consisted of rice, dal (split peas), and fried fish. For dessert, he ate fruits like bananas, mangoes, and whatever he secured. He sometimes made kheer, like his mother had done in India.

Because he was a model worker and because of his good behavior, he was very well liked both by his peers and the estate supervisors. Hence, he had no problem getting passes to leave the premises for the evening outings to catch some fish and acquire some fresh fruit. He generally went to bed early and was up by 4:00 a.m., when he did his morning cooking, ate his breakfast, drank his sweetened tea, packed his lunch, and got ready for his daily assignments. As the sun rose, Desai, with his shovel, cutlass, and lunch pail, was on his way to work. The overseer would have his task measured, and in that manner, he had an early start during the cool morning breezes. He wasted no time. His callused hands and broad shoulders powered the shovel like a well-timed steam engine as folks admired his rhythm one scoop at a time. That was how he managed to get the work done earlier than most, allowing him time to catch fish and gather fruit. The shovel gang offered one of the highest wages paid to field laborers bound to the various plantations. It took strong men with stamina to perform such a task in the intolerable heat and humidity of that tropical environment.

During that period, some of the young men at the Port Mourant Estate were no longer bound to the plantation, but they stayed in the area along with many Negros who were descendants of African slaves. Those independent people worked for the estate as independent paid laborers. They worked there out of necessity because their options were limited. Most were illiterate with limited skills. With money and plenty of free time, many got into mischief when any opportunity presented itself. They generally stole estate supplies and sold them on the black market to men operating like Jahaj did at Ruimveldt.

One of those boys at that plantation was a son of Kangal and Kalya. His name was Jaman, better known as Juman. He was a troublemaker and had a gang of young men composed of East Indians and Negros. They wanted to befriend Desai and tried to recruit him as a member of the gang, but that did not happen because he was legally bound to the estate. Desai did not appreciate their lifestyle or their unacceptable and unethical behavior. Juman then proceeded to tease Desai about his long hair, telling him that the hair made him look like a girl. Desai paid no attention to him. He kept doing his daily tasks and lived a simple reclusive life. In the evenings, he bathed and put on clean clothes. He cooked his meals, which he ate by himself. On Sundays, he went fishing at faraway trenches, where the diverse fish population was plentiful and of better quality. He traded most of those fish for fresh vegetables with neighbors. He generally sat under a nearby tree by the roadside, outside of the estate confinements. From there, he could observe whatever the sights had to offer. He was a loner.

Then one evening, he was doing his usual daydreaming under his shade tree. He had finished supper and was selecting what fruit would be his dessert. He slowly fumbled with a mango, an orange, and a ripe yellow banana, and then chose the orange. He would eat the rest later. It was a pleasant evening, and inside the fenced area, many workers were shuffling about hurrying to get supper eaten before the mosquitoes arrived. The swarms were severe after dark, and the bats knew their schedule. Birds that knew no boundaries flew about with missions unknown to the people. People waved at him as they hastily passed by. He was eating the orange.

Then Desai saw her! He could not believe his eyes. A girl of East Indian background, about fourteen years old, was walking down the dirt road carrying a pail of water on her head. She was slim and had long black hair in a single long curl down her backbone, which swayed from side to side in harmony with her wiggling walk. She was neatly dressed in a colorful sari. From behind, she looked exactly like the goddess he had loved so dearly years ago in India. He scrambled to his feet, spilled the fruit, and ran toward her. But when he came face-to-face with her, it was a slight disappointment. She was pretty enough, but not the one he thought she was. His disappointed enthusiasm and confusion surprised her. His wild, excited look mixed with long unruly hair made her scream. Soon, Juman was there. He explained to Desai that the girl's name was Mangrie, and she was his little sister.

He warned Desai that he better leave her alone. Desai apologized, and feeling silly, he meandered back to his shade tree, picked up the dishes and fruit, and hustled to his quarters. He washed the dishes in record time as the bats began their acrobatic flights and the birds ended their cacophony of twittering and went to roost. Desai tried to settle himself down.

He sat on the floor by his bed, thinking about the incident with a stomach full of butterflies. Cockroaches were scavenging about, but he did not notice them. With confusion as his sole companion, he fell asleep, probably dreaming about India and the family he had left behind. He dreamed of his mother's sobbing, his father's questioning, his sister and her new baby, and all the folks in his beloved village, especially the woman he so dearly loved. He woke up feeling homesick. He propped himself against the wall and cried like he never had before. His roommates inquired about his agony, and he explained that he was homesick. They understood those emotions and went back to bed. But in the midst of his confusion and tears, there was the image of Juman's sister carrying that pail of water down the dusty path. Her image pleased him, and the next day, after work, he went on a mission to find out more about that girl. He realized that he was a few years older than she was, but his curiosity encouraged him.

He slowly walked about and cautiously approached the family. He could see her doing the household routine in a fairly graceful manner. He liked her. After several more visits, he one day approached Kangal and Kalya about his feelings for their daughter. The parents did not object to having that fine, young man for a son-in-law, but Juman raised strong objection because he did not like Desai's long hair. He continued his mischievous behavior, and his small gang of hooligans continued playing dirty tricks on Desai.

It happened one Sunday when the gang got Desai to sit with them and offered him a drink. Not knowing that it was an alcoholic beverage, Desai drank it and soon was stumbling about and passed out. The gang got scissors and a razor and shaved all the hair off Desai's head. Then they shaved off his nicely groomed beard. After the haircut and shave, during their drinking and laughing, they wrapped Desai in a fish net and placed him by the roadside. They used vines to tie his hands and legs.

It was not a pleasant moment when Desai woke up. It was midafternoon, and the heat was unbearable. The yelling and screaming soon attracted the attention of the neighborhood. The people saw Desai's situation and quickly managed to free him from the net. He went crazy and started chasing the laughing Juman and his gang members. The estate police were called in, and they managed to wrestle him to the ground. Not knowing what to do, the authorities chained him and tied him to a cement pillar under the Port Mourant hospital. The magistrate at the court of law tried the case and fined Juman and his friends. Desai was released and ordered back to work digging ditches along the cane fields.

After that incident, Juman and his gang members lived in constant fear because every day Desai would seek them out and gave them a sound beating one at a time. The bald-headed Desai continued to inflict bodily harm on the gang members. Desai was summoned to court many times and was fined severely, but he continued beating up on those boys. Some of them had broken bones and other serious injuries. The estate police were tired of his violent behavior, and once again, they chained him to the pillar under the hospital. They claimed that he was mentally unstable and was a danger to society.

At the hospital was an English nurse whom Desai referred to as Missy. Slowly, she got to know Desai, and because he could communicate with her in simple English sentences, she started to counsel him. She soon learned about his misfortunes in India and about what Juman and the boys did to him. He explained that he wanted to maintain his long hair. He truly believed that his hair was what gave him an advantage in life, at least so he was told by the old pundit in India. He talked, and she listened.

Missy took pity on him, and soon she was spending more and more time during the day talking with and getting to know him. She convinced his neighbors that contrary to their belief, Desai was not crazy. He needed time for his hair to grow, and then he would return to his normal self. Missy found out about the letter Desai got from the captain of the *Lena* and discussed the subject with the estate management personnel.

Weeks passed, and Desai's post became an informal meeting place for his friends and neighbors. In the evenings, they came to visit and to keep him company. Many brought him food. Missy spent time there during the day when most of his neighbors worked in the fields. She ensured that he was well fed and that his daily needs were met. He requested a daily bath and that his clothes be periodically washed. She took care of such details. At nights, when all the visitors departed, he washed up in the darkness and changed his clothes. The chain was tied around his waist. It was long enough to allow him to walk around in circles and to let him use the latrine close by. The hospital provided crude bedding materials and blankets. Those items not only kept him comfortable during the nights, but they shielded him from the pesky bloodsucking mosquitoes. The hospital guards checked on him, minimizing their boredom and ensuring his safety.

Then one day, Juman, feeling guilty, came to visit. Seeing him, Desai was enraged. He backed up to the cement pillar and, with a roar, leaped forward at Juman. To the surprise of everyone, the little chain broke, and Desai was freed. The screaming Juman ran into the hospital with Desai and the rattling chains chasing after him. The word was out that the crazy man was loose. Surprisingly, even some of the so-called sick patients jumped up and ran. It was not uncommon for healthy people to pretend to be sick in order to escape from laboring in the fields for days at a time. It was a wild scene with Juman and the so-called sick people running about trying to avoid Desai and his rattling chains being dragged behind him.

They stumbled over hospital furniture, dirty laundry, sick people, some not-so-sick people, medical personnel, security personnel, and other obstacles. It was total chaos along the narrow hallways. The larger chaser with anger as his propeller and the smaller, panicking Juman were like a hound dog pursuing a timid rabbit among numerous obstacles, both going as fast as the slow traffic allowed. The noise from the rattling chains blended with the banging of obstacles, and the screaming of the frightened observers created an environment of ongoing horror. People were scared.

At the end of the hallway, Desai caught the little Juman. He grabbed him by his ankles. He picked him up and pushed his head out of an open wooden window. Then he leaned over the windowsill and started swinging Juman like the pendulum on a clock, back and forth. Juman was crying and pleading with Desai that he would do whatever was necessary to spare his life. Desai finally spoke and told Juman that he would drop him headfirst unless Juman gave permission for him to marry his sister, Mangrie. Juman was literally in no position to negotiate, so he agreed. Then Missy came and ordered Desai to pull the man in, and Desai obeyed.

The magistrate decided that he had suffered enough, and Desai promised to behave. He told the magistrate, in English, that he had a wedding to plan. He was released and ordered back to work on the shovel gang. Many neighbors were happy because fish would be available to them again. Kangal and Kalya were pleased about the release and apologized for their son's behavior. They had several meetings together, and he got to know Mangrie. She was rather shy and tried avoiding him, but they had brief conversations. She explained that her brother was trying to protect her, and she told her brother that she did not want protection while in his drunken state. Kangal told him that their daughter was almost fifteen, and the wedding would be held after her sixteenth birthday. They all agreed, and Juman slowly accepted Desai. In time, they became friends.

Desai continued his duties on the shovel gang. He continued his routine except that he now had an adopted family. He caught large amounts of fish, which he shared with Kalya. She had large quantities of different types of vegetables from the now expanded garden. She and Kangal had several children and lived in their private home close to the estate compound. The overseer understood the situation so he granted daily passes to Desai to go visit his future in-laws. He enjoyed the company, the home-cooked meals, and the fish that were prepared in various ways. That continued for a year, and one day, as the calendar revealed, it was Mangrie's sixteenth birthday and her wedding day. She and Desai were married in 1905. He was twenty-six, and she was sixteen.

It was a simple wedding. The tall, handsome Desai, wide at the shoulders and narrow at the hips with a full head of black hair nicely groomed, accepted Mangrie, the daughter of Kangal and Kalya, as his wife. The pundit blessed them, gave them his usual marriage advice, collected his fees of coins and groceries, and sent them off to a plantation honeymoon. That meant a day off for the celebration and back to work the following day. He worked, and she took care of the home front still at her parents' house. They built an addition to the family house with mud walls and a thatched roof. And when he was no longer legally bound to the plantation, he and his wife slept in their cozy enclosure attached to the family house.

With time, Desai and Juman became very good friends, and to Desai's surprise, he was given a better job. Missy's campaigning had convinced the estate management, with the aid of the captain's recommendation, that Desai could better serve the plantation in a different capacity. To qualify for such a job, people had to meet certain criteria. They had to be fit and strong. They must speak English. They had to be able to shoot a gun with some accuracy. The overseer must approve of his loyalty and work ethic. Desai qualified in all categories and also had the captain's letter of recommendation. They studied him and observed his physical appearance, his bodily strength, and his ability to communicate in simple English. After a series of interviews, he was given the job as a guard during payroll transportation.

At that time, the laborers were paid with coins, mostly shillings. The coins were minted in England and brought to Demerara in the colonies on ships. From there, money was transported by horse-pulled buggies that were well fortified. They were susceptible to potential attacks by local thugs who loitered about, waiting to ambush someone and steal anything of value. It was Desai's job to help the security team guard against such attacks, starting from Canje and going southward. Almost all the attacks were unsuccessful because the guards were well armed and traveled with the galloping horses.

He was given a series of trainings in driving a team of horses and using guns. He liked the guns and took pride in handling them. He would place an empty quinine bottle on an elevated spot away from people and fire his weapon. He became a good shot. There were lots of quinine bottles because those dark bottles brought quinine to the plantations. Quinine was used to minimize malaria outbreaks. There was no shortage of malaria outbreaks in that mosquito-infested environment. Desai collected the empties and used them for ongoing target practice.

Because of his new position and his legal indenture to the estate ending, he was informed that he was no longer considered an indentured servant and would be paid a higher salary. On days when there were no payroll transport duties, he helped the overseer with general maintenance. When new workers were assigned to the shovel gang, he was their trainer. Generally, he stayed close to the estate and continued working as a guard when money had to be transported. The money was taken to various destinations, like the post offices for safekeeping, and was well guarded. Post offices were generally built close to police stations, and those local officers patrolled the area and guarded the buildings that housed the vaults. When the horse-drawn fortified wagons arrived, the station was notified. Desai and the local police carried the money and delivered it to the payroll personnel at the post office. From there, the money was given to the plantation personnel, and the paymasters delivered the money to the workers.

*   *   *

Mangrie was quite young and did not stay home alone. So when Desai was on duty on the road, Kalya and her older daughters spent time with the new bride. Most of the time, she went to their family home. Doing their usual chores, they entertained themselves with basic girl talk. Most of the time, they were in the family's vegetable garden, and the various discussions helped to minimize boredom for all. In the evening, they cooked and ate together, and after dark, they lit the little lanterns and talked themselves to sleep. Her older full sister, Budhnie, was married and had a daughter. But the marriage was a failure, so she returned to her parents' house with the daughter. That little girl ran about in the evening in the house and, in the garden during the day, chatting and chasing colorful butterflies. She kept the family entertained long after sunset until exhaustion consumed her and all slept peacefully.

The oldest (half) sister was also married and lived with her husband close by. They had small children, and they both worked at the estate. So on any weekday, Kangal and his wife babysat those and other grandchildren. So, when Desai was traveling on duty, his wife had plenty to do helping with all the work and the babysitting.

Kangal was pleased that his daughter was close by when her husband was on duty because women who stayed alone were prime victims for assault. It also allowed them time to talk about life in India and why they chose to migrate to South America. It was said that Mangrie was very fond of her father, and being with her parents allowed her to pamper her dad by making and sharing his favorite sweets called *meethai*. So, most evenings, she made him a fresh batch and served him that favorite treat with a cup of warm milk and honey. He was fond of his granddaughter and took pleasure in sharing the evening treats with her.

That was a fine life for Mangrie. She still had her family and a husband to boot. But it was a good situation for Desai, for when he came home, he got his wife's attention. Instead of sharing time with her family, they had each other. As time went by, the estate wanted Desai to relocate to a different location. He was asked to move to Canje because it was a starting point for the money deliveries. He was offered a pay increase to do the relocation. After several weeks of discussion, they decided to move on. They packed up their few personal belongings, and with the help of the estate payroll wagon, the young couple moved to Canje, another plantation site, where they rented a small house. Desai scouted about and found an older single woman and asked her to spend nights with his wife when he was out on estate business. The woman agreed, and Mangrie was happy to have the company while her husband was gone. They paid the woman with vegetables and fish.

It did not take very long for him to get acquainted with the new environment because there was a sugar factory there called Rose Hall. To Mangrie's surprise, she liked the freedom and independence. They grew a garden and supplemented their diet with fish that Desai caught in nearby rivers and streams. Fishing had always been a hobby for Desai, and most evenings when he was home, he and Mangrie spent quality time by the Canje River and caught plenty of fish. They kept some for themselves and traded some to neighbors. He caught them, and she cleaned and washed them with the clean river water. Then they hurried home to fry their catch in coconut oil and seasoned it with various spices. On the way home, they traded with others for coconut oil, vegetables, and various spices.

They became good friends and partners in life, and one day, Mangrie informed Desai that she was pregnant and that he would soon be a father. Some months later, in 1907, the baby was born at Kangal's house. It was a boy, and the local pundit named him Nandalall. They nicknamed him Luloon, but most of the time, they called him Nanda. When everyone was sure that mother and baby were well enough, the family of three returned to their home in Canje.

Mangrie spent most of her time taking care of the baby. During the day when Desai went to work, she took the baby along to tend her garden. She loved flowers and grew many colorful varieties next to the vegetables. She was a good wife and a happy mother. Desai earned a good living working at the estate and went fishing whenever he could. Some days, when he caught an abundance of fish, he continued to barter with the neighbors for household supplies. With the money he saved, he purchased a rocking chair, and in the evenings, when his wife was busy with household chores, in their humble home, he would sing to the baby in Hindi and rock him to sleep.

Four years later, they had a second son, whom they named Gopilall. They became a family of four, and like most families in the area, they continued to live by and work for the plantation. The indentured process still continued, and whenever a new person came to the area,

Desai was always trying to find out news about India and inquiring if any such person from the Agra area knew about his village. He still wondered about his family that he had so suddenly abandoned. But now he had his own family to support. In the evening, he still sat in his rocking chair with his two sons, humming and watching Mangrie as she hustled about like a hungry hummingbird.

Like most kids would do, the boys began tagging along with Desai. They were now three and seven years old, and Mangrie was once again pregnant. In the evenings, they went fishing with their father and enjoyed the outing and the excitement of catching fish. The black waters of the Canje River originated from the tropical rain forest and were pure enough for drinking. On calm days, the almost still surface reflected images above, including passing clouds and blue skies. The upside-down reflections of the immediate vegetation appeared to be growing roots up and shoots down. The fishing was great at Desai's favorite spots, and the kids would jump for joy as their father slowly pulled the net toward them, and the trapped fish struggled to escape.

One day, while they were fishing, the net got caught on a log in the river. Desai told Nanda to keep an eye on his brother, and he went into the river to rescue the net. He was a very good swimmer. The younger brother, not knowing the danger of the water current, followed his father to the edge of the river and was swept away by the current. By the time Desai understood the situation, the little lad was gone. The panicked father called for help as he jumped into and out of the water. Many people came running, and numerous swimmers tried to locate the missing boy. Eventually they found him and frantically tried to revive him, but it was of no use, the boy was dead.

Desai wrapped him in a cotton sheet that someone provided, and taking Nanda by the hand and cradling the lifeless body of his younger son, he and a small procession walked home to his pregnant wife. It was a slow and painful walk. His grief and guilt comingled with his slow pace. Someone called the pundit, and the neighbors gathered. A message was sent to Port Mourant, informing the relatives of the tragedy. Later the next day, a small grave was dug, and the three-year-old boy was buried. The pundit blessed his soul and sent him to heaven.

The shock was too much for Mangrie. Recognizing her mental instability coupled with a delicate pregnancy, her mother and sisters suggested that she and Nanda return to Port Mourant with them. They did, and Desai was left alone in that tiny shack with grief and guilt as constant companions. He worked during the day, and in the evenings, he rocked alone in the chair, humming his favorite tunes. He refused to go to his in-laws' house on account of his job and the guilt he felt for the boy's death. Neighbors came to visit, and the pundit spent time with him. The holy man told him that the incident was not his fault, that it was an accident. He told the grieving father that God took the boy for reasons unknown to mortals. He told Desai that his greatest strength came from prayers that God, who had his son, would show him the path forward. He said that it was okay to grieve but not to get consumed with grief. He had to be strong for his wife and the older son. They needed him.

Weeks passed, and one day, Juman came to visit Desai. He explained that Mangrie would soon be having a baby, and she wanted him to come and spend some time with her and their family at Port Mourant. He came back with Juman and was happy to see that his wife was doing well. It was a good reunion, and Kangal found them a place to stay. Again, they had some quality time together and tried to become the family they once were. They seldom spoke about the tragedy, and it appeared that they had, for the most part, moved on. Desai found temporary employment at the plantation, and Mangrie helped with the family gardening and took care of Nanda. Her sister, Budhnie, had remarried to a man named Lachman. Folks called the man Gunjay.

It was January 1915, and Budhnie had delivered a son. So, while the women were busy with household and baby stuff, Desai, Gunjay, and Juman entertained themselves by playing cards and checkers.

Some two months after Desai's return from Canje, the midwife was summoned on March 15, 1915. It was time for the baby. The men knew their duty, which was to vacate the premises and let the women and the midwife perform their respective duties. Later, in the darkness, there was the crying of a newborn, and the men standing patiently outside knew that those lungs were announcing the arrival of another baby at Port Mourant. It was a boy, and the pundit later named him Motilall.

The baby was fine. He was cleaned up and wrapped in clean cotton garments. Mangrie was, on the other hand, not doing very well, for they could not stop her bleeding. She was taken to the local hospital, but the bleeding continued. She did not recover. Two days after hospitalization, she died. Kangal, in his grief, called Budhnie, who had her baby some two months prior, and handed the little bundle to her, telling her that she now had twins and to go breastfeed her new baby. Then Kangal's family and Desai called the pundit to conduct the funeral process. That was the burial of Mangrie. She was placed in a wooden coffin and loaded on a donkey cart. All the men in the area followed the pundit who walked directly behind the cart as he conducted his rituals. They got to the cemetery where the grave was dug under a silk cotton tree. She was lowered into the site, six feet deep, and was covered with the pile of dirt that was excavated that morning by men with shovels.

Desai did not say much. What could he say? He stayed by the grave all alone and quietly prayed. He told Mangrie that he would take care of the two children on earth, and she could take care of the one in heaven. Then he put some of her favorite flowers on her grave and walked away as the gushing tears rolled down his dusty cheeks. Some of the dirt had accumulated on his now graying beard. His anger, fear, and confusion drove him to the water where he once again swam and cried like a madman. Nothing helped his situation. For the next several days, he walked toward the silk cotton tree that shaded his wife's grave, collecting flowers and soliloquizing about the subject at hand. He would sit by her grave and have a monologue; then he would place the flowers on the grave and walk home to his two sons. He suddenly became a single parent.

Kalya was a good mother-in law. She had always admired that young man and his strong personality. She and her other daughters made sure that he was fed and that he maintained his sanity. Budhnie gave one breast to her own son and the other breast to Motilall. The two babies had their dedicated breast from which they nursed. That continued for several months, and both babies survived. Kangal, now retired, still did his gardening with the help of his wife and daughters. His four sons and three sons-in law did the forking and tilling, and the entire family enjoyed an abundance of fresh fruits and vegetables. They also cultivated a small plot of rice. They acquired a cow that provided milk especially for the two babies. Desai still went fishing, and most days, he caught enough fish for the entire Kangal family. In the evenings, he played cards and checkers with Gunjay and Juman. Kangal, now fifty-six years old, walked with a slight limp, slightly bent forward, and he was completely gray. On hot days, he limped slightly about in his dhoti. The scar on his back was still quite visible. Most evenings, he sat quietly and watched as the men played their games and argued about who was cheating.

That extended family stayed together for another year. Then Kalya became ill. The estate doctor gave her some medicine and told the family that she had some incurable disease and would not recover. They did what they could to keep her comfortable, but as the doctor had said, she did not recover. She progressively got worse, and one night in 1917, two years after Mangrie died, she, too, was gone. She was sixty-one years old. The pundit again did his rituals, and she was buried at Port Mourant close to Mangrie under the silk cotton tree. She had a good life after leaving India. She had eight children. Her youngest son was now twenty-two years old. She had served her family well. Kangal said that she went up to keep Mangrie company among the clouds.

After Kalya's death, the family noticed that Kangal was becoming reclusive. He spent many hours in his hammock and did not say much. Occasionally he walked in his dhoti to Kalya and Mangrie's grave and sat there for extended periods of time, talking to himself and occasionally would toss a pebble about. He wondered about his mother's fruit trees in India, about his brother continuing the family business. He visualized his life in the homeland and realized that coming to the colony, meeting and marrying Kalya, and raising several children were the best blessings in his life, and he should be thankful. Then he would walk home to the security of his hammock where he held the little Motilall on his chest and quietly hummed an old familiar tune. His concerned family tried to console him, but it was of no use. He was a lost and depressed man. He truly missed his wife and daughter. Everyone understood his grief and gave him space to handle the situation at his pace.

Then one early morning, he got up, took a bath, picked some flowers, and walked to the burial site. He placed the flowers on the graves, knelt down, and prayed. He did not realize that Nanda had followed him and stayed far enough away where he could not be seen. The old man was performing some strange rituals that were alien to the boy. Then he walked home and called his entire family together. He explained that there was too much grief in that area and suggested that the family should move on. They all agreed. During the next several weeks, they sold their home and got their meager savings together. Kangal went scouting and decided to buy some land at Number 57 Village. Here, he hired some carpenters, gathered some lumber, and together, they built a small house. He also purchased two acres of land that would be used for cultivating rice. Then he returned to Port Mourant, disposed of some personal belongings, sold the cow, packed up his stuff, and moved his family to the new residence at Number 57 Village.

The entire family except Juman and Desai moved to the new neighborhood and started growing rice. Desai did not go with them. He had different ideas and took his two sons with him. They settled at a place called Maida because there was a good fishing river close by. He worked at various odd jobs and did what he enjoyed most, fishing. He traded fish for supplies and for babysitting services. An older woman in the area took care of the boys when he was out, and she cooked for them. In the evenings, he told Nanda stories about his home in India and about his plan to return there. He told about his parents and siblings and the wonderful farm that his father had maintained. His enthusiasm and excitement always got the boy's attention, and he kept repeating the names of the places and of the people who lived in that faraway land.

One fine day, when Desai went fishing, Nanda begged the old woman to go for a walk and to watch their father catch some fish. They did. She carried the one-year-old Motilall, and Nanda walked along, hanging on to her cotton dress. They found Desai, and during the casual discussion, Motilall crawled away, and like his brother, he fell into the river. The old woman saw him and yelled. The commotion attracted the local folks, and instantly, Desai jumped into the river and grabbed the youngster. It was a struggle swimming against the swift current with a drowning baby in his arm, but Desai was no ordinary man. He was strong. He was an excellent swimmer, and at that moment of panic, he paddled with a racing heart and with adrenalin surging. They came to a spot where a few people had gathered, and tying themselves with a series of vines that grew in the area, they managed to pull the father and son to safety. Desai handed the baby to the crowd that had gathered. Then he collapsed.

Everything turned out fine. Desai soon scrambled to his feet and rushed over to hug his two sons. The incident scared him so seriously that, during the night, he considered moving away from that neighborhood. He had already lost one son to drowning and was not prepared to live through another such incident. He sat there thinking and convinced himself that the move was a wise idea. Hence, within a few days, he packed up and returned to Canje. There, he bought a small house, and he and the boys settled in once again.

The first week was busy for him as a single parent, trying to get the home ready. He had a few kitchen utensils and some sheets and blankets, and of course, he had his prize possession, the rocking chair. For light, he used a small, open clay container that was called a *deeiah*. At night, he filled the deeiah with coconut oil and partially dipped a piece of rolled-up cotton as a wick. On the exposed part of the wick, a flame burned. It was an identical lamp to the one his mother used in India. After supper, in the flickering light, he cuddled his two sons, and they gently rocked in their favorite chair. When the boys fell asleep, he blew the flame out, and they all went to bed and slept together.

The bed was a crude structure. It was called a *khatia*. Desai had to build the khatia. He started by partially burying four sturdy posts in the dirt floor in one corner of the shack. Pieces of wood were tied horizontally to the anchored posts about a foot off the ground. Other braced pieces of wood were used as needed to ensure that the structure was secure and that it did not wobble. A series of ropes were tied in a crisscross manner that somewhat imitated bedsprings. Of course, there were no actual springs, it was just a flat structure. Then he sewed some gunnysacks together in the form of a large bag. He stuffed the bag with dried reeds and sewed it shut. That was the mattress, and it was placed on the khatia and covered with sheets and blankets. Homemade pillows stuffed with cattail flowers were added, and the bed was completed. On that khatia and pillows, Desai and his sons slept.

Desai went out shopping for food one day and found out that a single woman lived close by. She had no children. He knew of the woman when he first lived in the area. She was a Muslim, quite attractive, and very polite. She had a large and productive garden, which she kept neat and clean. She also had several chickens and ducks. There, he purchased several items, and she thanked him for the business and suggested that he should come again and bring the children along.

Desai casually found himself visiting the woman and was soon helping her with the garden in exchange for vegetables. As their friendship grew, they bought several additional ducks and chickens and became business partners. When things seemed to be in place, he went looking for work. He was told that the estate was looking for an experienced person to guard the payroll wagon. He hurried over and applied for the job, and once again, Desai found employment as a payroll guard for the plantations.

The boys called the woman Auntie and stayed with her when Desai went to work. Nothing had changed; the payroll was still transported to local post offices and then to regional estates. That caused Desai to be gone for short periods of time. But at times, between pay periods, he was home for several days at a time. Auntie took care of the kids and grew fond of them. When Desai returned, he brought tasty treats like his father did when he was a child in India. So like all children, the boys patiently waited for father and his goodies to arrive. On days when Desai was home, he took the boys and Auntie fishing. He also did odd jobs for local farmers, who paid him with low-quality grains. Desai would pound the grain with his wooden pestle assembly and feed it to the ducks and chickens. Nanda collected the eggs daily, which they sold to neighbors and at the local markets. The hens were kept for egg production, and the roosters and drakes were also sold at the local markets. In addition, Auntie sold vegetables from her garden. All those things gave them a decent income, and the four of them made the most of what could be eked out from the various streams.

One day, a farmer asked Desai to help him with repairs on his granary. The two men walked around the wooden structure and worked out a plan. They agreed that prior to repairs, the floor needed to be chinked because the grain was spilling out through the wide cracks. The farmer told Desai to handle that, and for payment, he should take all the spilled grain for poultry feed. The next morning, Desai packed his lunch pail and headed out to fix the leaks at the granary. Upon arrival, he crawled under the structure and started pounding away. The foundation was in bad shape, and with the constant pounding, the support beam at one end slipped. The entire structure came down upon Desai. It was not a very large building, but with the weight of the grain, it was quite heavy. Desai grabbed the beam and screamed for help. Many neighbors came running, and with brute force and with the aid of prying logs and blocks, the panicked workers managed to pull the suffocating Desai out. He was hurt but alive, and the group of helpers took him to Auntie's house.

He was bruised and bleeding, but the estate doctor assured them that he had no broken bones. The doctor suggested that he should stay in bed for a few days, and his condition would be evaluated the following week. It was tough for him to stay in bed, but Auntie insisted. She made him chicken soup with fresh vegetables, and for supper, they had rice, dal, and curry. She also grated cassava that she had uprooted from the garden and used it to bake a tasty dessert. To minimize the boredom, he hobbled along with Nanda as he gathered up the eggs. For breakfast, they sometimes ate spicy fried eggs and fried cassava and plantains. Auntie and the boys loved having him home, but he was restless and bored.

The doctor examined him the following week and diagnosed him with cracked ribs. He said he should not return to work for at least another week. It was during those days that Auntie discovered the money belt that Desai wore. He explained that the belt was given to him by the captain of the *Lena* when he crossed the great waters. Nanda was again fascinated by some of the stories and asked many questions about the long journey and about life on the farm in India. Like most nine-year-olds, the boy kept asking questions and wondered why his father did not want to take him and his brother to that wonderful farm across the waters where many relatives lived. To satisfy their curiosity, Desai would sit under a tree and tell stories, especially to Auntie, about his departure from India. He told about the girl he wanted to marry, about the death of the neighbor, about the stay at the church, about the trip to Calcutta, about the arkathies, about the *Lena* and the captain, about his village where he grew up herding cattle, and many other things. The boy was genuinely interested in the stories and kept asking questions over and over again. Desai, being bored, was unusually talkative and found himself repeating the stories with more and more details. Then Auntie would tell about her life and about her ancestors in India. Her Muslim ancestors came to the colony a long time ago. Her parents were born in British Guiana, so she knew little about India.

She was about thirty years old. Her name was Nazmoon. Most people called her Naz. She got married when she was twenty. It was an arranged marriage, and she did not like her demanding mother-in-law. Her husband drank a lot, and she felt like an outcast in that home and was treated like a servant. By the time she was twenty-five, it became obvious that she could not have children. That infuriated the mother-in-law, and she demanded that Naz be sent away and her son should find another wife who was fertile. Nothing happened for another year, and she came to the realization that she must move on and that she would never have children. So she packed up and left. She acquired the little house and lived there all alone, planting her garden and raising poultry.

Desai never recovered fully from the accident. He did return to work, but during the long trips, he had occasional pain in his chest area. His lungs seemed congested, probably from all the grain dust he frantically inhaled when the building collapsed. More and more, he found himself daydreaming about his childhood home. He wondered if his parents were still living, if his brother was managing the cattle herd well, if his sister had more babies, if his little sister ever got married, if the village had changed much, and most important of all, what happened to the girl he loved so dearly. He tried to convince himself that that was long ago and far away. But memories knew no distance, and time was irrelevant. Day by day, he wondered with more curiosity, and when he was home, he told the more detailed stories to his son. He was getting more obsessed about the return trip, but his resources were limited. It would cost more than he could afford to travel with two children to India. Then they had to survive there. If he could not earn a living in India, he and the children would end up on the streets, homeless and hungry. That scared him. But he still dreamed about returning someday.

Then one day, he had a great idea. He started thinking about robbing the payroll wagon. It was risky, but if handled properly, he could steal some of the coins. With that loot plus the savings in his money belt, he could pay the passage for the boys to India. He figured that he was guaranteed and qualified for a partial return trip for himself. He did not discuss the subject with anyone, but the idea intrigued him. When the deliveries were made at the various stops, he studied the process and started to devise a plan on how best to rob the wagon. He also had to plan where to hide his loot because he knew that he would be a prime suspect. He decided that the best place was at Port Mourant. The stage occasionally traveled there toward evenings, and the drivers were generally tired. He knew the area well and picked out a secluded ambush spot.

He studied his plot time and time again until he figured out a master plan with all the details covered. Because of his good shooting, he was sometimes invited to go hunting in the interior forests. So, one day, when the jungle hunters came to town, Desai bought a large jaguar skin from his hunting buddies. He paid the hunters extra and asked them not to discuss the purchase with anyone. The hunters were puzzled and asked what the big secret was. Desai told them that someone was stealing his chickens and he needed to scare them off pretending to be a jaguar. The hunters had a loud laugh and assured Desai that his secret was safe with them. They also appreciated the good price for the skin. The hunters walked away, laughing at the man pretending to be a jaguar in an attempt to scare away the chicken thieves.

For the next several days, Desai dried and modified the jaguar skin, using a large needle and some course twine. He filled in the void parts with some type of fabric and buttons to ensure that it fit his body. It was not pretty, but in the dark when he got on his hands and knees, the figure had the appearance of a jaguar with a big head. The next thing he had to learn was to make a growling sound like a jaguar. He studied jaguar behavior and learned how to make sounds like those fierce cats. At nights, he lay in bed thinking about all the details. During the day, when time permitted, he walked into the woods, practicing his jaguar growl.

The hijacking day came like any other day. The money wagon had to make the periodic scheduled run past Port Mourant. Desai woke up early that day. He packed his feline skin in a gunnysack and securely tied it with some twine. He cradled the package under his arm and went to work carrying his lunch pail in the other hand. The traveling payroll staff was curious about the sack, but Desai casually mentioned that he had to deliver the contents to his brother-in-law, Juman, at the Port Mourant stop. During the waiting period, Desai, as usual, casually inspected the gun. When he was sure that no one was watching, he removed the bullet cartridges, put them in his pocket, and returned the gun to its usual spot. With everything in place, on schedule, the wagon started the journey. The men did their normal duties as the well-fortified wagon traveled down the road, making its occasional scheduled stops. Nothing seemed out of the ordinary, and the nervous yet stoic Desai waited for his moment. The wagon arrived at Port Mourant on schedule. When they reached Desai's designated spot, he told the men that he needed to relieve himself in the bushes because he was suffering from a mild case of the stomach flu. They came to a stop, and Desai, grabbing his gunnysack, ran into the bushes as the others tried not to laugh at his perceived urgency.

The sound of a jaguar was followed by a cat man leaping into the wagon. The sight scared the men, who scrambled for the gun, only to find it nonfunctional. Instinctively, they all jumped off the wagon to avoid the prowling beast. The commotion scared the horses, and they bolted into a frenzy. Desai wasted no time. He grabbed two sackfuls of shillings and halted the horses. He then stashed away his disguised garments and the money into a hollow tree trunk that he had previously identified as a good hiding place. He then replaced the bullets into the gun and turned the team around in search of his fellow travelers. He called for them, and one by one, they came out of the woods totally scared. He explained that having finished his bowel duties, he heard the vicious cat and saw it jumping onto the wagon, so he started to run and eventually found the wagon after the team got snagged by some tree branches. He questioned them about not shooting the cat, and the men explained that the gun did not work. Desai grabbed the gun and fired it, telling the men that in their panic, they could not fire the gun. He took the gun along and pretended to be searching for his gunnysack while explaining to the men that in his panic, he had dropped it in the bushes. It was getting dark, and the petrified traveling team yelled at him to forget the bag and get on board before the hungry cat made a meal of him. He gladly obeyed, and they went about their travels down the dusty path and to the next destination. One of the men had a slash from the cat's claws, and they took him to one of the estate doctors for treatment.

The next day, the discovery was made. Some of the money was missing, and the incident was reported to the proper authorities. On the way home, Desai asked the men to drop him off at Port Mourant to see if he could find his brother-in-law's sack. They did. Once the wagon was out of sight, he wasted no time finding the hollow tree. He grabbed his loot and his gunnysack and hurried toward Mangrie's grave. He quickly got his hidden shovel and buried everything at his wife's gravesite under the silk cotton tree. After disposing of the shovel, he washed up in a nearby stream and went to visit Juman. He told Juman that he was bringing something for him, but they were attacked by a jaguar and he had lost the sack in the woods. Juman had already heard of the lost shillings and looked at Desai with suspicion, but instead of further inquiries, he offered him a drink. Then they had supper, and Desai spent the night with that family.

The next day, when Desai arrived home, he found the authorities waiting for him. He was arrested and hauled away to jail, where he shared a cell with all his coworkers. There were a series of investigations, and the men were repeatedly questioned, but there were no answers. The men told of the attack by a large jaguar and wondered if they could have dropped the money during their mass confusion and panic. Desai told his story about being in the woods for a nature call, and during his return, he saw the large cat attacking the men and the horses galloping away. Two of the men had claw marks, though one was a minor scratch, which confirmed that they were really attacked by the beast. All the threats and mild torture revealed nothing, and the men were returned to their cell while the investigating team huddled around the table in an effort to get the men to talk, but it was of no use. They tried everything, including bribery, but the men continued telling the same story over and over. They were then separated and placed in solitary confinement for several days, but the story did not change. There was a major search along the road in the Port Mourant area, but the money was not found. There was a reward for information about the lost money, but there were no leads.

The solitary confinement was a good thing for Desai. He had time to think. He lay there for several days, dreaming about returning to India with his sons. His dream was to sneak into his village some evening and find his brother, Dashrath. If his parents were alive, they would be living close by. Then they would send a message inviting the sisters and have a quiet reunion with them. If all went well, he would eventually buy some land in the area, and the two brothers would acquire a large herd of cattle. He would find a woman like the one he knew there years ago who would be a good mother for his children, and life would be spectacular. They would all live happily ever after. With each passing hour, his dreams got more and more splendid. He would close his eyes and visualize himself and his brother walking along the old familiar ditch bank, admiring that enviable herd of cattle as they grazed on the luscious green grasses. He did not suffer from the confinement; instead, he rather enjoyed the solitude. He could dream for hours at a time about his return to India. There, he would be able to give his children a stable home and a good education using the stolen money and his savings to do so.

The investigations finally halted, and the men were freed. The children were glad to see their father, and Naz was very sympathetic with the whole situation. They had supper and went to bed with Desai hugging his two sons in the rocking chair and continuing with his wild dreaming. The next day, when Desai returned to work, he was told that he no longer had a job, that the whole crew had been fired on account that due to their negligence, the plantations had suffered a severe loss. There was a new crew with better bodyguards to move the payroll coins around. Desai pretended to be sad and protested, but it was of no use; he was fired. He went home to gather feed for his chickens and ducks, walking along with a smile on his face. He still maintained his relatively long hair, which was receding and thinning. He was mostly gray with a graying beard and moustache.

Some days later, Juman went to visit the graves of his mother and sister. He noticed that the dirt was disturbed in one area and wondered what could cause such a situation, but being a superstitious man, he did not investigate further. Some weeks later, Desai came to check on the site. Satisfied, he went to Juman's house. Juman discussed the situation of the disturbed soil at the grave site. Desai told him that he was aware of the soil disruption because he did it the evening that he spent with Juman. He explained that his late wife loved flowers so much that he intended to plant hibiscus and oleander plants there that would serve as grave markers. The flowering plants would further please his late wife's spirit. He explained to Juman that he wanted to work the soil so it would be ready when the plants arrived. The superstitious Juman questioned no more but suggested that he would help with the planting. Within a week, the smiling Desai and the ghost-fearing Juman planted flowers at the spot where the soil was disturbed, and as the plants grew, the matter was closed.

Juman had a suspicion that Desai had had something to do with the robbery, but it was just a hunch, so he went about his daily business. He had an unusual situation. He was married to an Indian woman named Chenia. His job at the sugar factory was to fuel the boiler that generated steam to power the factory. He shared his job with a Negro man named Phingol. Those two men had been friends for many years and were members of Juman's rebel gang that had shaved Desai's head several years before. Juman and Phingol had the same job but worked on opposite shifts. One worked the day shift, and the other worked the night shift. Every two weeks, they changed shifts, and the night man went on days and vice versa. They not only shared jobs; they also shared a house. What was more interesting was that they also shared the woman, Chenia. It was a workable situation because the men were not home at the same time. Chenia had four children. Two children were of Indian descent, and two had Negro characteristics. It was quite obvious that the two girl children were fathered by Juman and the two boys were fathered by Phingol. The Phingol boys were named John and Reggie. The Juman girls were named Julie and Maggie. An interracial child like the Phingol boys was called a *dougla* by the Indian community, and the elders referred to them as dougla boy or douglin gal. Hence, all of Juman's relatives called John and Reggie dougla boys.

That was why when Kangal's family moved away from the Port Mourant area, Juman did not accompany them. During those days, there were other douglas and douglins in the plantation area where they were better accepted, but in the villages, like Number 57, where

Kangal and his family settled, Chenia would become an outcast for having children of mixed races; and the children would be victimized wherever they went. Juman, Chenia, and Phingol were fine with their situation and their jobs. They saw no reason to migrate to a village to become rice farmers and to be humiliated by the ignorant neighbors. In fact, Kangal encouraged them to stay at the estate because he did not want to deal with the fact that his son lived such an unacceptable and sinful life. Juman did not care what others said. He was always revolting against the establishment, like the plantation system. Sharing his home and his wife with a Negro was another way of bucking against the East Indians and their rituals and beliefs.

Desai did not care about Juman's lifestyle. Ever since he arrived at the estate, Juman had been a troublemaker. He would occasionally visit Juman but never brought his children there. His occasional visits were excuses to visit his wife's grave and to tend the flowering plants there. But the main reason was to ensure that his loot was secure and that the site was not tampered with. When he was satisfied that things were in order, he paid his respects and returned to Juman's house, where Chenia would have a meal ready for him. On occasion, when Juman accompanied him to the burial site, he paid careful attention to Desai's nervous behavior, and as the months passed, he became more convinced that there could be more than bodies buried at the site. He often contemplated investigating further, but his superstitions and fear of ghosts kept him from doing anything. It was during those months that Desai began making arrangements for his return trip to India. The year was 1917. His sons were ten and two years old.

The year 1918 came, and Desai hosted a party and invited all his friends and neighbors. They butchered ducks and chickens and bought delicacies from the local store. The women helped Naz with the cooking and food service as the men enjoyed refreshing, cold alcoholic beverages, which soon resulted in clapping hands and stomping feet and finally erupted into a noisy dance party. It was during the celebration that Desai made his announcement about going back to India. The drunken men cheered and congratulated him on his bold move, but the women were concerned about Naz's situation. Desai assured them that he and the boys were going first, and when they got established, Naz would join them. That took care of that situation, and the drunken mob resumed their dancing, singing, and shouting only to be interrupted by a cheer for the family's upcoming return trip. It was a fun occasion, and all had a grand time at Desai's expense.

The years 1918 and 1919 were not good ones in the world, and British Guiana was no exception. There was an epidemic of influenza going around, and people started dying. It started out suddenly and soon became a horror. The first case was diagnosed in November 1918 in Georgetown, the capital of British Guiana. Shortly after that, people started dying by the thousands from that pandemic. There were so many corpses that the public could not bury them in any traditional manner. Coffins brought premium prices that only the wealthy could afford for an unfortunate victim. In order to dispose of the bodies that decomposed rapidly in the tropical heat, they started digging mass graves. The bodies were dumped in the trenches, which were filled with dirt as rapidly as possible. Day by day, the numbers of dead increased, and the number of trenches increased to accommodate them. The bodies kept piling in on top of one another. When one trench was full, they covered it with dirt and moved on to the next recently dug trench, and that continued. Nobody knew who would be next. Some families escaped without being affected, while several members of other families perished. In the colony, the poor and malnourished East Indian and the blacks between the ages of twenty and forty seemed to be most susceptible.

Then one night in January 1919, Desai began coughing. At first, he figured that he was getting a cold or that his lungs were congested. He went about his business the next day, still coughing and having trouble breathing. By nightfall, his symptoms made it clear to him that he was suffering from the deadly flu. He said nothing to Naz and started taking various homemade remedies, but it was of no use; his condition worsened to a point that he began moaning and shivering and sweating. He seemed to be gasping for air. Nanda piled blankets on him, but it did not help. He suffered through the night. The next morning, he went outside, hoping to minimize the symptoms. It was no use, his condition seemed to worsen. Desai really believed that he was strong enough to fight off the infection. But he wasn't. Naz saw his behavior and prayed for him. The symptoms became progressively worse by the hour. Late that night, Desai asked Nanda to help his brother along toward the main road where the carts went by frequently picking up people along the way and transporting them to the hospital. The locals called the hospital the sickhouse. Desai explained to his son that when they got to the road, he was to keep watch for the cart that went to the sickhouse. They slowly walked toward the main road with Desai coughing and gasping for breath. They took a few short breaks but needed to get to the road and secure transportation to the sickhouse.

The three huddled by the roadside for what seemed to be an eternity. Father was sick, and his sons were crying as they waited for a cart to arrive. Desai had a large black raincoat that he and the boys covered themselves with as they sat there into the morning hours. The flu symptoms became worse, and Desai began gasping severely for air. The father squeezed the boys as tears flowed from his eyes, sweat oozed from his shaking body, and a bloody mess foamed out of his mouth and nose. At that moment, they heard the noise of the creaking cart approaching. Nanda ran out in the fog to stop the cart as Desai cradled his three-year-old son, gasping harder and harder for air. The cart stopped, and the attendants helped Desai to climb in. He sat among other shivering, coughing, and gasping souls on their way to the sickhouse. With a groan, he told Nanda to take his brother to Naz's house as he tried to clear his throat. The drivers tapped the horses, and the cart creaked away into the distance as the morning sun crept out of the eastern horizon. The light of the flickering lantern on the cart was soon out of sight as Nanda held his little brother's hand, and together, they walked to Naz's house. By the time they arrived there, the sun was already up and consuming the dense morning fog that had lingered in the darkness.

When she heard the news, it was like being hit by lightning. She screamed and cradled her midsection. She found it hard to breathe, and in an instant, she fainted. The commotion got the attention of some of the neighbors, who came running and took her into the house, trying chaotically to keep her calm. Many of those neighbors had recently lost loved ones to the dreadful pandemic. They explained that Desai was a very strong man and that the doctors at the sickhouse would give him some of the miracle drug and he would be cured and come home in no time. She wanted to believe that, but she knew that Desai had not been feeling well for about a week, and he was weak from a stomach illness, from his respiratory concerns, and from lack of eating. They waited all day. No news came. Some friends tried to investigate but found out nothing. Three days passed, and Nanda insisted that he was going to the sickhouse to find his father, so he and Naz went. They did not find him. The sobbing woman and the crying boy must have made quite a scene, as they attracted the attention of numerous people in the area. Among them were some drivers who picked up sick people along the roadside. They asked the boy questions about when and where the subject was picked up. After a series of discussions, they told the boy that they remembered picking up his father that early foggy morning. They explained that when they arrived at the hospital, his father was among the dead. He died along the way to the sickhouse from suffocation. They asked about the body, but all the drivers knew was that he was loaded onto another cart and was hauled away to some mass grave where his body was most likely dumped and buried. Naz asked about the money belt, but there was no knowledge of any personal items. All they did was transfer the body onto another cart packed with dead bodies.

That was the end of Desai. All his dreams and plans to return to his homeland were buried with his bones in a ditch full of other bodies. He did leave two sons behind and joined his wife and their one son in a place unknown to mortals.

Naz took the boy by the hand, and they walked away from the sickhouse. They had no tears left and could not find words to communicate. They walked away in silence and went home. It was no use telling the almost four-year-old Motilall, who kept asking for Papa and wanted to go fishing. The neighbors had lives and grief of their own and soon went about their respective business, leaving a Muslim woman with two orphaned Hindu children in a land of limited resources, especially for such a family.

The poultry had to be fed, so Nanda went about the neighborhood trying to do odd jobs in exchange for some feed, but being only eleven, he was limited as to what he could do. They sold Desai's house and most of his personal items, except the rocking chair. Nanda insisted that he needed that to rock his little brother to sleep every night. With the limited sum they received from the sale, they managed to secure feed, and the eggs they sold subsidized their income. The woman tried to maintain the garden, but it was very hard work for her. Then one day, some estate personnel came to offer their condolences to the family. The woman explained the difficulty in making ends meet without Desai. She explained that she needed some support in order to raise the two boys. The sympathetic visitors told the woman that they could put Nanda to work at the factory bailing water out of the punts. They would pay him twelve cents per day. In addition, they would give her some groceries and some milk for the little one.

The next day, the men returned with a box full of various food items and an empty milk bottle. They explained that she should go to the milkman every morning and get one pint of milk for the little one, and the estate would pay the milkman on a weekly basis. Then they took Nanda and his little lunch pail and put him to work bailing water out of the punts with a two-gallon pail. He did that for six days per week, and at the end of the week, he was paid three shillings. Proud of his earnings, he hurried to the feed store and paid for his poultry feed. On Sundays, some of the neighbors came and helped Naz weed and fork her garden. So, it continued, and the three became a family with Motilall always waiting for Papa to come home and take him fishing. His Papa never came.

Pandemics and Global Disasters

Some historical facts need mentioning before our story can continue.

It is estimated that from 1918 into 1920, the flu killed some twenty to forty million people worldwide. Some sources estimated that the death toll was over fifty million. Nobody knows the exact count, but it was a lot of people. It was named the Spanish flu or la grippe. Many authorities now say that it was of avian origin, and it was a strain of the H1N1 virus. It was called the Spanish flu because the king of Spain became infected, and that nation made it public. The English-speaking nations then named the disease after that country. It is further estimated that a large fraction of the world's population was infected, and it was universally deadly to people between the ages of twenty and forty. The pandemic possibly killed more soldiers than actually died during combat in four major wars combined. Those four are World War I, World War II, the Korean War, and the Vietnam War. The initial infection in the United States was identified in March 1918. Soldiers from the United States deployed to European countries became the mode that rapidly spread the disease. Initially, the strain of the pathogen was somewhat mild, and many soldiers recovered after a few days of being under the weather. However, by September 1919, the pathogen seemingly mutated into a more deadly strain that took its toll on the global human population.

Many returning soldiers brought the disease home with them to their respective countries, and the death toll increased significantly from that source. It became obvious that the catastrophe was spread by humans. Outbreaks spread all across North America, Europe, Asia, Africa, and South America and to various islands around the world. Every continent except Antarctica was affected. It is also estimated that the mortality rate in India was fifty deaths per one thousand people. Death was due to a rapidly fatal bronchopneumonia. With such a high infection rate and ships coming into the colony on a regular basis from India, there was no shortage of the constant flow of infected people.

Desai was one more victim to the global catastrophe of 1918. He and all the global victims were fine people with dreams and aspirations. The majority who died were those in the prime of their child-bearing years. That pandemic left behind numerous single parents and countless orphans like Desai's children.

Nevertheless, the flu of 1918 was not an isolated pandemic. History has documented many other diseases that have slaughtered millions and millions of people in all parts of the globe, and diseases continue to create havoc on mankind into modern times. The world wrestles in a panic about the Ebola virus and about HIV. The 2020 pandemic is a reminder of historical catastrophes on earth.

In 430 BC, the plague of Athens killed an estimated one-third of the population in that area and was probably caused by typhus. The plague of Justinian took its toll from AD 541 to 542. The Black Death started in Asia and followed the trade route during that period into Europe in the 1340s. It killed seventy-five to one hundred million people globally and reduced Europe's population by 30 to 60 percent. It was possibly caused by bacteria or an Ebola-type virus. Smallpox, which is an airborne virus that infects through inhalation and by direct contact with bodily fluids, devastated the Aztec population in Mexico and spread to various tribes in North America, whose immune systems could not handle the deadly virus; and they perished. Between 1492 and 1900, the death toll from smallpox is not known, but it is estimated that between 50 and 90 percent of the native people in North America were affected. In 1793, yellow fever killed some five thousand people in Philadelphia and turned that city into a ghost town because people fled in order to avoid infection. That city was again devastated in the 1918 pandemic because of irresponsible political choices. Cholera became a global concern from 1817 to 1823. The disease that started from contaminated rice in India was contained in the Ganges area. But in 1817, British troops spread the disease throughout India and elsewhere. After the influenza outbreak of 1918, typhus became the major concern. It had a major impact from 1918 to 1922. Typhus was spread by mosquitoes, lice, and ticks that transmitted the bacteria that caused the disease in filthy areas with poor hygiene. Thousands died from typhus in Siberia, Poland, Romania, and other Eastern European countries. Malaria spread by female mosquitoes killed countless people in the world. It was after the introduction of DDT that the disease could be managed. DDT had other issues, especially with birds, but its function to almost eradicate malaria should be recognized. Although HIV can be managed today, the human race must remember that some twenty-five million people died from the disease and that an estimated 77 percent of cases are women who can pass the infection to their babies. HIV can be found today in every part of our planet.

Desai's death was one more unfortunate circumstance in human history. But it is a fact of life that rapid and violent death caused by diseases of global origin and mutations of various organisms has and will continue to have devastating effects on human lives. The world must also understand that infections know not nations or borders, nor do they favor affluence. However, effective treatments can and do favor affluence. Money talks! Proper nutrition, a good health-care system, and a healthy lifestyle can help one resist infections to some degree. These simple habits are not exclusive to affluence; they are equal-opportunity lifestyles. But there will always be some mysterious disease that can and will emerge in any part of our planet, at any time. With modern travel and trade, it becomes difficult to quarantine such outbreaks even in remote areas. It comes down to personal choices and safe habits. We should all adopt the Boy Scout motto: Be Prepared.

CHAPTER 10

The Orphans

When Desai died, Motilall was almost four years old. In fact, he could have been four years old if his birth records were accurate. His birth certificate reveals that he was born on March 15, 1915. But some of the relatives believed that he was born in January. In those days, the registration process for children of indentured servants was done when it was convenient for some of the families. When his mother died, shortly after he was born and his aunt began nursing him, the extended family did not see the urgency of such a registration process. They wanted to ensure that the child could survive simply because, in those days in that remote area, many children died from a host of diseases, malnutrition, accidents, snakebites, and to some extent, abuse by others. When it was obvious that the child was healthy and had a chance of survival, the birth registration process took place with someone estimating the birth date.

The older brother, Nanda, continued his job at the estate bailing water out of punts and made enough money to buy poultry feed and an occasional snack for the little one. Naz loved them both but totally favored the younger as if he were her own son. She had no living children of her own. It must have been difficult, but she managed to maintain the home with limited resources and the contributions from the estate. They continued getting the pint of milk daily and the weekly ration from the estate consisting of two pounds of flour, two pounds of sugar, one gallon of rice, one pound of salt, one pound of split peas, two pints of kerosene, and a bar of homemade soap. They gathered coconuts that fell from the tall trees and made coconut oil, which was their only source of cooking oil. She was not very good at fishing, but the three of them often wandered about the waters and tried their luck with a fish hook tied to a string. The string was attached to a piece of bamboo about an inch in diameter. They baited the hooks with earthworms and usually caught a few fish. They celebrated every catch by jumping about and waving their arms. The smaller fish were cleaned and fried in their coconut oil. But the bigger fish were cleaned, salted, and smoked. The smoking was done over an open fire smothered with green twigs and leaves. They crisscrossed some green sticks over the smoky fire and let the heat and the smoke do their jobs for several hours. The smoked fish were then tied to the clothesline and dried in the tropical sun. The dried fish were stored and periodically used to flavor the various vegetable dishes. Sometimes they caught shrimp in the swamps, and on those days, Naz would fry them and make a shrimp and vegetable stir fry that they ate with a plateful of rice. But the best times were those occasional Saturdays when Naz and the little one went to the local market to sell their poultry and eggs. After they sold everything, they would celebrate with sweetened drinks, sugarcane juice, and various pieces of candy. Those days concluded with purchasing the various spices and other necessary items. Then they returned home for a nice evening nap and to dream about the fun time at the market. When Nanda returned from work, Naz would share some of the sweets with him and explained how much money she got from the sale of the various items.

Day by day, they grew closer together, and although there were many grieving moments, they enjoyed being the family that they became. Naz sometimes took the little one for a stroll. They would sit by the river under a shade tree where she hummed various tunes, and they all enjoyed the whistling of the wind and the twittering birds that perched above on waving branches. They pointed and smiled as the parent birds brought food for their babies in the nests and danced as the chicks ravished the nourishment. Then they flew away as the chicks dozed and waited for their next morsels. They would watch the ripples in the river that gently bombarded the water grass that grew on the surface and reached outward into the river. They watched as the spurwings leaped from one water lily leaf to another and then flew away into the open air. They watched as an occasional monkey mother carried her baby on her back, leaping from branch to branch and tree to tree. Then Naz gave the boy a small treat and hugged him in the presence of Mother Nature. She loved that child. On the way home, they searched for and picked wild fruits and berries, which they ate as slow steps meandered them home.

Months passed, and Juman wondered why his brother-in-law had not been there to visit him. He decided to pay Desai a visit. Upon his arrived, he found strangers living at Desai's shack. The occupants informed him that they bought the site from the woman down the lane. Juman went to investigate and found out that Desai had died months before. He was shocked. Nobody informed the family of such a tragedy. He went to the estate to protest the situation and was told that the woman who took the children in said that as far as she knew, there were no immediate relatives alive. That infuriated Juman, who instantly marched to the woman's house in a rage. The woman explained that she had no idea that the family existed because they never came to visit, and Desai never spoke of them. In fact, since Desai left Port Mourant, he never took the boys to visit Juman, who was now seeing the boys for the first time in three years. He was at least happy that they had a home and seemed to be well cared for. So he introduced himself to the boys, and while he was leaving, Motilall told him to go find Papa because they had to go fishing. Juman smiled at the innocence of the little chatterbox and went back to Port Mourant.

Weeks went by after Juman visited the boys, and he went about his daily business fueling the factory boilers with bagasse in the usual alternating schedule with Phingol. As he slowly scooped the fuel into the mouth of the blazing boiler, he kept thinking about Desai and his tragic death. He kept thinking about the boys, especially the little chatterbox who wanted to go fishing. Occasionally he would think about his beautiful sister and her sufferings during her last days. He also wondered about the money that Desai possibly stole. But he figured that the boys seemed happy and he should leave things as they were. He periodically visited the grave site and wondered if the loot was under those blooming hibiscus and oleander plants. But he was too scared to investigate.

Then one day when the factory was down for routine maintenance, he and Phingol were home together with Chenia and the four children. It was a rare occasion when that happened, so they had a small celebration. They ate a good meal, and the children were given money to buy sweets at the local candy shop. People referred to those establishments as cake shops. The two men opened up their liquor (rum) bottles. In crude tin cups, they blended the rum with coconut water. Together, they swallowed their drinks, shook their heads, grabbed a piece of curried duck, and chewed away. Shortly after, they began singing and dancing together as the family laughed at their silly drunken behaviors. They took occasional breaks in order to catch their breath and to refill their cups and make nature calls behind a nearby tree. If there was something to talk about, they sat, sipped their drinks, shook their heads, chewed on duck meat, and discussed whatever was appropriate for two drunks at that moment.

It was during one of those breaks that Juman told Phingol about Desai's tragedy. The news stunned Phingol, and the two sat there drunk and crying for the deceased Desai. The conversation went on about the welfare of the children and their future. After all, there was no money left for them, and now, they were at the mercy of a strange Muslim woman. Phingol was talking, and Juman started to think. He wondered if Desai really stole the money from the payroll wagon and buried it at his wife's grave site. He knew that the soil had not been disturbed since he and Desai planted the flowers there. Phingol was still babbling as Juman shouted out in a typical drunken manner that there might be some money. That got Phingol's attention. He paused and started asking a series of questions in order to understand the details. Juman, in his drunken state, revealed his suspicions. Phingol asked why he did not dig up the area and investigate. They had the superstitious discussion about digging up a grave site. Juman had the worst fear of ghosts, and Phingol knew that.

After a few more drinks, the men passed out and fell asleep under a mango tree. The family brought out two pillows and some sheets and tried to comfort the drunks. It was easier for them to do that than to try to haul them to bed. They had done that duty before. It became very inconvenient when they were both home at the same time. To avoid the situation, they would drink and sleep together under the mango tree. On rainy nights, they both slept on the floor, leaving the woman to herself.

The next morning, they both suffered from serious headaches as they sipped sweetened hot tea and copious amounts of water. Their discussion soon continued about Desai's alleged robbery as both men held their heads and whispered. The family laughed at the whispering, speculating that their heads would hurt too much if they spoke any louder. Phingol told Juman that he had no fear of digging up a grave site if there was the possibility of finding buried treasure. They agreed to go together, and Phingol would do the digging. After lunch, they grabbed a shovel, a garden fork, a cutlass, some water, and a shoulder bag and walked toward the burial site. For a long while, they stood under the silk cotton tree. The many hibiscus and oleander flowers were red and white, and the green plants had grown to several feet. A few cows were grazing close by. High above, the vultures sailed effortlessly on the ocean breeze, circling about in search of any carcasses below. The men stood there sweating in the tropical heat and high humidity.

Finally, they both knelt and prayed—Phingol praying to Jesus and Juman praying to Krishna. At the conclusion of their prayers, Juman stepped back, and Phingol slashed the branches, casting aside the beautiful flowers still attached to the stems. Having cleared the area with the cutlass, he started the digging. The flower plants had turned into small trees with large deep, penetrating roots. Phingol, with a slight headache still, labored and perspired in the tropical heat, swallowing water and chopping away the roots. It was hard work, and he questioned his own sanity for believing such ridiculous story. Then he found something. It was a rotting gunnysack wrapped around a decayed animal skin. He held the fragile skin up with a puzzled look on his face, and Juman began to laugh. He finally understood the jaguar mystery. His hilarious behavior annoyed the tired digging man, who started shouting out profanity to the laughing Juman. The excitement eventually brought him to the site, and the two dug away with shovel and fork in the tropical heat, gulping warm water from the rum bottles that they had emptied the night before. They found the money! Not saying much, they buried the evidence carefully at the site and took the coins home in the shoulder bag. After dark, when they were sure that the children were in bed, they nodded that it was time. In the darkness with the aid of a kerosene lantern, they divided the shillings. Half the money was set aside for buying a new home and some furniture. The other half was divided between them. Juman got three quarters, and Phingol got one quarter.

They told no one, but soon thereafter, the family had new clothes, they moved to a nicer, well-furnished house, and their spending habits increased significantly. They spent their money incrementally to avoid any suspicion. Their story was that the children were growing up and needed more space. Juman told his friends that he planned to spend his life savings while young and healthy and to enjoy life to the fullest.

Both men soon thereafter quit working at the factory and did other less stressful jobs. A few weeks later, Juman, now with money and a flexible working schedule, went to visit his father and brothers, and he told them about Desai's death and about the fate of the children. He said nothing about the money. Kangal was infuriated about the fact that his grandsons were being raised by a Muslim woman. He immediately called his sons together and told them to arrange transportation so that they could go and rescue the boys from such an environment. For some unknown reason, Kangal did not like Muslim people. Speculation was because his wife's immigration papers had classified her as Muslim, and he was occasionally harassed by his

Hindu associates as a traitor to Hinduism. He probably had other reasons for his hatred, for such feelings ran deep in the history of India and eventually created the country of Pakistan. So to find out that his two orphaned grandsons were in the company of a Muslim did put him into an uncontrollable rage. He never told anyone that his wife was basically enslaved by a Muslim bully prior to arriving in British Guiana. That was their secret, and he wanted to keep it that way.

His sons had families of their own, and resources were limited. They were not eager to bring more mouths into their homes. But Kangal was adamant. He wanted the boys to be rescued from a Muslim environment. Juman made it clear that he would not take the boys because of his domestic situation, and Kangal agreed. Going from a Muslim environment to a Negro environment was beyond his tolerance. He despised the fact that his son shared his home and wife with a Negro man. But Juman had that discussion many times before and told his father very emphatically that at that moment, he was not the subject of the discussion. They should be making living arrangements for the two orphans. He called a meeting with his father and brothers and told them what they would do. Juman agreed to pay all expenses for getting the boys to their new homes, and he further agreed to pay his brothers a small fee to care for the boys for one year. Kangal was pleased to hear Juman's offer, and he also offered to help in any way that he could. He explained that he was an old man with some money and intended to use the money for the benefit of the children. It was the least he could do for his wonderful daughter, who departed at such a tender age. He was on the verge of crying. Two of his sons agreed to take the boys into their respective homes.

On New Year's Day 1920, Kangal and two of his sons picked up Juman at Port Mourant and went to Canje to get the boys. At Canje, Juman purchased a donkey, a cart, and a kerosene lantern and drove the donkey and cart to Naz's house. It was almost dark when the four men disembarked from the cart and tied the donkey to a tree where it could graze. Juman called out to Naz. She was not at home, but the boys came running out. Seeing his grandsons, Kangal could not help his emotions. He began to cry as he hugged the two and, through the tears, explained that he was their grandfather (Nana). The boys recognized Juman, and the little one asked him if he had found his papa. He was explaining that Papa must come home and take him fishing. His innocent chatter brought tears to all the men, and Kangal chuckled through the tears about the little chatterbox. He instantly loved the little talker, and he looked to the heavens as if to give his daughter a message that he had found her sons.

It was a peaceful moment as the sun was setting. Flocks of blackbirds flew from tree to tree, singing in the twilight in search of a suitable place to roost. Frogs began their evening mating calls, owls were celebrating the approaching darkness, and bats dotted the sky.

Then Naz came home. Seeing Juman and the others, she suspected that they were there to visit the children. But Kangal wasted no time. He explained that they were there to take the boys home where they could be cared for by real blood relatives. He did not wait for a response. He stated his purpose for being there and walked out, telling Juman to handle the details. Shocked and angry, she told the men to leave her house and not to upset her children. Kangal heard that part about "her children," and the fighting began. The four men realized that nothing could be accomplished on the evening of a holiday and proceeded to climb onto their cart and drive the donkey to some place with food and lodging. As Naz lit her lamp in the house, Juman lit his and tied it to the axel of the cart, which soon disappeared into the darkness.

The next morning, the four men went to visit the estate manager. They explained that they had every legal right to claim the orphans and raised them in a sound Hindu environment. Kangal further explained that the woman was a burden to the estate and, in her lazy manner, was avoiding working for a living because of the subsidy she was receiving. They pleaded their case, and the manager told them to return the following day to hear the final decision, which would be made by the local magistrate. The men once again used the donkey and cart to travel to the place with food and lodging. They called the restaurant a cookshop and ensured that the establishment did not serve beef or pork. They figured that no good quality Hindu cookshop would serve such forbidden meats. They had a good meal of fish curry, fried vegetables, dal, rice, and roti. They drank tea and enjoyed come kheer for dessert. Juman paid for the meal and lodging.

That afternoon, January 2, 1920, the estate manager met with the magistrate. They had their usual social get-together and casually discussed the orphans' case. It was not much of a discussion because the laws favored the relatives as legal guardians. So, the next morning, when the manager summoned the woman for a private meeting, she knew what would happen. She took a bath, put on her best clothes, combed her hair properly, and went to see the man and to hear the decision. She took the boys along with her. The manager had Kangal and his sons wait outside while he discussed matters with Naz and the children. She cried and begged and pleaded, but the manager informed her that she had no legal right to keep the children. They belonged to the relatives. The manager also told her that her being a Muslim complicated things even more because she had to decide the faith and religion of the children. He asked the question about church. He asked her if she could keep the boys, which religion they would be? Her response stunned the manager when she told him that God made man, and men made religion. She further explained that she planned to raise the children in the name of God, for God did not favor religion. The manager, not knowing what to say, called in Kangal and his sons for a discussion with him and the woman. The boys sat quietly and listened.

The discussion soon escalated into a shouting match, and the estate police were summoned to keep the peace. The angry woman shouted and screamed only to be silenced by the police. Then she told the group that they could take the older boy, but she wanted the little one. The answer was still no; the children must both go with the blood relatives. Then she told the manager that she had an investment in the little one because she had cared for him for almost a year. She finally requested fifteen dollars' reimbursement for the care she provided for Motilall. Kangal protested, but eventually he and Juman quietly said that they would pay the fifteen dollars if that would solve the whole matter. The woman reluctantly agreed.

Together, they walked back to her house to gather up the boys' personal things. Nanda hugged her and told her to keep the rocking chair as a memory of Desai. Then the boys went out to feed and water the donkey. They went and said goodbye to all the chickens and ducks. Kangal kept an eye on them and was quite impressed as to how responsible they seemed to be and how polite and mannerly they appeared. He wanted to go to the house and compliment the woman on the fine job she did in raising the boys, but his pride was in conflict with his emotions, and he allowed his pride to be the driver at that moment.

By the time all the details were handled, it was getting late, and by the time the cart was loaded and the passengers climbed aboard, the sun was setting. Juman lit the lantern and tied it to the axel of the cart as the donkey struggled to pull the heavy load. The boys sat at the back with their bare feet dangling below the knees. They watched as their crying Auntie kept pace with the slow-moving cart. Her friends and neighbors stayed a few paces back, walking along in support of the unfortunate woman. She kept walking and talking to the boys until darkness surrounded them and the road came to a gradual descent. There, the donkey broke into a trot, and the woman and her friends tried to keep up. They started to fall further and further behind, and through her gasping and wailing, she sounded like an animal in agony. The boys yelled back at her as she hurried, but finally, in the darkness, on that dusty trail, she stumbled and fell. Her friends picked her up and tried to comfort her. They could see the distant flickering of the lantern on the cart's axel as the donkey continued his trot, and with a few slight flickers in the distance, the cart vanished into the darkness. The boys were gone to their new homes, and she was left with her loneliness in her little shack, fifteen dollars, and Desai's rocking chair. She checked on her poultry in the yard. A few neighbors kept her company. Eventually, she went to bed. The boys never saw her again.

*   *   *

The traveling group stayed at the hotel that night and again ate at the cookshop. After breakfast, on the public road, Kangal drove the cart and the other three men found other means of transportation. By the third day, they arrived at Port Mourant, where Juman traded the donkey for a fresh one. The boys had a brief moment with Juman's daughters, Julie and Maggie, but at Kangal's request, "dem dougla bys" were not welcome to visit with his grandsons, and neither was Phingol. There, they said goodbye to Juman and left him at his new home at Port Mourant. The two uncles went ahead to make arrangements for the boys' arrival, and after two days with the fresh donkey pulling the cart, Kangal and his two grandsons arrived at Number 57 Village. It was raining when they arrived, and everything and everyone was wet. They unhooked the cart, put the harness away, penned up the donkey, put on dry clothes, and went to bed listening to the thunder and seeing the bright flashes of lightning in the tropical darkness. It rained all night, and the boys could hear the dripping of water from the thatched roof, which collected into metal buckets strategically placed on the floor. Although it rained all that night, the two boys, exhausted from the trip and the weather, soon were fast asleep as their grandfather sat next to their bed tired, excited, and concerned about their future. He fell asleep sitting up in the chair as the drips of water collected into the partially filled metal buckets one drop at a time. Drop, drop, drop.

Morning was greeted by calm winds. Bright sunshine had chased the storm away. The boys slept on the home-made bed, and their grandfather was snoring on the floor. The noisy thunder and howling winds were replaced by singing birds and crowing roosters. There were barking dogs, mooing cows, and braying donkeys. Occasionally, gravity pulled drops of residual water off the leaky grass roof and plopped them into the overflowing buckets on the floor.

The smoke from the kitchen and the clanging of dishes informed all the occupants that it was time to get up and face the day. Kangal got the boys up and emptied the buckets out of a wooden window. In his dhoti, his scar was quite visible down his back. He got the boys up, and with sleepy eyes, they followed Kangal to the kitchen area.

After gazing around in the smoky haze, Kangal sat on a wooden bench and leaned against the wall. He was soon joined by the two newcomers. They wore long cotton garments that were more suited for girls than boys, but at least they had dry clothes. They were given warm sweetened tea in white enamel cups by the woman in the kitchen, who was trying to get breakfast ready. There was a girl child about two years old and a crying baby. Kangal went and picked up the baby as the shy little girl tried to hide behind the busy mother by grabbing onto the mother's cotton skirt and getting dragged about as the woman hurried about in the tiny kitchen. Kangal explained to the boys that the baby belonged to the uncle next door and that he would be babysitting while the women cooked breakfast.

The yard was flooded. Chickens were perched on fences as the ducks paddled about with bobbing heads, wiggling tails, and cheerful quacks. The boys looked out of a wooden window and saw the two barefooted uncles clothed only in little white shorts, milking cows by hand in the mud and having a discussion. They both had wooden twigs in their mouths that served as toothbrushes. The water was now slowly receding, exposing patches of shrubs and grasses and plenty of manure and mud in the backyard. The woman went out the front door, followed by the little girl. The boys followed and found her in a neat vegetable garden next to numerous flowering plants. That area was on higher ground, and the flood did not have much impact there. Kangal came out carrying the baby. They picked some vegetables.

The high humidity and blazing morning sun were becoming unbearable outside. Inside, the little kitchen was even hotter from the cooking smoke and fire. The smoke from the fireside made it almost unbearable as one of the half-naked uncles handed the woman some milk in a metal bucket. She strained the raw milk with a piece of cotton and poured it into a large pot. The pot was placed on the hot fireside. The little girl was still being dragged along by the woman as Kangal fed the baby with a bottle filled with warm cows' milk.

After breakfast, the uncles and Kangal explained to the boys about the arrangements made for them. Motilall would stay at that house, and Nanda would live next door with the other uncle and his wife. So their wet clothes were hung out to dry, and the boys were separated as discussed. The humble houses with thatched roofs were adjacent, and the two uncles shared a common yard where they grew vegetables and tended their livestock, which consisted of cows, chickens and ducks, goats, sheep, and donkeys. They also shared a pair of oxen that were used for working the rice field and for pulling heavy loads. Between the houses in the back lot was a small storage shed that also served as a granary. They called that structure a *khotilla*. The A-framed roof was made of several layers of braided coconut branches that extended almost to the ground, and the walls were made of home-sawed lumber of various dimensions. Adjacent to the khotilla were pens for the goats and sheep and a small enclosure for two donkeys. The chickens and ducks had their own little enclosed structures that kept them protected from various predators during the night. During the day, the feathered creatures roamed about freely. Those were some observations the boys made that first day as they were separated into their respective new homes.

The boys also noticed that the pair of donkeys did not get along, and now the arrival of a third one made things quite unsettling in the small confined area. Kangal explained that they would have to sell the older one and keep the younger, more aggressive one for pulling the cart. Within a few days, two donkeys and the extra cart were sold to the neighbors. He gave some of the money to the two uncles as partial payment and sent the rest to Juman to offset the fifteen-dollar cost incurred for the purchase of Motilall. He thanked Juman for being so generous with "his" money.

No one really knows what happened to the Muslim woman, Naz. Stories were told about her coming to the village to visit the boys. But she was met by the roadside and emphatically told to leave. When she insisted on seeing the boys, she was dragged and pushed about, probably beaten, and sent away. She must have left with another broken heart. She must have cried all the way home to Canje. No written words can do justice to such emotions. She must have taken those memories to her grave and buried them with her body. One hundred years later, family members still talk about her and the agony she lived and died with, in that remote Canje village in Guyana. This story can immortalize Naz for her kindness and generosity to those two children in need and for all the joy she brought to their young lives.

CHAPTER 11

Thumru

Being an orphan can be difficult for a child. Some orphans are fortunate to be living in good homes with loving parents who adopt them. But many are not so lucky. Motilall was not one of the lucky ones. It did not take him long to realize that he was going to be a servant to his uncle and his family. His uncle's name was Somwaru (he was also known as Raghoonandan or Raghoo), son of Kangal and Kalya. He was born at Port Mourant on January 21, 1893. His wife's name was Seelochanni (also known as Mularie). She was born in Number 56 Village on March 22, 1900. Her father came from India when he was six years old on a ship called the *British Monarch* that landed at British Guiana on February 27, 1870. The little boy's name was Poonoyeah, and he was called Poonai. Poonai's wife's name was Mutchowa, and she came from India when she was three years old. She and her mother, Tejia, came on a ship called the *Clarence* that arrived in British Guiana in 1874.

Motilall called his uncles and aunts by the customary name of Mamoo and Mammi, meaning maternal uncle and wife. Hence, Somwaru was Mamoo, and Seelochanni was Mammi.

The five-year-old Motilall was a constant talker compared to his older brother. He was given daily chores, which he rather enjoyed mostly because he got help from his grandfather, Kangal. The gray, old man with the scar down his back loved the little talker, and as the boy babbled away, the grandfather stroked his long, gray beard. He was now sixty-one years old but had the appearance of an eighty-year-old. He was only five feet five inches tall, but now due to hard work and poor diet, he walked slightly bent forward, which made him appear even shorter. He walked with a cane because his knees had issues. But he hobbled along with the little talker, habitually pulling on his long, gray beard when they had a reason to stop. They made quite a pair and brought comfort to each other. The boy brought good memories to the old man about his deceased beloved daughter, and the old man brought comfort to the scared little boy in that new environment.

Other than talking, the boy loved to eat and to climb trees. He could not get enough food at the table, so Kangal would have the women (his daughters-in-law) give him extra food at supper because he claimed that he usually got hungry during the night. All the extra food went to the boy, who sat in the dark behind the khotilla and ate. Kangal knew where wild fruits and berries grew. During the day, he found them, and they picked and ate together. The boy climbed various fruit trees and vines and secured the ripe ones, which he and Kangal shared. It was a symbiotic bond between grandfather and grandson in one little corner of our world.

The months passed, and the boy became very familiar with the neighborhood. He could wander about without Kangal and gather up various wild fruits and berries to share with the old man. He recognized that the old man had difficulty walking on the uneven terrain, so he would have him sit and wait as he loped about in search of some prized fruits. It was obvious that Kangal's legs were getting progressively worse for when it was time to get up, he would lean on his cane and painfully push with a groan until he was standing. Then he slowly hobbled along. It was quite obvious, too, that his breathing was not normal, for as he hobbled along, he was constantly gasping for air.

The boy still had daily chores, which included getting milk from the Poonai family. He was told that their cow did not have milk anymore and would not until she had another calf. So, every morning, he gathered the milk pail and went to Number 56 Village to get milk. Mr. Poonai had many cows. His family worked at the plantation, and after their bounds were fulfilled, they worked and invested in farming and bought several cows. Within a few years, the herd grew significantly, and Mr. Poonai hired local men to help with his various operations. He made sure that his daughter, Mammie, had enough milk for she was again pregnant. Mr. Poonai, in his mid-fifties, also loved the little talker and named him Thumru. No one knew where the name came from, but all the hired cowhands soon got to know the skinny little orphan boy named Thumru. While Mutchowa got the milk ready, the milking men gave the little Thumru fresh, warm milk straight from the cow.

The boy grew fond of the Poonai family and their cattle operation. Every day, when he went to get milk, he would linger about and watch the men milking the cows by hand. He enjoyed petting the cows and occasionally tried to ride the smaller calves. That usually turned into a miniature rodeo, which brought laughs and chuckles to the cowhands. He carried around a coconut shell, and the milking men would fill the shell with warm raw milk, and he would drink as much as he could. Sometimes he carried a calabash, which could hold larger quantities of milk for his morning consumption. Such behavior infuriated Mamoo because the boy was not home to perform his chores in a timely manner. But when he tried to discipline the lad, Kangal would come to the rescue, claiming that he, Kangal, had done the morning duties for the boy, and there was no harm done if the boy socialized with the cowboys at the Poonai residence. Mamoo would not show disrespect to his father, and the boy seldom got disciplined.

One day, during the hunt for fruit and berries, Kangal began his usual gasping for air. The gasping became so intense that he finally discarded his walking cane and crouched down on the ground. The scared lad, not sure what was happening, ran home for help. The two Mamoos and other folks followed the panicking boy as he ran back to the site where the old man had collapsed. It was too late. Kangal was dead. The two Mamoos had their wives rush home for some sheets.

In the sheets, they wrapped the corpse and carried it home. It was a wild scene, as everybody had an opinion as to what must be done. The scared boy started looking for his brother, but he was in the rice fields and could not be found. So he ran to the Poonais' house and shared the news. Mr. Poonai grabbed his hat and hurried over to the scene where he managed to calm the family down and took charge of the funeral arrangements.

The local pundit was called to offer prayers, and the village carpenters were summoned with instructions to build a coffin. Some of the neighbors were sent to town to get some ice. Kangal's corpse was then placed on a galvanized metal sheet with the ice covering his body to avoid rapid decomposition in the tropical heat. Then his entire body was covered with a sheet as messengers departed to notify all the friends and relatives. Motilall sat by the bed in total confusion, listening to the drips from the melting ice that went into a metal pail— *drop, drop,* and *drop.* All day long, people shuffled about like working bees doing whatever was necessary. Night came, and the kerosene lanterns were lit. Some folks sang and prayed around the corpse, and outside, some of the men gathered with no objectives in mind. They just came to show support for the family and to discuss issues with the neighbors. They sat in small circles rolling chipped tobacco and inhaling smoke from their homemade cigarettes. Some played checkers, and others shuffled and played card games. Occasionally someone passed out crackers and tea. It was a typical scene at a village wake house. They gathered there to "keep wake," meaning that they did not sleep. They stayed awake to support the grieving family.

The morning sun replaced the kerosene lanterns as the relatives, friends, and neighbors filed into the yard at the "dead house." The men congregated among themselves, and the women sat together on cotton sheets that were spread on the ground under a temporary shelter. The prayers, chanting, and singing continued. Soon, the wooden coffin arrived. It was time to bathe and dress the dead. Then there was the funeral. The coffin containing Kangal's corpse was placed on a donkey cart, and the procession of men followed to the cemetery. Women traditionally did not go to the cemetery.

It was midafternoon as the donkey labored along, pulling the cart, especially on any slight incline going uphill. On the descent, the donkey came to a slight trot as the driver ensured that they did not get too far ahead of the small groups of men who marched along, trying to keep pace with the donkey. Far behind, the two crying orphaned grandsons followed the procession holding each other's hand.

At the cemetery, the grave diggers had done their job. With shovels in hand, they dug the grave deep enough and wide enough for the coffin. The dirt was piled on both sides of the hole. The coffin was carried to the site where the pundit did the rituals and instructed the men to lower the body into the hole. With ropes in place, the coffin was lowered while the pundit continued his rituals. The ropes were removed, and the grave diggers were instructed to shovel the dirt back into the hole. The grandsons were asked to throw a handful of dirt on top of the coffin, to say a prayer for the departed soul, and to ask the Almighty to guide him into heaven as the shovel men did their thing.

As the hole was being filled, the men began to meander out of the cemetery. They all walked toward a nearby ditch, where they washed their hands and bare feet. It was customary to leave all cemetery dirt in the area. Taking such dirt would encourage some lonely ghost to follow the transporting party, and that person would be haunted for carelessly removing dirt that belonged to the dead. It was one more tradition that was created by persons unknown, and the men knew better than to lead a perceived ghost to their homes. After the washing, a small handful of water was sprinkled over the individual, ensuring the final cleansing to that individual. The grandsons were instructed to do the same as the men did, and they obeyed. Then they all walked back to their respective homes. Many went to the house where Kangal had lived, where the friends and family had prepared food. The singers soon began their traditional familiar tunes, and the pundit did some ritualistic details. The singing and talking continued late into the night, and the darkness found the lonely Thumru sleeping on a rice sack in the khotilla with his brother sitting next to him. And just like that, there was no more Kangal. The year was 1924. He was sixty-five years old.

The neighbors gathered every night at the home where Kangal had lived for several more nights. Juman was there with his two daughters and helped to pay for the groceries and beverages that fed the visiting neighbors who came to keep wake and to partake in the food provided. Juman's daughters, being bored in the strange area, followed their little cousins about during the day, and they picked and ate fruits and berries that grew in the woods. As they wandered about, Motilall told his cousins stories about Kangal and how they usually went in search of ripe fruits. The girl cousins, Julie and Maggie, loved their little cousin as he sprang about the tree branches with monkey-like motion, picking wild fruits for them.

After the departure of Julie and Maggie, Nanda returned to the rice fields. The visitors to the wake house became fewer and fewer. The little Thumru became sad and lonely. He had lost his Nana and best friend. Poonai noticed his sulking and pitied the little orphan. So he called the boy over, and they sat under a fruit tree close to the fowl coop. He talked, and the boy listened. He talked about living and dying. He explained that Kangal had been old, with bad legs and other health issues. He told the boy that God took Kangal to heaven to fix his legs and his illnesses, that Kangal would be living with God above the clouds. He explained that every living creature would die someday and go to the hospital in heaven to get cured. He needed to pray for his Nana during his journey and for his recovery. When he was completely recovered, he would be happy and healthy again in God's house.

The boy listened to the wisdom of the elder, and when the talking stopped, the boy looked at Poonai and commented that God must have a very large house to accommodate so many people because that was where his Papa and Mama lived with his brother, who drowned in the Canje River. Mr. Poonai laughed at the innocent wisdom.

The sons of Kangal had their heads totally shaved except for a few hairs in the back called a *churkie*. Those few hairs were saved because if an evil spirit should possess that individual, the local exorcists would cut off some of those hairs, which would separate the ghost from the possessed. The hair would be sealed in a bottle and discarded. Most people, especially children, during that time would not open any sealed discarded bottle for fear of letting a ghost out and possibly being possessed. There were numerous explanations for the bottle ritual, but that was the popular one. After two weeks, the family gathered by the running river water and offered various food items to the departed on lotus leaves that drifted away with the water current toward the Atlantic Ocean. Motilall, hungry as usual, figured that it was a waste of food and wished that some was given to him. But at the conclusion of the ritual, they turned away and walked home being careful not to look back at the departing food because looking back would be dishonoring the soul of the hungry deceased who might be partaking in his favorite foods.

With Kangal gone, there was no one to protect the little Thumru, and soon Mamoo became a tyrant toward him. He had the now nine-year-old boy doing all types of jobs around the farm. One of the responsibilities was to ensure that the donkey was penned up every night. Their male donkey was released every morning for grazing. Being a stallion, he occasionally went in search of females for breeding purposes. Hence, he wandered about all day, and Thumru had to find him in the evening and bring him home.

One day, the boy had too many chores to do and did not get out in time to find the donkey. In the dark, he ran from place to place in vain. He did not find the animal and finally came home. He gave the news to Mamoo, who looked at the boy with anger and whispered something to his wife before stomping off to bed. Mammie told the boy that the penalty for not finding the animal was no supper and that he had to sleep in the khotilla, and she, too, stomped off to bed. He was puzzled, scared, and hungry. He stood there alone in the dark for some time and slowly walked toward the shack. There were no sheets or pillows, so he rummaged about in the dark and found a few old mice-infested sacks, which he managed to assemble into a make-believe bed. He slept there that night.

In the morning, he noticed that an angry neighbor was in the yard yelling at Mamoo. He could not understand what was happening until he asked Mammie for some breakfast. He was just starting to eat when Mamoo came into the kitchen and took his plate away. Then Mamoo removed his belt from his waist and began striking the lad with all his might. After several lashes, the man threw the belt aside and told the boy that last night the donkey wandered into the neighbor's yard and beat up upon the neighbor's donkey that was tied to a post and could not escape or defend himself. The neighbor claimed that his donkey was badly injured and could not pull the cart so Mamoo need to pay for him to rent another donkey for the immediate future.

To avoid any more beating, he ran away to Poonai's farm. Mr. Poonai, upon hearing the complaint and seeing the belt marks on the boy's body, became angry. They fed him a good meal and told him to go home and attend to his chores. He did as he was told and was pleased to find out that Mamoo was not at home when he got there. He had learned his lesson. His number one priority was to ensure that the donkey was penned up every evening. So he hurried about all day getting all the domestic chores done on time and then hurried out to find the animal. He was lucky that day, and the donkey was close by. After getting a rope around the animal's neck, he tied him to a tree and then went searching for fruits and berries. It did not take him long to see the complaining neighbor's watermelons, so he hesitated until the man went home. He stashed his wild fruits and took the donkey home. Then he went and asked for supper. There was no supper for him. Mamoo made it clear that he should not be fed until he said that it was okay to feed the boy again. In addition, he was not permitted to sleep in the house anymore. So the boy wandered out, gathered some sacks, and made himself a bed in the khotilla. Then when he was sure that no one was watching, he slipped away in the dark of night, grabbed a watermelon from the neighbor's garden, and ate the whole thing. Then he gathered up his fruit that he had stashed away earlier and took it to his new living quarters.

He woke up early the next morning and ran to Poonai's farm. Again, they fed him and gave him some roti and fried vegetables wrapped in a piece of cotton. Then he hurried back to his quarters from where he slowly emerged and started his morning chores. On that day, Mamoo had to use the donkey for pulling the cart, so he told his wife to have the boy take the grass knife and cut some grass for the donkey to eat when they got home. After he left with the donkey and cart, Mammie gave him some food and warned him not to tell Mamoo about it.

In the afternoon, he went to cut the grass for the donkey, which he piled up into a big heap. Then he stuffed the grass into a sack, tied it with a piece of vine, and leaned against the sack. It felt quite comfortable. So he cut some more grass and spread it out to dry. Then he managed to pull the sack onto his back and carried it home. Tired and exhausted from hauling the heavy load, he sat in his quarters and ate the food that the Poonais had given him that morning. After eating, he went to the local ditch and drank some water. Through the reeds, he saw Mamoo coming home, driving his donkey and hauling some lumber on the cart. Quickly, he ate a few wild fruits and went home to feed the donkey. He could hear the neighbor cursing and screaming loudly about the thief who stole his watermelon. He smiled and went about his business, justifying that if the neighbor had not complained about his donkey, the watermelon would not have been stolen. That night, he was fed a small bowl of rice and some dal.

After a few days, things seemed to be back to normal, but he was not allowed to sleep in the house. He anticipated that, so he gathered up some old sacks and stuffed his dried grass into them. One, he used for a bed, and the smaller one, he used for a pillow. On a third sack, he cut holes for his arms and head to go through and wore it as a blanket. It was quite comfortable, and that night, he slept in relative comfort and soon began to dream.

He dreamed that a man and a woman came and took him to a wonderful place with bright lights and plenty of food. The handsome couple were very well-dressed, and everyone at the establishment knew them. Pretty women dressed in fancy garments came about with more food and all sorts of exotic drinks, and they told him to eat and drink as much as he wanted. The women were truly beautiful, and they gracefully walked about with smiles on their faces. After the meal, the couple took him to a beautiful palace and tucked him into a nice soft bed, and she sang him a Hindi lullaby. It was the nicest place he had ever seen, and as he dozed away in his fantasy bed, the man told him that he would return and that they would go fishing. But he soon woke up in that dark, dirty shack wearing an oversized rice bag and lying on two grass-filled sacks. It was back to reality. He heard the rooster crowing and the dogs barking. Birds were twittering about the trees that were rustling in the morning ocean breeze. He was cold. He cradled himself and tried to savor his wonderful dream, but it was of no use. He just cried as the morning sun began to appear on the eastern horizon and absorbed the morning dew. He sat up and wondered what was going to happen that day.

Time passed slowly for an orphan with no purpose in life. He tried to join the neighborhood kids in various games, but not knowing the rules and having no practice, he was a liability to the teams, and nobody wanted a loser on their team. His place of refuge was the Poonai farm, where the cowhands became his buddies, and although those men were poor in material things, they were wealthy with their generosity. Any time the boy was among them, they gave him food, attention, and lots of milk. Little Thumru cherished their attention, and he felt at home among that family of hardworking men.

It did not take long for the boy to find a lasso, and he began practicing his roping skills. He was clumsy at first, and the men laughed at his techniques but admired his tenacity. Soon, they were all willing to help with his beginning lessons on how to rope a calf. Occasionally, he would manage to rope one only to be dragged about over dirt, thorns, cow pies, and fire ants. The men would again laugh and explained that those were the beginning lessons on the road to becoming a tough cowboy.

It was during one of those playful days that he forgot about the donkey. In the sunset, he ran as fast as he could, looking for the animal. He found him. It was getting dark. The donkey was grazing in the cemetery. In a land ruled by superstitions, most grown men would not venture into such a ghost-filled environment. For a kid, the fear must have been many times worse. He sat some distance from the land of the dead with his eyes closed in order to avoid seeing the hovering ghosts. Peeping occasionally, he kept wishing that the animal would come out, and he could grab him and take him home. No such luck. The stubborn ass kept on grazing. An owl began to hoot. Other strange night birds made haunting sounds, forcing the scared lad to run for home. He dived into his bed with his eyes tightly closed, hoping that something evil would not grab him in the darkness. Realizing that he was finally safe, he relaxed and fell asleep.

The crowing rooster woke him up. It was still night. He began to think about the punishment Mamoo would inflict upon him if the donkey attacked another animal that night. Torn between the ghosts and mortal abuse, he decided to go out and look about for the animal. To his surprise, the stubborn beast was standing by the gate of his pen. He wasted no time. In record time, he had the animal penned up. He grabbed handfuls of manure by the gate and carefully carried the piles into the pen. He washed his hands in the nearby pond. He once again nestled himself among his grass-filled sacks as the roosters kept on crowing and dogs were barking about.

The shouting, cursing, screaming neighbor was in the yard again. His donkey was again molested, and he was lodging complaints with Mamoo and seeking compensation. The two men walked toward Mamoo's donkey pen to find the animal comfortably resting on three legs with the fourth leg partially cocked and his head lowered toward the ground, cradling a pair of sleepy eyes. The evidence on the ground proved that the animal had been there long enough to make the deposits. The irate neighbor saw the boy walking about the yard doing some morning duties. He began yelling at the boy, but Mamoo intervened. He asked about the situation, and the boy replied that he put the donkey in the pen last night and went to sleep. Frustrated, the cursing neighbor returned home. Then Mamoo asked the boy why he did not show up for supper the past evening. The boy explained that he ate at Poonai's house with the cowhands.

The angry Mamoo abruptly paid a visit to Poonai's house. Of course, Mr. Poonai was his father-in-law and did not take kindly to the accusations. He calmly explained that they fed a hungry kid and would continue to do so. Not to be disrespectful to the elder relative,

Mamoo walked home, grabbed the boy, and gave him a sound thrashing with his cowhide belt. With the belt still swinging, the boy managed to escape and ran to Mr. Poonai, who inspected the bruises and cuts. He told his wife to take care of the kid, and he paid Mamoo a visit. Seeing the approaching elder, the cowardly Mamoo tried to escape, but it was too late. Mr. Poonai simply asked why the boy was beaten so brutally. There could be no reasonable answer. Mammie tried to keep her father calm, but it was of no use. Mr. Poonai sat the couple down and spoke forcefully about child abuse, especially for no reason at all. He told them that they should be ashamed of themselves taking money from Juman for child support and treating the boy like an animal, starving him and not allowing him to sleep in the house. He finally told them that the boy would not return for at least a week, and they must perform all the daily chores. Mammie protested, using her pregnant state as a reason not to do the heavy lifting. Her father told her to have her abusive husband use some of his energy to do all the heavy lifting and other daily tasks, and then he would not have time and energy to beat up on little defenseless boys. Then he departed, leaving the embarrassed couple wondering how Mr. Poonai knew about the money that Juman was providing.

The little Thumru was having a great vacation at the Poonai farm. He was well fed, and he played with the cowboys and the calves during milking. During the day, when the men were out, he walked about the pastures with a lasso trying to rope the goats and sheep and of course the calves. But his number one priority was finding wild fruits and berries. He drank water form a nearby canal and went in for swim sessions. Then he ate the fruits. Relaxed and somewhat tired, he fell asleep on the banks at the edge of the water. It was a calm day with a gentle ocean breeze. Carrion birds were circling on air currents high enough that they appeared to be the size of pigeons. Clouds rolled about above the carrion birds displaying a host of shapes and patterns. The environment was perfect for sleeping.

As he slept, his dream took him back to the handsome couple. The man asked if he wanted to go fishing, and together, they got the bamboo rods and some bait on the hooks. The fishing was great, and the boy managed to reel in some large fish as the man coached his techniques. When the fishing was over, the man went to clean the catch while the woman sang a beautiful melody as she cradled the boy. The song was great and the meal was delicious. The boy woke up in disappointment at the edge of the water. He gazed at the passing clouds and admired the various shapes that were formed. He closed his eyes, said a simple prayer, and thanked the handsome couple for the wonderful dream. He invited them to come back often.

When he got to Poonai's house, supper was being prepared. They were having fish that night. It was a great meal, and he was encouraged to eat as much as he wanted. They gave him warm milk with some honey, which he relished, and then he finally went to bed. He slept in a real bed with clean sheets and soft pillows and huddled and cradled himself with the soft blanket. He had a great vacation at that residence, but it finally came to an end, and he went back to Mamoo's house.

The angry Mamoo became even more irate when he was informed that Juman would no longer send child support money. Now with two children, Mammie spent most of her time with the kids and with the kitchen and garden duties. Mamoo increased the boy's duties, which now included gathering firewood. So the skinny Thumru spent part of the day pulling branches and cutting them into small sections with a machete. He used vines and tied them into small bundles that he carried home on his head. On occasional rainy days, when the wood got wet, Mammie could not get the fire going in a timely manner, resulting in supper being served late. Of course, the blame was put on the boy, who was given a beating for bringing home wet wood. To solve that issue, he started keeping a stack of wood hidden at the base of a hollowed-out dead tree.

He did not have much for clothes. All he wore was a long shirt that went down to his knees. He had no pants, nor was he given any underwear. That manner of dressing was not unusual. Many poor boys wore similar garments and walked about. One of the games that the village boys played was called enter hole. That was when they rolled marbles of various sorts into shallow holes in the ground. The winner collected buttons. Once when Thumru was given a new shirt, the marble gang noticed the nice new buttons. He was befriended and was asked to participate in the games. Flattered to be asked and starved for friendship, he agreed and soon found his new shirt with no buttons. With an open shirt and no underwear, his front area was fully exposed, and that triggered a loud laugh with the button-rich gang sending the crying Thumru home. Of course, Mamoo saw that and gave him a sound thrashing for losing the buttons from his new shirt.

He was given no supper that night, and he went to his khotilla bed crying himself to sleep. But soon there was the handsome couple again. They carried him to the wonderful mansion again and provided sweet-smelling soaps and warm water in a room of marbles where he splashed about like a fish and sniffed the perfumed soap. He used the soft towel to dry himself, and the lady fitted him with garments that were alien to him. His hair was combed, and he put on the new sandals provided. He looked in the mirror and saw a handsome lad that he did not recognize. All dressed up, they walked to a fancy chariot pulled by two graceful horses that took them to the establishment with the bright lights and endless tables of food served by those beautiful women. He ate and ate and then was driven back on the chariot to that elegant mansion with the marbled decor and sweet-smelling soap. The man carried him to that soft bed again, and the woman sang him to sleep. To him, she had the most beautiful voice, and her song ended with a quiet hum. Then the rooster crowed, and the sad little Thumru woke up in the shack wearing his shirt with no buttons. His trembling hands felt all the places that the belt had made connection with his body, and he cried in the dark all alone, trying to suppress his physical and emotional pain.

Not being able to sleep, he could see the red eastern horizon. It would soon be dawn. He got up, wrapped the shirt about his body, and walked to the see Mr. Poonai. Daylight found him on the doorstep as Mr. Poonai made his morning walk to the outhouse. Shocked and angry, he called to his wife and sent the crying lad into the house. When he returned, the boy was drinking warm sweetened tea with milk. They wrapped him in a sheet and gave him breakfast, and she sewed new buttons on his shirt and sent him home. He was doing his morning chores when Mamoo noticed that the shirt had buttons. He questioned that, and the boy told him that an angel had mended his shirt while he slept.

All day long, he kept imagining the handsome couple walking about with him. He could smell the sweet perfumes, and wherever he lay down for a rest, he felt the nice soft bed. He could almost hear the sweet melody that the woman sang, and he hummed along in harmony. He could taste the sweet tea when he drank from the ditch, and in his loneliness, he found comfort knowing that he was never alone. And as the months passed, he accepted that Mamoo would punish him for whatever reason, but he knew that others cared about him too.

The years passed, and the once little Thumru slowly found his place. He spent more and more time with the cowboys and followed them about. He spent less and less time at Mamoo's house because of the repeated abuse and because they had more and more children who could do some of the duties that he performed. The cowboys taught him to ride horses and to rope cattle. He helped with the roundups and the milking. Many nights, he slept among the cows, and on cold nights, he huddled close to an old pet cow that tolerated him. When occasional confusion and fear surrounded him, the handsome couple always arrived and took him to that lovely mansion with marble and perfumes and to that exotic place of food with the beautiful women dressed in fancy garments and exotic jewelry. They would ride the chariot to places unknown to most, and the woman always sang that sweet melody that he hummed about among the cows. He grew up to be a tough cowboy and refused to return to Mamoo's shack that housed so much misery for him. But nothing can last forever, and as the years passed, the little Thumru became a teenager and graduated from the school of experience taught by some of the best hands, who survived in an environment where luxury was not yet invented.

Some days, he worked with the road-building crews. He got paid eight cents per day for carrying pails of bricks from the brick-making site to the road construction areas. He carried the pails on his head, which was rubbing the hair off his head. So the Poonai family made him a padding from rags to minimize further injury. Mrs. Poonai kept his money for him.

There was a school close by that taught the Indian children Hindi. The Poonai children attended that school. Classes were held in the evening because some of the children went to English school during the day. Mr. Poonai encouraged his Thumru to attend. They bought him a slate and pencil, and in the evening, after his construction job, he went to school to learn how to read and write Hindi. The schooling did not last very long, but he learned the basics, and through self-teaching and occasional tutoring, he became literate in Hindi. He could read and write. When he had spare time in the fields, he practiced his writing on the ground with a pointed wooden pencil. He did not go back to his uncle's house. He hated and despised that man. For years to come, he referred to him as Cruel Mamoo.

CHAPTER 12

Moving On

By 1920, the importation of indentured servants from India to the west came to an end mostly because of political pressure from London, from efforts started by Mohandas Karamchand Gandhi (Mahatma Gandhi) and from other sources. As a result of that law, several of the immigrants became wage earners at the estates. Some took their savings and returned to India. Some became farmers, and some became tradesmen and businessmen. Those who could not handle things became beggars. The colony was referred to as the land of six peoples. They were the native indigenous people referred to as Amerindians; the Negroes, who were descendants of African slaves; the East Indians, referred to as coolies, from India; the Portuguese; the Chinese; and the other Europeans. Each group found their respective niche and had to survive with whatever resources they had saved and or inherited. For most, it was basic survival, except for the few whites who monopolized the sugar and other industries and dominated the colony's political arena.

Pyroo and Radha's daughter, Doormatie, was frugal and smart enough to use the resources given to them for business purposes. She got money from Radha, and Lalla inherited land and money from the Singhs, his adopted parents. She and Lalla farmed the land, growing rice and vegetables. They inherited and invested into cattle. Lalla was the worker, and Doormatie was the brains. Together, they had thirteen children. Ten survived into adulthood. Although they were illiterate, Doormatie decided to start a retail business. In 1933, they opened a store across the street from their home, and their oldest son, Bissesar, who was born in 1902 and went to English school, became the store manager. He initially helped with the basic recordkeeping and accounting, and as the years passed, it more or less became his store. They left their other older sons to handle the farming and the cattle operations.

In 1927, Nanda had a wife named Mahadey. They had their first child one year later, a boy they named Baboolall. They went to the now teenage Motilall and asked him to abandon the life of a wandering cowboy and to come live with them. He did. In 1929, at the age of fourteen, he moved in with them. Together, they built a grass hut in Number 61 Village that had three rooms—one room for the kitchen and two small sleeping quarters fitted with khatia like the one that Desai had built. They used dried reeds and cattails for making pillows and mattresses with jute bags that were sewed shut and covered them with sheets of cotton to minimize the roughness. The whole thing was quite simple, but it was home and reunited the two orphaned brothers. They ate basic meals, and every day after supper, they discussed and planned their future together.

They were both hardworking men and soon acquired oxen and a plow. Land was available, and the two sons of Desai went about clearing the land and planting rice. Like most folks in the area, for them, growing a garden was essential for survival, and before long, the men had a parcel of land fenced in and had a flourishing garden. During slow times, they went to the Skeldon estate and worked in the cane fields, cutting and loading the cane to be processed into sugar and rum. Mahadey had two sisters, and they got married to two Dutch brothers. So, the three sisters lived in the same area. One married Nanda, one married Ramouthar, and one married Rampersaud.

Those two brothers came with their father from Dutch Guiana (now Surinam). People referred to those brothers as "dem Dutchman." They spoke some broken English, but most of the communication was done in Hindi because that was the common language among them. One was Mr. Ramouthar, and the other was Mr. Rampersaud. Those two Dutchmen were obsessed with making a living in the British colony. They and their father embarked into a working frenzy. Now there were five men working together, and through a division of the labor, they accomplished remarkable amounts of farmwork every day.

Their father's name was Muna Singh. He was a rather large and rugged-looking man who had emigrated from India to Dutch Guiana. After his wife died, he and his two sons left the Dutch colony and came across the Corentyne River to settle in the British colony. He only spoke Hindi and walked about wearing just a dhoti, which exposed his impressive physique. He had a large nose and a raspy voice that was intimidating to most people. Nobody dared to upset him because he had a temper that matched his ruggedness. He was a very tough and scary man. Most of the time, he wore a white turban on his head.

After the first harvest, the two orphaned boys bought four cows from the Poonai farm. With their future accumulated wages from the estate and additional farming, they soon had a dozen cows, and Motilall was the designated cowboy. He did those duties during his so-called spare time. He borrowed a horse from the Poonais and went about daily checking on the cows. It was like vacation for him, riding horses and checking on the herd, which continued to grow. Within three years, they had some twenty-five head of cattle, and within five years, they had about forty. People were amazed at how animals trusted Motilall. Whenever a neighbor had a difficult cow, they called on him to tame the animal down, and he usually could. If someone had a cow that was considered hard to handle, he would buy the animal at a much-reduced price and could generally earn its trust. Before long, he could be seen leading the once ferocious beast like a puppy on a leash. The other four men applauded his skills and went in search of "wild" cows to buy. Then they turned the cow whisperer loose on them to do his foolproof thing, turning the animals into manageable commodities.

Soon, the Dutchmen's wives started having babies, and Nanda and his wife also had their second baby. As with most partnerships, the disagreements escalated. Finally, they agreed to maintain their friendship but to dissolve the partnership. In order to acquire better living quarters with some basic household furnishings, they sold some of the cows and divided the remainder among the three families. The disappointed Motilall found that they only had fifteen cattle, and he was told that they would focus more on the rice fields and the vegetable garden. Some of his time would be devoted to babysitting on account that his sister-in-law (Bhowji) got tired in the evenings. There was not much time for rebuttal. The lady of the house, his sister-in-law, Mahadey, was now making the rules and controlling the business and the finances. Motilall began to feel like a hired hand in the home that he helped to build, but those were the new rules. He reluctantly obeyed.

The following year, one of their prized cows had an impressive-looking bull calf. Within a week, he became a sight to be admired. He danced and pranced about the yard and around the neighborhood. All the neighbors agreed that he would become a prize ox someday. By the time he was three months old, they could harness him with pieces of rope and had him pulling logs home to be used for firewood. Sometimes, he struggled and strained with the heavy load, but he kept on pulling. There was no question, he was going to become an ox that would be used for pulling the plow and hauling the carts. He was branded and castrated, and they named him Maloo. He generally wandered about with his mother. One day, he could not be found. Both he and his mother were gone. The men searched on foot and on horseback, but there was no Maloo around. He was gone. It was not unusual for animals to wander off because there were no fences to keep them confined. They went farther and farther in search of better pasture and eventually found themselves in the savannah areas, where they roamed freely among other cattle that belonged to various families. The men agreed that he was branded and earmarked, and when the time was ready, he would be found. They informed the neighbors that the animals had wandered off and asked if anybody saw them, that person report it. The owners would go in search and verify the animals' identities and their habitual grazing territory.

With Maloo gone and the search abandoned, the men went about their usual business of farming. They acquired a donkey and cart, and all the necessary harnesses, which they used to haul their produce to market. Periodically, they harvested coconuts and made coconut oil, which was used for cooking. Occasionally, they sold some of the oil at the market. For the most part, things were fine. The months passed, and work was completed. They understood the seasons and planned their farming operations to match them. There was the rainy season and the dry season. It followed a pattern every year. They planted the rice in the wet season and harvested it in the dry season. There was no need for meteorologists, and they did not need one. They worked according to the seasons.

Periodically, when the Poonai cowboys went into the savannahs for a cattle drive, their little buddy Thumru went along. They traveled on horseback and carried trained dogs along to aid in the roundup. It was during one of those trips that he discovered the remains of Maloo's mother. He recognized her from the curve of her horns and from the faded letters of her brand. That day, he told the men to leave without him because he wanted to go in search of Maloo. They left him some food and drove their heard homeward.

He built a fire and secured some fish from a nearby pond. He roasted the fish and ate it with a roti that his friends had provided. After supper, he went walking about, admiring the cattle grazing in the tall lush savannah grasses. An occasional half-wild bovine would spot him and take off in a full gallop with its tail rolled up on its back. An occasional mating bull would toss his head about as warning not to interfere with his business. There was an abundance of birds of all sorts, each species making its inherited sound. Occasional trees of varying sizes dotted the flat landscape that housed troops of monkeys. Some ran with babies on their backs, and some bellowed warning signals to him. They behaved like wild monkeys, and the observer smiled at their varied behaviors.

There were scattered ponds dug out that served as watering holes for the cattle during the dry seasons. Those bodies of water housed an abundance of fish. The fish did their water dance, creating ripples that gently caressed the banks where an occasional alligator basked in the warm sunshine. There were fruits like monkey apple scattered about, and Motilall chose prized ones and feasted on them. The diversity of countless bees and butterflies sailed in airborne motions, ensuring pollination and continued life for the numerous species. He saw many cattle but no Maloo. That night, while the jaguars roared and nocturnal creatures made their programmed noises, he built a fire, smoked a homemade cigarette, and slept where the cattle congregated.

Motilall grew up tough and hard and could outwork most men. Folks admired his work habits and his dedication to neatness. But most of all, they had great respect for his ability to handle and tame animals, and as time passed, he became a much-respected neighbor who grew into a handsome young man.

In 1935, the local matchmaker approached Nanda and the two Dutchmen about Motilall's future. He informed them that the boy was now almost twenty years old, and he should get married. He further informed them that there was a girl at Number 64 Village, a daughter of Lalla and Doormatie, who was a fine girl from a good family. If they were in agreement, he would approach the girl's parents, and if they agreed, he would schedule a meeting to see what could be arranged. The older brother, somewhat surprised and stunned, did not say anything, but Mr. Ramouthar asked for some more information about the girl. The matchmaker told him that she was a fine-looking girl and that she was almost fourteen years old. Her parents were doing well financially. Not knowing what else to say, they agreed that the man should do the proposal, and if the girl's parents agreed, they would pay a formal visit to the family.

When Motilall came home from the field, his brother waited until after supper and then gave him the news. He was not surprised because some of the cowhands were already teasing him that being almost twenty-one years old, he should have a wedding soon. His only objection was that he did not have a home and that he was in no position to support a wife. His chattering sister-in-law could no longer hold her tongue. She took over the conversation, claiming that they would all live together in the grass-thatched, mud-walled hut. She continued babbling that another woman in the home would relieve her of some domestic duties, allowing her to rest occasionally. It was obvious that she saw an opportunity of becoming a surrogate mother-in-law with a chance to acquire a "servant" girl. There was no more discussion, and she made it clear that the meeting must take place and started coaching the men as to their respective behavior during the whole ordeal.

Within a week, the matchmaker was back with the good news. There would be a meeting after two Saturdays at the girl's parents' house at Number 64 Village. The Dutchmen and their wives, the Motilall household, and a few other friends began preparing for the meeting, and at the scheduled time, the group of men arrived at the designated house. Women did not participate in such meetings. The handsome Motilall, all dressed up, was escorted into the yard, where he was greeted by the girl's parents. They all exchanged greetings, and they were invited into the house. Motilall was very impressed at how nicely the wooden house was painted, and he admired the varnished furniture. They were invited to sit around the table, and a beverage was served. Doormatie left the men alone and went into a bedroom from where the men could hear whispering and giggling. It was obvious that the girl was in there with some other women. They were busy getting the girl properly made up, and occasionally one of the women would peep through the cracks in the wooden wall and give a summary of her observations, which generally resulted in quiet, silly giggles.

The men were having their casual discussion when two of Lalla's sons joined them. One was pleasant and talkative, and the other was very grumpy. The discussion continued, and finally, the grumpy one spoke. He wanted to know why his family was wasting time discussing the subject with that *lungera*. A good interpretation of that word would be something like "a useless, lazy bum." To minimize the tension, Lalla told his son, whose name was Bholanauth, to leave the table and to show some respect for the guests in his house. He immediately got up and walked out, and his talkative brother followed him. The angry Motilall stood up and told Lalla that he was a poor orphan, but that did not make him any less of a man. The tension was increasing when one of the Dutchmen spoke to Lalla, explaining that they should not forget the purpose of the meeting and that he would vouch for the young man to be the hardest working soul in the entire neighborhood. Lalla smiled and nodded. He finally told the Dutchman that he knew all about the work ethic of that young man and would be proud to have him for a son-in-law. That took care of the tension, and immediately Doormatie came out of the room, leading a tall, slim, barefooted teenage girl wearing a nice dress, some fancy jewelry, and a veil over her head that partially covered her long black hair. Motilall gazed at her with utmost admiration. Lalla stood by his wife and told him that the girl was their daughter, and her name was Finey.

Finey was quite embarrassed. She stood with the proper posture of a fine young lady, but she had her head bent forward and stared at the floor. The group had their usual conversations, and Doormatie took the girl back to the comfort of the room from where they had emerged earlier. There were whispers and giggles while Lalla excused himself and soon returned with a bottle of rum. They all had a drink, and the visiting party departed with nods, smiles, and handshakes. In the street, they all clasped their hands and bowed to each other, saying, "Namaste." They all departed to their respective homes to give a detailed report to the women, who anxiously waited.

The next morning after milking the cows, the family gathered for breakfast. The sister-in-law kept on prying for more and more details. She finally asked Motilall if he liked the girl. He kept eating his roti, dal, and fried vegetables and occasionally gulped down some warm sweetened tea. The nagging continued, and he finally told her that he had work to do and walked out. Taking his shovel and machete (cutlass) along, he was heading for the garden. When he looked back, he saw the three brothers-in-law, his brother, and the two Dutchmen, following some distance behind. The men caught up with him at the garden and suggested that there should be some discussion away from the women. It was a casual discussion, and his brother told him that he needed to make a decision about the girl. One of the friends asked if he could see himself living with that girl for the rest of his life. He gave the generic answer that he knew very little about such matters, and the group should help with such a major decision. The three men told him that she was a beautiful girl from a good family and that he should seriously consider marrying her. They were hoeing and pulling weeds. They would talk about various other things, but the subject proper kept creeping back into the conversation with the men telling Motilall that they truly believed that he should marry that girl.

The excited Motilall knew that the men were correct. But he had concerns. He had no money, he had no home of his own, he was offended by Bholanauth's comments and the name calling, and he was concerned about Mahadey's arrogance and bossiness. He also realized that he must start his own life someday and that start should be sooner rather than later. Hence after serious consideration, he asked Mr. Ramouthar to speak with him privately. He expressed his concerns, and the Dutchman agreed with him. He shared his concerns again but repeated that he must move along and start his own life. The Dutchman promised Motilall to help in every way he could and that his wife shared in that decision also. They had that discussion the previous night and agreed that if things did not go well with his brother's wife, he and his wife would do whatever was necessary to help.

The group reconvened, and Ramouthar told the other two men that the boy was in agreement. They should proceed with wedding plans. Motilall was not sure that he had agreed to that but was glad that the decision was made. He was excited to think that he was going to marry that fine-looking girl.

He did not get much work done that day, partly because of the nervousness and partly because he was concerned and scared to face the reality of being a husband. He left the garden early and went to spend time with his cowboy buddies. He shared the news, and the men were happy to hear the good news and offered suggestions but mostly teased him with lessons about the birds and the bees. It was all in good fun, and they spent the evening drinking and just being goofy drunks. It was his unofficial engagement and bachelor party spent with the people who were near and dear to him. Some of the men had their wives prepare food, and the lot of drunken cowboys celebrated the good fortune for the now grown-up Thumru.

He was quite sick the next day from excess consumption of alcohol and stayed in bed most of the morning. It was not peaceful there, for he heard the constant complaining of his sister-in-law. He finally got up, walked to the ditch close by, and washed up. Feeling a little better, he walked to the local shop and bought some pastries and lemonade. The shop was owned by a man they called Mackerel Maraj. He was supposed to be a spiritual Hindu person, but in the shop, he sold pickled mackerel. Those fish came in a wooden barrel drenched with brine to keep them from spoiling. Being a Hindu man of God, he was supposed to be a vegetarian. He was not supposed to handle fish and meat. Because he sold the imported mackerel, most people did not know his real name. Everybody called him Mackerel Maraj. The man had already heard the news that the boy was now unofficially engaged and told him that there was no charge for the pastries and the drink because of the special occasion. He thanked the man, ate, drank, and walked toward the ocean. There, he sat on the sandy beach, tossing seashells about and watching the waves as they came tumbling toward the sand dunes. He eventually leaned against a coconut tree deep in thought as the howling wind blew past him, causing the tree branches to wave in obedience. He was tired and still felt sick from the liquor and spicy foods from the previous night. He soon fell asleep. Cattle and horses walking along the beach must have noticed him but casually plodded along toward wherever. The high tide brought the waves farther into the beach as plovers scurried along the dying waves in search of food. An occasional fishing boat went by, and women were in the distance with nets gathering fish and shrimp. The onshore breezes whistled past him with occasional gusts. But he noticed not.

His conscious thoughts soon turned into a dream, and there were the man and woman, that handsome couple who always took him to the beautiful mansion. But that day, there was no food, nor mansion, nor chariot. They took him by the hand, one on each side, and walked along the beach. Nothing was said, but he felt the peace and tranquility as they walked gently and effortlessly, and he felt the warm sand squeezing between his toes. On that day, he was not carried, and the woman did not sing her famous melody. They walked along as three adults as the waves continued their ebb and flow, and the sun maintained its perfect schedule toward the western horizon.

It was dusk when he woke up, feeling strong and invincible. His troubles all seemed to have vanished, washed away with the receding tide, and the gentle evening breeze commanded the coconut branches to wave gently at him like servants fanning an ancient king. He knew that things would be fine now, so he said a silent prayer, thanked the handsome couple for the solitary and empowering visit, repeated a few mantras, and walked home.

A week after New Year's Day 1936, the matchmaker had the men visit the girl's parents, and they agreed that there was going to be a wedding. The local pundit was called in to bless them and to use his astrological books to pick the date for the wedding. The book helped with the date, ensuring that there were no evil or other superstitious concerns. They picked Sunday, March 8, 1936, for the wedding date. The young assistant pundit's name was Diaram. He was Lalla's nephew. He was the son of Lalla's sister, daughter of Kumar and Shanti, who was adopted by Bhagwat Singh and his wife, Gulabia, from the Ruimveldt orphanage.

They all thanked the pundit and his assistant for coming and for consulting the holy book, the Patra. The pundit then blessed the occasion, collected his fee, and departed. The others did their usual Namaste partings and returned home. It was official. Motilall and Finey (Brijrani) were scheduled to be married on March 8, 1936.

CHAPTER 13

The Couple

The two brothers and the two Dutchmen and their wives acted like one big family. They had their own homes and their own lives and did their respective work during the day, but in the evenings, they all gathered, men and women, and talked about whatever seemed important at that time. Most of the conversations in January and February 1936 centered on the wedding. There were agreements and disagreements as would be the case with any small group, but they always managed to compromise and made decisions based on the principle of majority rules. They did agree that Nanda and Mahadey would act the part of father and mother on behalf of the groom.

Time was scheduled for gathering enough firewood to be used for cooking during the wedding period. Occasionally, Motilall was invited by his future in-laws to share a beverage of ice-cold lemonade and some pastries. Anything cold in the tropical heat and humidity was greatly appreciated; adding homemade sweets to that was almost a luxury for the young man. Those brief visits encouraged the girl to become marginally acquainted with her future husband, and caution was taken to ensure proper supervision during the short meetings. It must have been quite uncomfortable for all involved. Finey never said much, and the men had general conversations about the crops and livestock. There was always tension when Bholanauth was around, so the family tried to ensure that he was working in the fields when the occasional meetings were scheduled.

Two weeks before the big date, the tailor was summoned to sew up the wedding clothes for the groom (*dulaha*). Finey's mother and sisters went into their store and picked out fine linen with matching buttons, laces, and all the other materials that the local seamstress requested. She was measured and fitted into a fine dress and all the necessary items and jewelry that would make her a fine bride (*dulaheen*). According to custom, she would be married in a beautiful sari. The dress was to be worn for occasions after the wedding ceremony. As far as Doormatie was concerned, that was another rehearsal, for she had three of her older daughters already married. But for Nanda and the Dutchmen, it was all new to them. They had many suggestions from friends and neighbors, and the cowboys, who were ever present, rum bottles in hand, chopped wood and offered all kinds of ideas. Muna Singh split most of the wood, and the men admired the power of his arms as he swung his ax and the pieces of wood flew in all directions. They even took up a collection that would help offset some wedding expenses, and the Poonai family returned his savings from his construction job. They also donated a handsome amount. They all believed that their little Thumru was their little brother, and they would ensure that the celebration would be a gala event. With every little sip from their bottles, the ideas and suggestions intensified to match their slightly intoxicated states. They did not drink much rum because of the danger involved while swinging axes. The abusive Mamoo did not participate in the discussion, nor did he contribute any resources for the event. He was angry because he and his wife were not asked to act as parents to that ungrateful orphan in whom they had invested so much (according to them). They did not attend the wedding, but Juman and his other brothers did. Juman was now fifty-three years old. He was short and completely gray. He did not age gracefully. He looked like a little old man. But he acted as a true elder of the family and supervised most of the cooking. He still drank plenty.

Those rowdy cowboys started the celebration one week before the wedding. Every evening, when their respective chores were completed (in record time), they congregated around the Dutchman's mud-walled hut with bottles of rum and some fish and meat. As they were Hindus, fish and meat were not tolerated at the dulaha's residence during that sacred period. It did not matter to the friends; they came every night to drink, dance, eat, and celebrate their little buddy's stepping into holy matrimony. A few of them drank too much and found themselves sleeping under trees the next morning. They went to do their daily routine, and by evening, they were back, bottles in hand, ready for celebrating again. Most were social drinkers who came to show support for and to celebrate their little buddy's upcoming event.

The wedding events started on Friday, March 6, 1936. The matchmaker, the pundit, his assistant, and anybody who was somebody participated in the traditional events like rubbing turmeric over the entire body of the person to be wed. Local drummers and musicians were ever present, showing off their respective talents. The women at Finey's house did their traditional rituals with the dulaheen, where men were not allowed to participate. Friday night was called *maticoor* at the dulaheen's house. That celebration was exclusively for women.

Shelters were built at the dulaheen's residence. Tall bamboo plants were cut, brought in from downriver, and planted vertically under the ceremonial shelter. Saturday was treated like a special holiday in the dulaha's neighborhood. The entire lot of partying cowboys and most of the neighbors, young and old, loitered about patiently waiting for the music. When the drums began their accelerated beats, the self-invited male friends tried to keep up with their wild and not-so-coordinated dances. Their women cheered them on and had lots of laughs to see the men so happy. It was fun for all, and Motilall felt blessed for having all his good friends feeling happy, getting rowdy, and celebrating on his behalf.

Like fireflies in the dark, more neighbors came later, walking with their families and bringing their kerosene lanterns along.

The lanterns were hung on various tree branches that collectively caused the whole yard to be bright enough for the crowd to walk about without stumbling on various obstacles, like cooking utensils, firewood, and any other items scattered about. The party went late into the night. Eventually, the neighbors retrieved their lanterns, and like vanishing fireflies, they dispersed in various directions. Even the cowboys went home early, partly because they were exhausted from dancing but mostly because they wanted to be ready for the main event the following day. The happy lot went home singing in a chaotic manner along the dirt road.

Women congregated at Finey's house after their chores were done. Saturday night was literally the big dance for them. Selected women tied pillows on their bottoms that their dresses covered. With clapping hands and crude instruments' sounds, they sang "wedding house songs" as the "big-bottomed women" wiggled their enlarged bottoms and showed off their respective moves. Such rituals were more for fun. It was time for the women to advise the bride-to-be about being a wife. It was very embarrassing for Finey, as the women occasionally got carried away with the discussions on the bedroom duties. Doormatie would intervene when the discussions and advice got out of hand. Then all would laugh and continue with theoretical sex education 101 to a fourteen-year-old girl.

Sunday morning was like a beehive at both homes. The cooking was in full force, and the pundits were busy arranging all the colors and various ingredients necessary to perform the rituals that their Hindu traditions had dictated over the centuries. Many people did not understand the significance of some of those rituals, but tradition and superstitions that followed their ancestors from India were strong forces in that area and were not challenged or questioned. People followed them out of fear and ignorance with strong beliefs that they were the right things to do, and they participated wholeheartedly, knowing that the rituals must be followed with no exceptions. The pundits exercised their authoritative power and mandated that every detail was followed to the nth degree. There were severe reprimands from those unofficial Hindu authorities for any deviations from the norms. They were empowered to do so and emphatically exercised their position powers.

The dulaheen stayed at her house. The dulaha and his male friends and family went to the dulaheen's tent for the wedding ceremony. The men, all dressed up, left the dulaha's home by various means in a procession called a *baryat* toward the wedding house. The dulaha was all dressed up in his fine tailored clothes and decorated headgear called a *mowr*. The Poonais brought a nice horse-drawn wagon to transport him for the almost one-mile journey to where his dulaheen waited in her fancy sari and expensive jewelry borrowed from her mother and sisters. Most of the men walked along, bottles in hand, as the horse clip-clopped along in a slow dancing trot. The drinking mob clapped their hands, beat on tin cans with pieces of sticks, sang various tunes, and ran about in wiggly dancing motions as the decorated gentle horse pranced along. The loud commotion encouraged neighborhood dogs to be alarmed, and occasionally, one would charge with vicious intent in an effort to chase the crowd away. Every few minutes, someone would propose a toast. That created an excuse for a momentary silence as they sipped some warm rum together. They made agonizing sounds and wrinkled their faces in personal protest to the effects of the ingested liquid, then resume the noise-making, anticipating the next toast and upsetting the dogs. Upon arrival, they met with men from that village, Number 64, and began discussing the various topics proper and sharing drinks. There, the dulaha and his family were greeted in the traditional manner and taken to the tent where the ceremony would be performed. Nanda led his brother, followed by the two Dutchmen. Women traditionally did not accompany the baryat. They came and sat separated from the men.

In 1936, a few cars were available in Berbice, but only the very wealthy could afford them. The Poonais had a rented motor car, a black Vauxhall, in the event of bad weather. They did not want the couple getting wet on their special day. As it turned out, the car was not needed because on that fine Sunday morning, the sun was shining bright, and there was a cool ocean breeze that caused the tall coconut trees to sway back and forth above the rustling shorter trees. It was a fine day.

The two to be wedded, in traditional manner, had their garments tied together while the pundit and his assistants performed the ceremony. The audience strained their necks and bobbed their heads so as not to miss a single detail. On that bright, sunny day, between the sounds of the preaching pundit, crowing roosters, shouting drunks, barking dogs, braying donkeys, twittering birds, mooing cows, rustling leaves, and whistling winds, the young couple, with garments knotted together, slowly walked around the tall vertical bamboo and the short banana plant, obeying the commands of the pundit and his rituals. They selectively listened to his perceived words of wisdom. There were the ringing of bells, the banging of brass instruments, and the occasional blowing of a seashell. The dulaheen, with her sari tied to his suit, had too much to handle, so as she walked around the obstacles barefooted, her little helper made sure that her garments and head cover stayed in place. With head looking down, she admired the various colors and patterns that decorated the circle around the bamboo and banana plants. Raw rice was stained with various colors and arranged in creative patterns. The bride and groom, with their traditional garments tied together, slowly walked in a circle around the decorations performing the various Hindu rituals as directed by the pundit. Their audience was mostly women sitting on sheets that lined the bare ground. Some of those women had small babies and many of them breastfed their infants to keep them quiet during the rituals. Finally, the pundit pronounced them husband and wife. It was a ritualistic marriage. No legal documents were signed. It was not until May 26, 1946, ten years later, that they were legally married.

It was a beautiful wedding, and the guests presented their gifts of dishes and cash. Most gave two enamel plates, two cups, and fifty cents. Lalla, with head bent down, occasionally cried because his little girl was leaving his house and moving on to the next phase of her life. It was a bittersweet occasion for Lalla that lasted some two hours. It was then time to move on. As tradition dictated, an old woman called a *lucknie* was sent along to chaperone the bride, and the young couple embarked into the horse-drawn wagon, heading toward his house, followed by the baryat, consisting of mostly drunk men dancing their way home and being chased by aggressive dogs. She had the red *seindoor* spread along the part of her long black hair and a dark red tikka on her forehead, signifying the status of a now married woman. Banging drums followed behind the disorganized procession. It was a loud and crazy scene, and the newlyweds enjoyed the attention and the rocking motion in the decorated horse-drawn buggy clip-clopping and rattling down the dusty road. Mr. Poonai's son drove the wagon, laughing all the way. His little brother, Thumru, whom they loved so much, was now a married man. His body language revealed his pride for his family being such a part of that young man's life. They considered one another as family.

At home, the women greeted the new bride, and the lucknie escorted her child bride into the mud-walled hut. Outside, the singing and dancing continued as the groom joined his rowdy, partially drunken friends, each wanting him to have a drink. Inside the hut, the women congregated, anxious to meet the new bride, and offered hilarious lessons about birds and bees. The lucknie ensured that things did not get out of hand with the teasing women. That was her primary duty. Outside, the singing and dancing continued until the exhausted men found a convenient spot and retired for the night. Those who were sober enough walked home and thus ended the celebration on that Sunday, March 8, 1936, that unofficially united Motilall, son of Desai and Mangrie, to Finey (Brijrani), daughter of Lalla and Doormatie, granddaughter of Pyroo and Radha, as husband and wife.

Almost drunk, the groom slept at Ramouthar's house, and the bride tried to sleep with the lucknie in his bed with uncertainty being her constant companion. It was the first time that young girl ever slept in a stranger's house.

Monday was the final celebration (*kakan*) for the guests with almost no exceptions on the menu. The men butchered a ram sheep and some chickens and someone brought some wild meat. They were not allowed to eat pork, but some of the men cooked up some pepper pot pork away from the crowd. Many had a taste of the hot pepper pork, chewing the fat that had small pieces of meat attached, which they washed down with warm rum and green coconut water. Beef was absolutely not tolerated. Food was served on oval lotus leaves, called *pooraine*, that were harvested from local ponds. The used leaves were discarded with any residual morsels that waiting dogs, poultry, and pigs ravished. They all chased and jostled about in search of discarded morsels. There were squeals, clucks, quacks, growls, and barks as occasional birds swooped down from branches above to get their helpings. The guests ate well, drank their fair share, danced to their hearts' content, and wished their friend, the dulaha, the very best. While the men celebrated outside, the women secretly did some celebrating inside the mud-walled hut. Then later that Monday morning, the lucknie, in traditional manner, took the confused fourteen-year-old dulaheen back to her parents' house, where she stayed for another week. They walked and talked as bicycles went past them in both directions. Many riders rang their bicycle bells, congratulating the new bride.

Tuesday was cleanup day. At both homes, people were actively picking up garbage and returning borrowed stuff. The spilled food was consumed by loitering dogs and cats and by occasional roaming pigs. The lotus leaves were left for nature to decompose. The people were all exhausted, and when things appeared somewhat normal, it was time to relax and enjoy the peace and quiet after several days' tension and excitement. It was a fine wedding, and all involved were thankful for the good weather. They were glad that things went well. They looked forward to resuming their regular schedules, taking good memories of the wedding along as they resumed their respective routine.

Juman stayed for a few days. After the cleanup, he called his two nephews and had a discussion. He told them about their father's arriving at the colony and their early years. He laughingly talked about the incident at the hospital when Desai attempted to throw him out of the window. He continued, "Desai was the hardest-working man at the estate. He was big and strong with long black hair that blew about in the wind. My sister, Mangrie, was a beautiful girl who learned to love and admire Desai for his tenacity and determination. She adored her babies and grieved bitterly for the son that she so tragically lost in the Canje River."

During the discussions, Motilall was called away by one of the Dutchmen. Alone with Nanda, he addressed the money that Desai had buried at the grave site. He wanted to tell the older brother only, in order to contain that secret. He knew that he would not live forever and wanted at least one of the sons to know the truth. He explained about paying the moving expenses, buying the donkey and cart, and using some of the money to pay their uncle Raghoo child support for several years. He told Nanda about his arrangement with Phingol and a host of other stories about family and historical facts that he knew about. The next morning, he returned to Port Mourant, where they still lived.

There would be no honeymoon for the groom. On Wednesday afternoon, he resumed working in the fields and weeding his garden. It was good for him to be away from all the noise and excitement during the wedding. But he really became increasingly annoyed at his sister-in-law's constant bickering and nagging about all the work that she had to do for the men and her children. She could not wait for the new girl to return and help with some of the domestic chores. She also complained about the wedding expenses and wondered about getting reimbursed for all such expenses. Nanda kept reminding her that the expenses were paid by friends and neighbors. He also told her repeatedly that the two brothers had worked together without pay and that the groom was entitled to something. But she chose to ignore his logic and continued her bickering, and the costs kept escalating with her imagination.

The Sunday following the wedding was referred to as second Sunday. On that day, the groom walked to his in-laws' house to escort his wife home. They were given some cash, some jewelry, and the wedding gifts, consisting mostly of kitchen supplies. Her little brother, Prem, loaded the stuff on a donkey cart and drove them and their supplies home. She wore her new dress and a pair of shoes.

Prem was an energetic, tall, and skinny twelve-year-old who loved to talk. He chattered all the way, telling his new brother-in-law, called *dabit*, about the cattle and the farm that he was already actively working. He knew of his dabit's riding ability and suggested that they should go riding horses soon and inspect the cattle in the savannahs. It was a short distance, and the speedy Prem, with the galloping donkey got them home in a short time. He helped to unload the boxes, said goodbye, jumped on the cart, and galloped the donkey home.

The sister-in-law saw all the boxes and smiled. She told Finey that the men had work to do, and the two of them should get busy with the housework. Finey, who was used to doing such household jobs, wasted no time with the assigned duties; and within an hour, she was outside carrying pails of water, washing clothes, and hanging them out to dry. After the washing, they gathered some wood, made supper, and had the family meal. The Dutchmen and their wives came for their evening visit, stayed long enough to welcome the new member of the family, and suggested that it was time for all to go to bed. Then they departed. Soon the lantern was blown out, and in total darkness, all went to bed.

It was the first time that the couple had time alone together, and in that dark room, they sat on the khatia and talked. He did the talking, and she did the crying. She missed her family and wanted to go home. He tried to console her, but it was hopeless. He stuttered, and she trembled for a while until he had the courage to compose himself and start talking. He explained that he was a poor boy with nothing to give other than his loyalty. He promised to be a good husband and that someday they would have a fine home, acquire some land and cattle, and have many wonderful children. Still sobbing, she lay on the pillow and finally went to sleep.

Tension continued to escalate between the two women, and everyone realized that the two brothers and their wives could not live in the same house. It was painful for Nanda, who really wanted his brother with him. He had dreams about putting their efforts together and, through hard work and frugality, building a nice house and acquiring some land.

By the time 1937 came, the situation was so toxic that something had to be done. One day, during an extremely vicious bickering session, Finey walked out of the house and went to the garden where her husband was working. She cried and explained that she could no longer take the abuse from the other woman, and they must move on with their own lives. That evening, during supper, Nanda informed the young couple that he had purchased one gallon of rice to feed his family. There was no food for anyone else. Sniffling, he further explained that he needed the other bedroom for his children, so there was no place for the new couple to sleep. He finally informed them that they must move out and start their own lives together.

Early the next morning, Finey packed up some personal items and suggested to her husband that they should go to her parents' house. She explained that there was plenty of room there because two of her brothers had recently built their own houses and had moved out of her father's house. She suggested that he could help her father and brother Prem with their farming and cattle herding. He picked up her bag, took her by the hand, and walked her to her father's house.

At the gate, he saw Bholanauth and could not stand the embarrassment. He told Finey to go tell her parents that she came for a visit and that he went to explore their various options. He slowly walked back toward the hut where he no longer lived. With no place to go, he wandered into Mackerel Maraj's shop and loitered about. Maraj saw him and wondered why that hardworking young man was not in the field that day. But he figured that it was none of his business and tried to ignore the situation.

By midmorning, he found his brother in the field. Seeing him, Nanda began to cry. Soon they were both crying and understood that their love for each other was still genuine. They also knew that wedges now existed between them that could not be removed. He asked Nanda about his share of their money. Nanda explained that there was nothing he could do about that. His wife had control of everything, and she would not part with anything. Nanda did explain that the only thing she did not know about was Maloo. He told his brother to find Maloo and keep him as a working ox. Nanda then shared his lunch with his brother, hugged him, wiped off the tears, and resumed his farming duties. With no place to go, he wandered back to Maraj's shop, where he perched himself on a wooden windowsill. Maraj knew that something was definitely wrong. Customers came to and went from the shop and wondered about him just sitting there. Toward evening, Maraj told him that it was time to close the shop for the day, and he must leave. He said nothing. Maraj began to pry, and soon the situation was revealed. The sympathetic Maraj closed the shop, took him into his kitchen, and asked his wife, Marajin (female for Maraj), to bring food for them. She did. As they ate the simple meal of rice, dal, and fried vegetables, Maraj explained the situation to his wife. She did not say much. She cleaned up the dishes and told Motilall that she would get a bed ready for him. In the morning, he would have breakfast with them. All she requested was that the young man help Maraj with lifting the heavy sacks of flour, sugar, salt, and some miscellaneous heavy boxes. In addition, she requested that he split some wood for her. Maraj was a middle-aged man who had difficulty lifting heavy loads and chopping wood.

In the morning after breakfast, he helped Maraj with his wife's requests and wandered out. The only place he could go was to the Poonai farm. They were happy to see him and gave him his old job back herding cattle. He worked there, ate there, slept there, and rather enjoyed the freedom from the bickering that he tolerated at home. A week later, Lalla visited the Poonais, and together they gave Motilall some money. Some was for wages, and the rest was a dowry. The lady of the house offered to keep the money for him. He kept one dollar and gave the rest to the woman for safekeeping.

As Lalla walked away, it was obvious that he had a limp. He appeared to be in serious pain, and the observers wondered what caused such discomfort. Motilall hurried toward him and questioned the situation. He explained that he would be making a trip to Georgetown soon to see a special doctor. The local medical personnel suspected that he was diabetic. Not knowing what else to say, he climbed into his cart, gave his Namaste greeting, and drove the donkey home.

At home, Finey noticed the sore on Lalla's foot and decided to play the part of nurse, cleaning and dressing her father's sores. It must have been painful for Lalla because after the dressing he sat on his chair and quietly winced. Finey sat with him because she loved him dearly and because it gave her a purpose in life during those lonely days. It was during those lonely days that she really got to know about her father's life. He told her about his parents' situation in India and their struggles with poverty there. He told her about their journey to British Guiana and the difficulties they faced at the Ruimveldt Estate. He told her about their unfortunate deaths and how he and his sister became orphans. And he discussed the adoption process that brought him to that village. He talked and she listened. She fed him, tended to his every need, and tried to ignore the winces that increased as the days passed.

After Lalla left the Poonai's farm that day, Motilall asked his boss for a couple of days off in order to handle some personal business. He went to Maraj's shop, where he bought some bread, some pastries, some sugar, some salt, some matches, and some rice. He noticed that there was a large empty butter can there, and he offered to buy it. Mr. Maraj told him that he could have the can and all the supplies if he would split some wood for his wife. He did. Then he purchased a cutlass, which he sharpened with Maraj's file. Finally, he installed a wire handle on the can, packed up his supplies, and walked away, waving the can by the handle on one hand and carrying the cutlass in the other hand. He picked some lime off a tree in the neighborhood, gathered some hot peppers, and continued walking toward the savannahs.

Lizards and birds went about their business, and an occasional alligator plunged into the water at the sound of his footsteps. He was determined to go find Maloo. He walked for several miles before taking a rest. There in the can, he put some water from a nearby stream, squeezed some lime juice into the can, and added some sugar. The lemonade and pastries made a hearty snack, and after a short nap, he resumed walking toward the western horizon. He walked toward the setting sun, crossing shallow ditches and swimming across deeper canals. He was an excellent swimmer. With his left hand holding his clothes and supplies, he paddled away energetically with his right hand, and while crossing, he saw the abundance of fish in the water. In a short time, he secured some for supper. A troop of monkeys suspiciously paused to look at him and continued with wild acrobatic leaps from branch to branch. They hurried away to whatever destination awaited. Canje pheasants were many, and they noisily darted about as he walked along.

Before darkness gathered, his fire was blazing, and as the sun was setting, he built a shelter with brush and reeds. Soon, water was boiling in his can, and fish were roasting on a bed of hot burning coals. He cooked up some rice, added some salt and hot pepper to the fire-roasted fish, and had himself a hot meal. All alone, he sat there listening to the sounds of the crackling logs and occasional sounds from night creatures. Occasional lightning flickered in the distant horizon, which distracted his gaze from the stars. He rolled some tobacco in special paper and had a smoke. The roaring fire kicked out small sparks with occasional popping sounds that soon found him sleeping in the simple shelter that he had earlier constructed.

By 4:00 a.m. the next morning, he awoke. The fire was reduced to a pile of ashes and some smoldering logs. In the foggy, chilly morning, he heaped dried grass and some kindling on the anemic fire, which generated a stream of smoke that created a ghostly image in the still morning. The rising smoke blended with and disappeared into the morning fog. He began blowing on the pile, which almost instantly erupted into a blaze. The warmth and light from the flames brought comfort to his loneliness as he boiled water in the wire-handled butter can, added sugar to it, and enjoyed a warm, sweetened drink. To satisfy hunger, he ate some of the bread he acquired from Maraj. He sat there in the fog, mesmerized by the flames and dreaming about the future. Then somewhat angry, he started visualizing himself as a wealthy man with a big white house and a large farm with countless cattle and many sons to manage his empire. He liked that vision and dwelled there while sipping his warm liquid from a coconut shell and staring at the blazing fire that crackled and expelled sparks into the morning stillness.

Before long, his warm beverage was almost gone, and the tropical sun lit up the eastern horizon, which soon devoured the lingering ghostly fog. The young traveler ate his leftover rice and fish, drank the last of his warm sugar water, washed up his can, gathered up his supplies, put out the fire, and resumed his western journey. He cut a twig from a black sedge plant, which he chewed and from which he made himself a fine toothbrush. The troop of monkeys watched with curiosity. As he walked barefooted along, his vision of the future intensified, and his dreams of the future accompanied him for most of that day.

It turned out to be a hot and humid day. On several occasions, he had to swim in order to minimize potential heat exhaustion. As he walked, he inspected small herds of cattle, and that evening, he inspected the gathering places where the animals slept. He built a simple shelter and slept close to a small herd that night. He continued his search the next morning, snacking on wild fruits and berries. He ate fish and rice for supper again, and on the fourth day, in the distance, he saw an animal that resembled Maloo's marking. Their sleeping quarters was close by, and the seeker figured that by evening, those animals would congregate in their familiar sleeping area.

Those animals slept in groups for two main reasons. First, the ratio of mosquitoes per animal was much lower than if the animals slept alone. Secondly, especially to young calves, the adult animals collectively created a strong defense against any intruding jaguar. Motilall knew all the habits of cattle and perched himself on a comfortable branch of a tall tree along the cattle trail. They called those trails cow tracks. There, he waited. As evening approached, the animals instinctively started meandering toward their sleeping camp. They walked along the trail, following the one ahead, and their pace accelerated as the sun began to set. The cows bellowed at random, calling for their calves, which emerged from their seclusion in the tall grass, answering their mama's call and galloping to their respective mothers to get their fill of milk. The older calves stayed with their mothers during the day.

Motilall patiently waited and inspected the animals as they walked past him. It was a pretty sight for him, and he again dreamed of someday having a fine herd like the one he was observing. He was in his daydreaming session when he saw the animal he was waiting for. In the twilight, the impressive animal came walking toward him. It was Maloo. He was even more impressive looking than anyone could have imagined. He appeared to have all the characteristics of a fine ox, and the jolly observer could not help himself. Dismounting from his perch in record time, he ran toward the animal calling, "Maloo! Maloo!" That scared the herd, and with tails curled on their backs, they made a wild stampede and raised a cloud of dust that blanketed the twilight. The only sound was thundering hooves in the distance. Motilall was still in a trot when he kicked up a piece of leather. He stopped, picked it up, and unfolded it. To his surprise, it contained several tarnished silver coins. Almost in disbelief, he inspected the coins over and over and then carefully folded the rotting leather case and placed it in his can. Happy and happier, he began his homeward journey, swinging the can back and forth from the wire handle and carrying the cutlass in the other hand.

In the warm moonlit night, he walked well into the morning hour until he came upon an abandoned camp. Someone had lately camped there, and with the pieces of wood left by the previous party, he made a fire and instantly fell asleep to the sound of the crackling firewood. Once again, he began to dream. The handsome couple sat next to him and seemed to enjoy the warmth of his fire. Nothing was said. The scene was like a family camping in the wilderness with the parents watching over a sleeping child. When he awoke, the sun was high up in the eastern sky. The fire was out, but the heat and humidity caused him to sweat profusely. He could not believe that he slept for such a long time. Then he remembered his treasure in the butter can and went to verify that it was not a dream. Satisfied, he gathered up some fish, roasted them, and boiled some rice. After the meal, he made some lemonade, and with a black sedge twig chewed at one end, he began to clean the coins. He carefully washed them, polished them with sand, and sat there admiring them. Satisfied, he put them back in the rotting leather wrapping, which he tied up with some vines. He then ate the last of his meal, drank up the lemonade, swam a short distance to cool off, and decided to head toward home. He once again put the coins in the can, which he swung on one hand. He carried the cutlass in the other hand and walked barefoot all day and into the night under the bright moon, constantly thinking about his good fortune and what to do with the coins.

He was gone for almost a week, and when he arrived at the Poonai farm, he was all covered in dirt and mud. His boss was torn between anger and excitement. He bathed, ate a home-cooked meal, and went to bed with his treasure tucked under his pillow. He woke up periodically to check on his coins and was happy when morning came. After breakfast, he asked the lady of the house for his money. She wondered what was going on but did not question him. He took the money from her and the coins and went to the post office, where he started a savings account. The post office personnel carefully inspected the old coins and mumbled among themselves but did not question their origin. They gave him a savings account book with English writings that made no sense to him. So he took it to Prem and asked him to verify that it was genuine. Upon verification, he and Prem went home to see Finey. She was happy to see that he was well and that he had a big smile on his face. He gave her the savings book and explained that he was making arrangements to buy the hut located a short way away from the Dutchmen's residence. Prem explained that he did have enough money to buy the hut and a whole lot more. They both smiled, and Prem began to laugh. He adored his dabit.

Within a week, he and Finey were the proud owners of a small hut. It was not much, but it was home. Prem, with his donkey and cart, transported their few items. As Prem loaded the cart, Motilall paid a visit to Lalla. He was not well. The doctor in Georgetown had confirmed diabetes. Lalla's sore on his leg got progressively worse, and there was discussion of a possible amputation.

Finey dearly loved her father and was sad to leave him in such agonizing pain, but fighting back the tears, she hugged him and followed her husband and brother to the loaded cart. Prem kept the donkey on a slow walk as to have time to discuss options for Lalla. There were no options. He had sustained a wound, which turned into a massive sore that got progressively worse. They all knew that he must go back to Georgetown and get the amputation done.

After unloading the cart at the new residence, they went to Nanda's shack to gather up their personal items that were left there. At the door, they were greeted by the sister-in-law. She was not pleased to see them, and when they announced the purpose of their presence, she went absolutely crazy. Her abusive language was not at all ladylike, and her screams soon brought her sisters, the Dutchmen's wives, to the scene. Her logic was that she fed and cared for Motilall while he was young and dependent, and after the wedding, she paid various expenses, and furthermore, the young couple lived in her house for months and did not pay one penny for food and lodging. For all those reasons, she was confiscating all the wedding gifts, money, and her wedding ring.

The two women tried to reason with her, but it was of no use. In fact, she told the women to leave her premises and to mind their own business. Insulted, her two sisters with quickened paces, left, muttering all the way back to their homes. The short-tempered Prem could not believe what was happening. He began arguing with the woman, who charged and slapped him, screaming that he was just a little boy and should know his place and not argue with adults. There was a stick on the ground. Prem picked it up and charged at the irate woman. Scared, she began to run. Prem, chasing her, kept beating the stick on the ground while his motor mouth shifted into overdrive. Down the dusty path, they ran, and her two sisters could not help laughing at the incredible scene. Not knowing where to go, she dashed into one of her sister's huts and crawled under the bed to hide. Prem threw the stick away and ran back to the donkey cart. Nothing more was said, he turned the donkey around, took the couple home, and then galloped the donkey home.

The disappointed couple began organizing their new home. They had a bedroom with a khatia fully intact. There was a cooking area with some old pots and pans hanging next to the fireside. They had sheets, pillows, and blankets, so Finey got busy making the bed while her husband was in the yard gathering and chopping wood with the cutlass. Soon, there was a rattling noise, and they saw Prem galloping his donkey and cart toward them. He unloaded his cargo, which had an ax; some groceries consisting of rice, split peas, salt, coconut oil, sugar, and spices to make curry; serving spoons; plates; enamel cups; and other miscellaneous items. He told his sister to arrange her house, and he and his dabit were going to the ocean to gather up some shrimp. As the galloping donkey was leaving, he yelled at his sister to beware of the witch. They all laughed.

It was a good shrimping day. They caught a basketful of shrimp and some mullets. They even managed to snag a few crabs. The women helped clean the seafood, and all had a good meal of rice, dal, shrimp curry, and fried mullet. Men and women perched themselves on a log behind the hut with platefuls of food and enamel cups of water, almost choking on each handful of food as they laughed at the scene of Prem, stick in hand, chasing the so-called wicked woman down the dusty road and her trying to hide under the bed. They had a wonderful first evening at their new home, and as darkness surrounded them and the mosquitoes made their buzzing appearance, it was time to retire to bed.

The following month, the Dutchmen and Motilall decided that they all needed better homes. They planned to gather and saw wood that would be used to construct such new houses. They gathered up their axes, saws, and supplies and departed toward an area called Blackbush to seek lumber suitable for home building. While they were gone, the three women kept one another company, alternating sleeping at the various residences. Finey was excited to have company at her home one night, and she wanted to make her friends a good breakfast the next morning. She spent all day gathering supplies at the store, checked on Lalla, and went home. It had rained that afternoon, and her wood was wet, so she went out gathering some better wood. She found some pieces of boards in the weeds and grabbed a few pieces. Realizing that everything would be wet, she decided to put the wood on top of the warm fireside, and after some casual conversation, they went to bed.

The three women awoke to flames and smoke in the house. The wood that she had put on the fireside to dry ignited, and soon the sparks reached the grass roof and set the house ablaze. In their slips and undergarments, they managed to escape with minor burns and a good dose of smoke that caused them to gasp for air between sputtering and choking. The hysterical Finey ran and screamed on the banks of the drainage trench close to the inferno. It did not take long, and the entire structure was consumed by the flames. One of the women got a sheet from her hut and covered Finey as they tried to keep her calm.

Things got worse when the sister-in-law arrived. She accused the women of gathering the boards from Pagalya's grave site and said the evil followed them home. The story was that there was a woman whose name was Pagalya (crazy woman) had died a few years before. Shortly after her death, tales evolved about a ghost that haunted the neighborhood. The scared neighbors came to the conclusion that it was the ghost of the recently deceased woman because she did some evil rituals when alive. The village called the local ghost buster (Obyaman), who did his rituals and had the people build a fence around her burial site. The rituals and the fence supposedly kept the ghost penned up, and that kept the village safe. Finey, ignorant of that story, grabbed some of the wood from the broken-down fence and took it home. Now the sister-in-law was yelling that the women had unleashed the evil ghost and that the village would once again be haunted. As the abuse continued, more and more people gathered, and as dawn approached, the three women went to Ramouthar's hut to continue with their crying.

Shortly after dawn, Prem arrived to console his hysterical sister. Not knowing what to do, he held her hand as she wrapped the cotton sheet around her body, and they rode the donkey cart to their parents' house. Doormatie had many concerns during those days. Lalla had scheduled his leg amputation surgery, and he was quite ill. Finey had burns on her body and appeared sick. So Finey's sister, Rampatie, who lived in Number 65 Village, was called to help. Her little sister, Guytrie, was only seven years old and appeared totally confused about everything that was happening. Finey took a bath and was given some clean clothes to wear before seeing Lalla. She could not believe how sick and scared he seemed, and he was shocked at how frail she appeared. But like most stressed people, they greeted each other with forced smiles and sat in quiet corners, not knowing what to say. That evening, Doormatie, her three daughters, and Prem had supper with Lalla and discussed the upcoming medical procedure. After the discussion, Prem informed them that he and some friends would go to Blackbush the next day and bring the men home.

When the men returned, they built a lean-to on Ramouthar's hut. The roof was thatched with braided coconut branches, the walls were lined with wattle and daubed with mud, and the floor was filled with clay and daubed with mud. Within a week, the young couple moved into their new quarters. Cooking and eating was done at the two friends' home.

Lalla had his surgery, but things did not progress well for him. He became progressively sicker and more delirious. The three men returned to Blackbush to finish their log harvesting, and Finey spent most of those days caring for Lalla. He screamed constantly from pain. When the men returned with the logs, they all agreed that Lalla was dying. The doctors confirmed that he had blood poisoning and that he only had a short time to live. It was during those stressful times that Finey informed her family that she was pregnant.

In 1938, Lalla died at his home with his ten living children by his side. He was fifty-eight years old, and all agreed that it was a blessing in disguise, for now he had no more pain. The pundit told them that his pain was buried with his bones and that he was dancing in heaven with two youthful legs. He was buried in the cemetery of Number 66 Village.

CHAPTER 14

The Worker

After Lalla's funeral, the family gathered at his house to perform the various rituals and to keep Doormatie company during her period of sadness and grief. All her children and their spouses loved Lalla because he was a kind, fair, and generous man, and his family being there was testimony to their respect for him. It was during that time period, while the siblings discussed just about anything to minimize boredom, that Rampatie asked Finey about their future plans. Among other things, they discussed building a house, but Finey confessed that they must find a suitable and affordable lot. Later in the discussion, Rampatie and her husband suggested that they had a vacant lot across the road from their home, and if Finey and her husband wanted to build on that lot, they were welcome to do so. After several more discussions, it was agreed that Motilall and Finey would build their new home in Number 65 Village, on the west side of the public road, across the road from her sister's house. The news got the Dutchmen so excited that they also decided to buy lots in the same village and build their new homes there too. In that way, they would still be friends and neighbors. It was also a good excuse to escape from the constant nagging and bickering of Nanda's wife. In addition, the Dutchmen wanted to get their father to live with them.

Their plan was to build attached living quarters to one of their houses for the senior Dutchman, Muna Singh.

The months that followed found the three men hauling logs from Blackbush. They sawed the logs into lumber to frame their new homes. They used crude instruments like axes, handsaws, and chisels for cutting, splicing, and dovetailing pieces of wood to firmly secure the beams and rafters. To avoid buying nails, when necessary, they grooved and notched the pieces and hooked them together. Those were banded together to ensure stability. The siding was made from a type of palm locally called manicole. Those palm trees were fierce competitors in the dense foliage of the tropical environment. In order to compete for light, the plants compensated by growing several feet above the dense canopy. The trunks grew tall and straight, forcing the leaves upward to reach the abundance of light. From a distance, they appeared to be skinny coconut trees.

Those trees were chopped down with axes and dragged to an open area where they were stripped into siding for houses. The rough, curved sides were toward the outside, and the straight inner parts were on the inside of the house. Those inner parts were plastered with a special type of mud to minimize slivers, and the mud also served as chinking. The caulking materials also served as insulation. The floor was made of crabwood boards that the men bought from local sawmills and sawed and planed by hand. Occasionally, the tapered ends did not totally merge together, thus leaving open spaces, creases, and gaps in the floor. Because of the tropical heat, small creases and occasional wider gaps in the floor did not matter to the occupants.

The plan for the roof was to use cattails and coconut branches. Those materials were harvested and left to dry in the tropical sun. At nights and during rainy periods, they were covered up by whatever materials were available. Then at the fleeting moments when the vegetative structures seemed ideal for flexibility, they were carefully braided by the skilled hands of the women. When fully dried to perfection, they were stored away under cover.

Motilall used up all his savings, and his house was only halfway built. He had planted two acres of rice that year on land provided by

Rampatie and her husband, Samaroo. That couple's oldest son, whose nickname was Name, followed along and was quite eager to be the resident gofer and errand boy. So when some simple tasks had to be done, a message needed to be sent, or lunch had to be delivered to the field workers, the seven-year-old Name was ready, willing, and able to hurry along, feeling proud of his contributions to building the new house and helping with the farm duties.

The rice crop was a month away from harvest. Motilall hoped and prayed that diseases and insects would not harm his precious crop because he needed the proceeds to buy additional building materials. In addition, they would require food, and rice was the standard diet. In addition to the rice crop, the pregnant Finey and her two women friends had their large vegetable gardens in peak condition, and on Saturday mornings, one of the women took some of the produce to the town of Skeldon and sold it at the market. The money they earned was used to buy supplies from the market that would last for the coming week. The women did the cooking together, and three times daily, when convenient, the three couples sat together as one big family and ate their simple meals.

They all needed additional income, so periodically, the men went to the Skeldon Estate and worked in the sugarcane fields. The job title was "cut and load." They cut the sugarcane, trimmed off the excess vegetation, and loaded the cane into punts. Those punts were hauled away in the canals to the factory, which squeezed them and converted the cane juice into sugar, rum, and molasses. The pay was not very good, but sitting at home was not an option. Between selling vegetables and working at the estate, they managed to save a few dollars each week to buy a few pieces of building materials, nails, and other necessary items.

By the time harvest came along, Finey was definitely showing her pregnant state. She did most of her daily duties and struggled to keep up with the other women. It was difficult for her, and her mother and sister grew increasingly concerned about her working too much. So Prem came to the rescue. He loved his dabit and having the opportunity to help with the rice harvesting was a joy to him. But he had his own work at home. With Lalla now gone, he had to grow up and step up to being the man in his mother's house. With help from his two older brothers, he managed to fill in for all the cleanup jobs that did not get done.

Long Prem, as he was called, could run, and he was fast. In fact, he was by far the fastest runner in the area, a skill he demonstrated at several local competitive sporting events. So he got from place to place in record time. For longer distances, he rode his bicycle with two speeds: fast and faster. People made fun of him, saying that he could go that fast because he was so skinny; he had no wind resistance. But skinny as he was, he was a hard worker, and at fourteen, he tackled several jobs that only adult men performed.

On days when he came to help with harvesting, he conveniently found room in his lunch pail to stash a nutritious snack for his pregnant sister. She would give him a cup of sweetened tea, and as he drank, she snacked on the surprise he brought along. After his chat and the snack, the morning sun found him and his dabit heading for the rice field, carrying their grass knives and lunch pails with them. The grass knives were used to harvest the rice. The straw was cut about twelve inches below the grain heads and left in the field to dry in small piles called *lehene*. When the cutting was done, they stacked the lehenies together and tied them into bundles with ropes made from rice straw. The bundles were later hauled away on a homemade flatbed drag (*draga*), pulled by oxen to some central areas to be threshed. Those central locations were called *kharyans*. There, the bundles were loosened; and the oxen, with their heads tied to a center post, were driven in a circular pattern as the hooves severed the grain from the straw. Driving the oxen around and around the center pole was a job for young lads like Name. The straw, which they called *pyra*, was removed by pitchforks, and the grain was collected in pails and dumped into sacks. Those sacks were hauled away by ox carts to the rice mill for processing. It was hard work that had to be done in the tropical heat.

With harvest completed and the grain processed, Motilall sold a portion of his average crop and kept some for consumption at home.

With money in hand, he resumed building his home. As usual, he and the Dutchmen shared labor and the kitchen as the neighbors heard constant hammering and other construction sounds. Finally, it was time to install their thatch to the roof. They were hauling the materials out of storage one bright sunny day when the local sanitary inspector arrived. He inspected various construction aspects and approved everything except the roof. He informed them that a new rule had recently passed by the local authority personnel stipulating that all houses built along the public road could not have grass roofs any longer. Those houses were fine on lots away from the public road, but houses along the road must have the roof built with galvanized material, locally referred to as zinc. The inspector apologized for bringing the bad news but emphatically stated that his job was to fully enforce the new law.

That news stopped everything. There was not enough money to buy the new roofing materials, and the baby would soon be there. The couple had hoped to move into the new house before the baby was born. Totally confused and disappointed, the three couples were standing by the roadside discussing options and passing time when a neighbor who was walking by stopped for a chat. Motilall shared the bad news that he received from the inspector about the roofing materials. The neighbor asked to inspect the materials that they intended to use, and after careful consideration, he offered to buy the grass. He explained that he recently purchased a herd of goats and a flock of sheep and would be building shelters for those animals. He explained that buying the materials would save him time because he would not have time to harvest, dry, and braid the new materials and was eager to get his pens built. He offered a fair price, and by midafternoon, he and his sons and the three builders hauled all the dried cattails and coconut branches away to the neighbor's yard.

With the cash, they purchased sheets of galvanized material and some nails and immediately began installing the new roofing materials. They used up all the sheets and realized that more materials were needed. Problem was there was no more money. Motilall went to his brother-in-law, who was managing the family store, and asked for the materials. He explained that he would pay for them after the house was completed. He said he would seek employment at the sugar estate. They tallied up the total, which was a few pennies over five dollars. The store manager told him that he would give him a family discount, and he would pay a total of five dollars. But he further explained that there would be no charging. It was a cash transaction, or there would be no transaction.

Motilall went home and shared the news with his wife. Frustrated, Finey went to visit her sister across the road and shared the news with her. Angry, her sister went and complained to their mother. Doormatie was furious but did not want to overrule her son's business decision. So the next day, she came to visit Finey. She explained that her son, Finey's oldest brother, was an excellent businessman, and that was why he was put in charge of the store. But she further explained that it was not his business. That business was started with money from Pyroo and Radha and from the Singhs and that all her children should have a stake in the business. Then she removed her white head cover (*rumaal*), and from the fold, she pulled out a five-dollar bill. She told Finey not to tell anyone that she provided the money, but her husband should go and get the necessary materials and complete the house before the baby and the rainy season arrived. Finey gave the money to her husband, and to be discreet, she told him that she had saved it from selling vegetables and eggs and was planning to use the money for baby stuff. So Motilall proudly marched to the store and secured the materials that he needed. Before sunset that day, Finey and her sister, with smiles on their faces, proudly inspected the completed house. It was a fine little house with a shiny roof that glittered in the tropical sun. That night, the three builders got a bottle of rum, butchered a chicken, and celebrated their success of building a fine house. They chewed every bone in the curried chicken, and by the time the bottle was empty, the Dutchmen sang and beat on an old metal drum while Motilall danced to the noise. He was an excellent dancer.

The next day, it rained. It was a major thunderstorm called a squall, with gusty winds that swayed the coconut trees almost to the point of breaking. In the wind, the large raindrops appeared to be traveling horizontally, and the flashing lightning and cracking thunder were testimony to the severity of the storm. As the little streams and small ponds' levels rose, the three builders were busy inspecting their workmanship. They checked for leaks on the roof and on the sidings. They checked the foundation and all the corners of the house. And just like that, the storm subsided. There was no more pattering on the roof, no more blinding lightning, no more deafening thunder, and the tall coconut trees resumed their steady vertical postures with trembling leaves. The three builders walked about slapping each other's backs and shaking hands, congratulating themselves on a fine job of building a sturdy little house. They laughed as some ducks landed in the yard, doing strange water dances and foraging for food. The house weathered the storm well with no leaks. One of the Dutchmen laughed and said that God sent a test for the house, and the house passed with flying colors. It was a total relief for all of them.

Within a week, the couple was fully settled in the house. They had few possessions and almost no money. But they felt like millionaires. Motilall still had his wire-handled butter can, which they used to cook the rice, and her sister gave them a cast-iron pan that they used for frying fish and vegetables. In another metal pot, she boiled split peas and made dal. In their new home, they cooked and ate, and in the evening, they drank sweetened tea from cups made from used tin cans and from the enamel cups that they so treasured. Some days, they invited the Dutch folks for supper, and some days, they went to their homes for a meal. They were truly good friends, and that gave Motilall a kind of family that he never had. Finey had her sister and her children across the road, and they had constant visits from boys like Prem and Name. Prem always teased them because they always cooked dal. Motilall generally commented to him that "rice and dal meck coolie man tall." He had a great sense of humor.

In November 1938, Finey delivered a baby girl at her mother's house. They named her Leela. It was customary for the mother and baby to be confined in a bedroom for nine days, and the father was not allowed to visit them during that time. Motilall, missing his wife, went off to see his old friends at the Poonai farm. He shared the good news about his baby, and they all celebrated that evening. As they sat around with the bottle of rum and some fried plantains, one of the men asked Motilall if he needed anything. There was a short silence, and then he answered yes, he needed something. He needed help to bring Maloo home and break him to pull a plow. There was a loud roar, and all the half-drunk cowboys started yelling and throwing their hats about. Within a couple of minutes, in the mass confusion, they agreed that on Saturday, they would go to the savannahs and bring Maloo home. It was the least they could do for their little buddy.

Early Saturday morning, the group gathered at the Poonai farm. The two boys Name and Prem also joined them. Doormatie and Rampatie packed food and snacks for the men and the boys. They carried their cast nets along with cooking supplies and, of course, a few bottles of rum. One of the men led a draft ox along with a rope tied to the ox's nose ring. The obedient beast, gentle as could be, walked along like a mammoth dog on a leash. Two men rode horses and carried ropes coiled around their shoulders. Two horses, an ox, six men, two boys, and a few bottles of rum and some tobacco left the farm that November morning, heading toward the savannahs in search of Maloo. They were a jolly bunch who clip-clopped, stomped, and marched westward with the rising sun and a gentle ocean breeze on their backs, as the chattering Prem and his little nephew Name scurried about in search of wild fruits and berries.

By late afternoon, they had reached the camp where Maloo supposedly slept at nights. They stopped and rested there. After a late lunch, they used the cast nets and secured a good supply of freshwater fish, and soon, the gathering turned into a fish-fry party. They ate some peppered fried fish with roti and rice that they had brought along. Then the rum bottles came out. Careful not to drink too much, they drank modest amounts while the horses and the ox feasted on the tall, luscious tropical grasses. They sat around sipping rum, rolling and smoking cigarettes, and snacking on fried fish.

Shortly after five o'clock, the two riders mounted and galloped away into the almost setting sun while the remaining men and boys built a shelter for the night. In less than an hour, into the twilight, the party could see a cloud of dust and hear the thundering hooves of horses. The riders were back. Maloo was spotted close to the camp. Again, there was a loud roar from the men as they passed the bottle and threw their sweaty hats about. The general consensus was that in the morning, they would take Maloo home and break him to be a useful ox. It was the least they could do for their little buddy, who was now the proud papa of baby Leela. Somewhat drunk and tired, they crawled into the crude shelter and snored away into the darkness, occasionally slapping at mosquitoes and other biting insects.

At 5:00 a.m. that Sunday morning, the two riders galloped their horses away into the morning fog. The grass was wet from condensation. The party at camp built their fire. The rising smoke jostled for space with the lingering fog, and the men cooked up a fast breakfast of fried eggs and made sandwiches using bread that they had brought along. They drank their sweet tea from coconut shells as the tobacco was rolled into cigarettes. The man with the ox hurried his breakfast, gulped his tea, put the rope into the nose ring of the ox, and headed toward the riders tracking the hoofprints as he hurried along. In record time, camp was abandoned, and the whole group went toward the cattle camp. The warm sun soon melted the fog away, and into the distance, they saw two horsemen dragging an excited bovine beast toward them. The riders soon came upon the ox, and with extreme skill and agility, they yoked Maloo by the horn to the neck of the draft ox and turned them loose. The riders dismounted when they reached the group, who handed them their breakfast. As they ate, they all watched the trained ox dragging the inexperienced Maloo toward the rising sun. Occasionally, Maloo would lie down, but the ox kept on walking, dragging him by the horns until he would scramble to his feet. He realized that it was easier and perhaps less painful to walk along stride for stride with the pulling beast.

Down the trail they walked toward the eastern horizon as they watched the two animals walking ahead. Maloo was confused, but the motivated ox knew that when he got home, there would be some good treats awaiting his arrival. They all agreed that Maloo was an impressive animal and offered opinions about how best to train him. They puffed away on their cigarettes, took occasional swigs of water from the ditches, and snacked on wild berries along the way. They made dangerous work fun! They did it for their little buddy, and he was thankful for their help.

With the house completed, Maloo well secured at the Poonai farm, and the baby still at Grandma's house, Motilall took advantage of the quiet time to care for his vegetable gardens. His brother occasionally came to visit and to investigate about the baby. But most of the time, he complained about his obnoxious wife. So he spent time on his farming and occasionally visited his brother and the Dutch families.

One morning, Prem stopped in to inform his dabit that it was time for Finey and the baby to come home. So he hurried over to greet his wife and daughter and thanked his mother-in-law for all that she was doing to help them during that early stage of their married life. They bundled up the baby, and the nervous seventeen-year-old Finey, her husband, and her mother started the southerly half-mile walk toward home. Prem was on his bicycle, weaving and bobbing about and showing off various riding stunts as most fifteen-year-old lads would do. Finey's sister was the welcome wagon as they walked toward the house. The local pundit met them there, did the routine rituals, and prayed for the young family. Before sunset, all the visitors had left, and the young couple and the baby nestled into their new home, occasionally slapping at the pesky mosquitoes. As the baby slept, Motilall told Finey about the garden and about Maloo. They took turns checking on the baby in the dim light from a kerosene lamp as creatures like frogs and crickets made their routine sounds that were occasionally interrupted by barking dogs and braying donkeys. The night passed with neither of them getting much sleep.

The next morning after breakfast, Motilall showed Finey his new acquisition. He had acquired an old bicycle and had it fixed up to the point that he could ride it. There was a little wobble in one wheel, and there were some minor squeaks. The seat was padded with an old gunnysack and tied together in a crude fashion with used twine from a rice bag that they called *bagtwine*. It was transportation. He hopped on his "new" bike and rode off to check on Maloo as Finey sat on the wooden steps, laughing at the squeaks while nursing baby Leela and appreciating the bonding process at her own home.

Maloo was in good shape. He was always a docile and gentle animal, and now fully grown, he appeared to have maintained that gentleness about him. He was a black steer with some white markings and medium-sized horns that had curved toward each other at the tip. There was something about him that even an ignorant observer would have noticed. He had a refined build and impressive-looking legs. The cowboys had a ring in his nose and said that he would be suited to be harnessed on the left side on a team of two. He planted himself there that morning, swishing his tail, occasionally shaking his ears as he chewed on a heap of freshly cut grass. Satisfied, Motilall paid his respects to the lady of the house and then pedaled his squeaking bicycle with the wobbling wheel toward home to be with his wife and baby.

Later that day, he and some friends gathered some lumber and built a small wooden pen for Maloo, and within a week, Maloo was dragged home by a draft ox and placed in his new pen. In the evenings, after working in the vegetable garden, Motilall would use his grass knife to cut a large bundle of grass and carried it home, on his head, for Maloo. They would eat supper and watch Maloo chew away at his grass and take an occasional drink from an old bucket located in one corner of the pen. Occasionally, Motilall walked around inside the pen until one day he got close enough to scratch the steer. It was the beginning of a bonding process that man and beast seemed to appreciate. Before long, a rope was placed in the animal's nose ring, and the man began to lead the beast around in the pen. Soon, he led Maloo out of the pen and allowed him to graze about on the lush green grass that surrounded them. Maloo would graze while Motilall petted and scratched him from head to tail.

After the grazing, Maloo was led back into the pen, where he found a small helping of rice bran rolled in molasses. The animal would devour every morsel of the sweet treat, and then he would stand by the gate bellowing for more. Motilall and Finey would watch as he slobbered, drooled, and stuck his tongue into his nostrils to capture any small flakes that were stuck there. He would use his tongue to get those remaining on any part of his nose and face. Then he begged for more. And within a month, he became the official family pet.

After the New Year (1939), as farmers were planning for the rice-planting season, Motilall rented two additional acres of land from his brother-in-law. During those days, he was working at the estate chopping sugarcane. His goal was to save enough money to buy another steer that would be compatible with Maloo. While searching, he used his brother-in-law's steer that was broke to pull on the right. He harnessed Maloo on the left side. With borrowed equipment, he slowly taught Maloo to pull lighter loads like logs until the ox understood the commands. Then he hitched them to a plow and slowly increased the depth of plowing as the team pulled harder and harder. It was no surprise that Maloo was an outstanding puller, and as his shoulders toughened up to the pressure of the hames (*sahilla*) and his muscles strengthened, Motilall knew that Maloo was everything that he had demonstrated as a calf that he would be.

The search was on for a new steer. One day, as Motilall was pedaling along on his squeaking bicycle, he saw a skinny brown-and-white steer tied to a stake in the ground. The animal was mostly brown rather than white, with long horns that grew straight up from his skull and turned inward halfway up. He leaned his bicycle by the roadside and went in to investigate the condition of the beast. It was shocking to him to see the animal with sores on his back covered with worms and flies. He was so amazed by the sorry sight that he did not see the owner approaching. The man greeted him, and they had a casual discussion about the animal covered with sores and tied up to the wooden stake. The man explained that the animal was lazy and wanted to lie down when harnessed to a plow. To keep the animal from lying down, the man would beat him and poke him with a pointed metal rod. When all his brutality did not get results, the angry owner tied him up without food and water and left him there to die. Motilall learned that the steer was broke to pull on the right side, which would complement Maloo as a team. His name was Kabra.

Motilall asked the man if he would consider selling the animal. The man said that the butcher offered twenty dollars, and he planned to fatten him for slaughter. After a long discussion, the man agreed to sell the animal to him for ten dollars as is. They agreed, and Motilall asked the man to feed and water the animal, and he would return the following day with the money to buy Kabra.

Early the next morning, Motilall, with a piece of rope, walked down the road, bought Kabra for ten dollars, fastened the rope to his nose ring, and led the animal toward home. People watched as the man led the skinny longhorn steer with sores along his back and flies buzzing about to feast on the infections. As he went past Number 64 Village, his brother-in-law Bholanauth saw the spectacle and gazed with disbelief. He started to laugh. He asked Motilall what he planned to do with such a bag of bones, and Motilall replied that he planned to use him for rice farming. Bholanauth laughed even louder and told him that his investment was not a total loss. When the animal died, his long rib bones could be used for peeling coconuts, and they could go into the coconut oil business. Many bystanders thought that that statement was funny, and they all had a good laugh about the whole matter.

When he reached home, Finey was very upset that he spent ten dollars on such a useless beast and insisted that he return that animal instantly and get his money back. He paid no attention to her either. Instead, he turned Maloo out to graze on his own and put Kabra in the pen. The first thing he did was offer the animal a helping of rice bran and molasses. The animal ate it up faster than Maloo could. He was given some grass and some water, and while he ate, Motilall started applying medicine to the sores that killed the worms and repelled the pesky flies. The black liquid medication was called jice fluid, and it was the standard treatment for animal wounds infested with various pests. Maloo stood by the gate and watched, probably wondering why the skinny intruder was getting such good treatment.

Day by day, the animal was well fed and watered and had his wounds attended to. The healing process was slow initially, but within a month, the wounds started to heal. With less pain, minimal pest provocations, and an abundance of food, Kabra started to gain weight. His ribs were less visible, and his sunken eyes showed great promise. As the weeks passed, Kabra grew into a well-shaped animal. Some of the hair on his back grew, but there were bald patches that exposed his hide as evidence of what had happened to him. He and Maloo then shared the pen and the treats and became friends and members of the family. The next challenge was to get them to work together as a team and to keep Kabra from lying down when harnessed to pull the plow.

In a land and time of few possessions, Motilall spent most of his spare time with the pair of steers. Finey carried Leela around and watched the animals and her husband as they created an unusual bond and seemed to appreciate one another's company. During the day, while the man was out working, the animals were turned out to graze. But by four o' clock in the afternoon, the pair of oxen came home and stood by the gate, waiting for their bundle of grass and to be treated with bran and molasses. By then, Kabra was almost as fat as Maloo and stood about two inches taller. His long, curved horns complemented his brown-and-white face as he proudly paraded about the village during the day in search of fresh grazing. He and Maloo followed each other about and became inseparable.

The day finally came for them to be harnessed as a team. With borrowed equipment, Maloo on the left and Kabra on the right, the wooden collar was placed over their necks, close to the shoulders. The wooden hames were tied together with twine, and the long shaft in the middle separated the animals. It was time for a practice run. Motilall hooked the shaft to a heavy log. He gave the command to go forward, and Maloo hustled along. But Kabra hesitated. With encouragement, he walked a few steps, mostly because Maloo was dragging him along until he went down.

Motilall left him alone and went to get his brother-in-law from across the road. By the time they got back to the team, Kabra was standing up. Motilall asked his helper to drive the team as he stood in front to watch the animals' behavior. It was obvious what the problem was with Kabra. He seemed to have a tender spot on his shoulder joint that was aggravated when the wooden hames pushed against that spot. Motilall then gathered some grass and leaves and used them to pad the part of the hames that seemed to cause the irritation. Then he gave the signal to go forward. Maloo went, and Kabra hesitated. He was encouraged, and realizing that he did not hurt, he kept on walking. They walked along for a short distance. There, Motilall removed the hames and collar and gave the animals their usual treats.

Motilall then went into the woods and secured materials for making his hames and collar. When the hames were carved and properly cured, he used soft rags and twine to pad all four hames. He bought a plow and a shaft, and before long, he was plowing his rice fields. The team worked well together, but Maloo was younger and stronger. Kabra was cured of his laziness to the amazement of the community and especially his previous owner. As the months passed, people in the surrounding areas recognized that Motilall indeed had special instincts that helped him to work with problem oxen, especially young and wild ones. People would hire him to break those unruly animals and train them to become gentle and productive. He broke them to pull on the right side because Maloo was on the left and managed to help train the unruly beasts. Together, they turned them into gentle helpers to work on their respective farms.

Motilall did not accept money for his services but bartered labor with the owners of the animals that he tamed. In such manner, he had help on his land growing his rice crop. Some generous people gave him an extra bag of rice as a gratuity for his services and to show their appreciation for him helping them. In such a manner, the once orphaned boy who turned cowboy had a family, became a farmer, and was respected by the community as a man with good instincts to train animals. Most of all, folks recognized him as a very hardworking and humble man and a dedicated husband and father who occasionally pedaled his squeaking bicycle with the wobbling wheel. When time permitted, he visited his good buddies at the

Poonai farm to tell stories and to socialize with them. Finey loved and adored him. His obnoxious brother-in-law did not make fun of him anymore. He had earned the respect of their community, and Prem and Name took pride in being with him.

And so, the little abused orphaned Thumru became Mr. Motilall.

CHAPTER 15

The Growing Family

The next rice crop was a major success. Soon, it was harvesttime, and with tools in hand, the young couple, with the help of Prem and the two Dutch couples, along with Muna Singh, cut and bundled the paddies. They built a wooden drag that was pulled by the oxen, and the bundles were hauled and stacked close to the community kharyans, where the animals did their circular patterns that severed the grain from the straw. The threshing labor was all bartered, and one early morning, the crew gathered and worked on Motilall's bundles. It was a windy day, and Finey, after ensuring that the crew was well fed and were resting, grabbed a pail and winnowed the grain, removing the chaff that blew away in the wind. The crew then used pails and placed the grain into sacks, which were sutured shut with bagtwine and a long needle called a *sucha*.

The lightning was flickering that evening as the crew was dismissed for the day. From the direction of the wind, it was obvious that rain was on its way. Maloo and Kabra pulled the drag loaded with the grain sacks to be stacked on higher ground. It was a difficult job for one tired man to stack those heavy sacks of winnowed grain weighing over one hundred pounds each. But with Finey's help, in the tropical darkness and brighter flashes of lightning in the distance, they pulled, dragged, and stacked the sacks in various fashions in a somewhat A-frame pattern. They used straw to cover the sacks and piled on pieces of wood and branches that had been secured earlier to keep the straw from blowing away. They finished after midnight, and by that time, the torrential downpour was upon them. Flashing and rumblings were ever-present, as if the heavens were angry. Finey, exhausted, sat on the drag, and her husband walked ahead of the two oxen as they slipped and stumbled along the dark and muddy dam toward home. By the time the animals were fed and all the details were handled, it was 2:00 a.m. Finey went to her sister's house to get the baby where she got yelled at for ignoring her baby all day long. They told her that the baby was sleeping, and they needed to rest, so she went in, nursed the baby, and stumbled home. They had a short discussion, changed out of the wet garments, and went straight to bed, totally exhausted.

There was a long and severe storm that night, and when the tired couple awoke late the next morning, all that was visible was water, water, and more water. The ponds and creeks were full, and the broken branches created ripples as the water meandered about in obedience to gravity. After tending to his animals, Motilall grabbed his cutlass and hurried to the fields to check on his grain sacks as Finey sat in the hammock nursing the baby. All the drainage and irrigation canals were full, and occasionally, water was pouring and gushing over the dams as the ebbing tide vacuumed the liquids eastward. At the various open sluices (*kokers*), the partially confined water gushed through the narrow open gates with uncontrollable rage and then gradually calmed into the wider creek, where it mingled and merged into the salty ocean water and deposited tons of sediment.

Many neighbors who had left their grain sacks in low-lying areas were anxiously and desperately trying to get the water-logged sacks to areas where there were no puddles or flooded fields. The whole area looked like a swamp more suited for waterfowl than for rodents. Even the large lizards were congregating on limited high grounds, jostling for space. The monkeys and canje pheasants were perched and parked on treetops next to iguanas, and carrion birds were circling on air currents high above in celebration of the feast to reveal itself as the water receded. Goats and sheep hurried about, feasting on broken branches scattered about by the wind.

When Motilall reached the spot where he and Finey had stacked their grain, he found instant relief. His sacks were safe, and the straw that they had piled on top channeled the water out. After removing the wet straw, he tugged and pulled the sacks by their ears and was elated to see that his efforts had generally paid off. He went home, shared the good news with his wife, ate a good breakfast, harnessed his oxen, and went to help the neighbors salvage their wet grain. It was extremely difficult work for those families. They had to open the sacks and get the contents dried to avoid sprouting. Men, women, and children labored with the help of friends and neighbors in a desperate effort to salvage whatever they could. Without the rice, those families would be limited for food and money. Their entire livelihood was dependent upon those sacks of paddies, and everybody understood that.

Motilall and his four-legged buddies got home after dark that evening only to find Finey holding the baby and crying. She was upset because someone had told her brother Bholanauth about her working in the fields like a man, handling heavy sacks of grain. Her angry brother marched to her house and yelled at her, saying that she was killing herself with the loser husband who was too cheap to pay a man to do a man's job. He was upset with their marriage, and his pent-up wrath exploded that day. His painful words left her crying as her exhausted husband came home to hear all about it. They consoled each other, and the three went to bed in silence.

That year, they processed the rice, sold most of it, and used the money to buy a donkey and a cart for the donkey to pull. Finey wanted that for hauling her produce to the Skeldon Market, where she would sell her various vegetables, eggs, and rice. Occasionally, she sold coconut oil that they made. They also bought some gardening tools. Finey bought some garments and a used the sewing machine on which she sewed a wonderful dress shirt for her husband and some clothes for the baby. When her husband protested that she deserved a nice dress, she said that she now had a sewing machine and could make herself a dress anytime. So Motilall had her mother hire a seamstress to make a fancy dress for her. Then on Sunday morning, he, in his new shirt, and she, in her new dress, and the baby, in her new clothes, went barefoot to church where people realized what a handsome couple they really were.

In 1941, they had a second daughter and named her Chandra. They still grew rice and cultivated an even larger garden. With the donkey and cart, Finey was selling stuff every Saturday at the market. When they had time, they went fishing and shrimping. Occasionally, if the catch was plentiful, they invited their Dutch friends to share in a meal, and the men were always ready for a few sips of rum and coconut water, and the women would giggle at their husbands' silly behavior after a few such sips.

Things went well until one day, Finey told her husband that Leela was not feeling well. They called in the local pundit to perform his rituals and to cast out any potential evil spirits. Things did not improve. The next day, they consulted the local doctor, who suggested that the girl be taken to a hospital in Georgetown. It took a while to get there, but the news was not very good. She was diagnosed with typhoid fever, and treatments began immediately. One of the Dutch couples had accompanied them, and the men suggested that the women should go home to care for the other children and handle the Saturday market duty while the two men would stay in Georgetown. That was agreed upon. The two men borrowed blankets from the hospital, and after eating a cheap meal at a nearby cookshop, they huddled in their blankets in the corner of the hospital and tried to sleep.

Leela was in the hospital for several weeks, which placed some major stress on that young couple. They took turns staying in town and juggled things about to keep up with the various details of their lives. Relatives and friends helped, when possible, but it was their responsibility, and they had to do what had to be done. Name took care of the animals. Apart from the emotional burden, the financial demand was intolerable. Their prayers were somewhat answered as, one day, the doctor in charge informed them that the girl was making a remarkable recovery, but she had to stay in the hospital for a few more weeks. The sympathetic doctor told them to go home and get their work done and that he would ensure that the girl would be well taken care of during her stay at the hospital. They agreed, and within two months, a relatively healthy Leela was home again with her family.

In 1943, they were blessed with another daughter. Motilall was hoping for a son but was happy to have a healthy baby girl. That year, one of their female donkeys delivered a handsome colt, and they named him Colombia. He was a feisty little thing with almost endless energy. He ran about kicking and braying, teasing the older donkey, and harassing the oxen by climbing on them when they went down to rest. He loved eating bran and molasses, and Finey complained that the little thing would get diabetes by the time he was two years old from all the sweets he was given.

Colombia did not stay little for long. He grew up to be taller and faster than most donkeys in the neighborhood, and like Prem, he loved to run. It was quite a chore to teach him how to pull the cart because to him, everything was a game, and he always wanted to play. But with determination and dedication, Colombia was trained to pull the cart. When harnessed, he did not walk along like most donkeys; he wanted to run. So, they loaded the cart one day with a few sacks of rice in an effort to get him tired and hopefully slow him down. Colombia still ran, struggling to pull the heavy load. The neighbors referred to him as "super jackass," and eventually, folks called him Super Jack, which, in their dialect, was pronounced Supajak.

In 1945, they got their wish. Their fourth child arrived, and it was a boy! Motilall and the Dutchmen celebrated with their usual beverage, and as the evening passed, Motilall was telling his friends about how he and his son would acquire several acres of land and a large herd of cattle and how they would become mega farmers and ranchers. The next day, he went and acquired a puppy. He named him Fury. And while Finey was busy with the new baby, he and his three daughters played with Fury, groomed Colombia, and fed the oxen. The girls took care of the chickens and ducks.

In December 1945, the old donkey died. Their second donkey had a leg infection and had to be euthanized. Colombia became the only one that could pull the family cart. He was, by that time, almost two years old and was quite capable of performing his duty. He still ran with the cart. On Saturday mornings, neighbors would load up their carts and take their produce to market. Most of them left home shortly after 2:00 a.m. with the usual lighted kerosene lanterns tied under the carts on the axles that swayed with the motion of the cart. Such motion created a flickering flame that sent signals like a lighthouse signaling ships in the water. Every time, Colombia would see one of those flickering lanterns in the distance, he would lower his head and gallop until he passed that light. Because of his speed and anxiety, Finey left home after 4:00 a.m. and got to the market before most of the neighbors who had a two-hour head start. Yes, Colombia was a real Supajak.

By 1942, Prem was eighteen years old. Tall and skinny, he could run like a gazelle. He competed in various races and always came in first. The issue with that was there were always new challengers. One such challenger was a Negro man named George. The Indian people called him Jaaj. He was also undefeated in his community, so it was just a matter of time before those two had to face each other. And that day did come. They were scheduled to run the one-mile race at a designated sporting event. Those events were held at the various cricket fields. The flag was lowered, and the race was on with Negroes and Indians screaming for their respective heroes. During the final lap, Prem was slightly ahead when the wife of the challenger stepped in front of him. Not wanting to harm the woman, Prem tried to go around her, and she pushed him out of bounds. He was disqualified. That infuriated the crowd, especially the Indian people, and it soon turned into a fistfight that evolved into a small riot. By the time the scene was under control, there were limping, bloody men with screaming women attending to them. The judges eventually called the race a draw, and all the grumbling spectators cursed their way out of the event field. Racial slurs and cussing phrases were common sounds all the way to the public road and beyond.

Prem was still very helpful to his dabit and sister. Together, they had acquired more land and were farming several more acres. Name's father became ill and eventually died, so the fifteen-year-old Name had to do his family farming duties. Hence, Motilall worked with the two teenage boys, and together, they grew many more rice acres. He became a substitute father to those teenagers.

By that time, Kabra was getting old and could not keep up with Maloo, so Prem found a steer that could be a replacement. The animal was a right-sided puller. The three of them went to look at the animal, and Motilall asked the owner what he called the animal. The owner said that he had various pet names but that one was "a fine boy." After buying the animal, they laughed about the fine boy, and eventually, they named the animal Fine Boy. Again, in their dialect, he was called Fineby. And so the new team was Maloo and Fineby. Shortly after that, Kabra died peacefully in their yard, waiting for his morning treats.

That year, they had a good crop, and after harvest, Motilall stacked his sacks on the dam. That same evening, a neighbor decided to burn his straw. Things went well until the wind changed direction, and most of Motilall's sacks of rice burned up. The three of them shared what they could, and several neighbors donated a sack of rice each, but the loss was significant and placed a large financial burden on the family. Not knowing what else to do, Motilall cried and prayed. He looked up to the heavens and asked the "why" questions. He stared into the perceived heaven and asked the higher power for some sympathy. He claimed that he was trying to work hard and to live an honest life. All he was asking for was some consideration for his sincerity and his work ethic. He mentioned that he could sure use some help and a focus on where to turn and what to do. Then he went home, gathered up his gardening tools, headed toward the riverbank, and started forking up his new fenced-in garden plot. To ease the pain of mental anguish, he kept on forking until his hands were bleeding. Eventually, exhausted, he put his fork on his shoulder, grabbed his water bottle and cutlass, and went home to bed. The next day, he went to the estate and signed up to chop sugarcane for some supplemental income.

To supplement, they also earned some extra cash by making and selling coconut oil. Motilall harvested and peeled the coconuts with a crowbar that was solidly anchored into the ground. The couple went through the whole process and eventually boiled the coconut milk using the shells for fuel. On Saturday, Finey took the oil and other produce on her donkey cart and sold them at the market. Colombia did his usual gallop on the eight-mile journey.

In March 1948, they had their fifth child, another daughter. While Finey was busy with the newborn, Motilall went to view the spot that he had forked up. To his amazement, the entire plot was covered with pepper plants. Those peppers were called bird pepper because the birds ate those hot peppers and passed the seeds unharmed. On the freshly tilled soil, the birds must have dropped countless seeds, and as Mother Nature would have it, the plants grew so thick that the weeds were suppressed. He laughed at the situation and went home, where he began to think. His conclusion was not to weed out the peppers; it was almost just as easy to start a new vegetable garden. That he did.

As the months passed, the pepper garden flourished, and as luck would have it, there was a shortage of hot pepper that year. Buyers at the market were bidding on any available pepper, and on the average, the price was about one dollar per pint. Such prices were unheard of during those days, and on Saturday mornings, Colombia would gallop into the marketplace with several gallons of pepper, some coconut oil, and whatever else on the cart. Finey was mobbed upon arrival, and she made it clear that anyone who wanted to buy her peppers must also buy her coconut oil. In such a manner, she collected her money, and within an hour, after feeding and watering the donkey, she was on her way home, getting pulled along by the galloping Supajak.

With Leela old enough to babysit the younger children, Finey hired some local women to pick and clean the peppers. She also bought up all the available coconut oil in the neighborhood for a reasonable price and added it to her own inventory. Those commodities, along with her eggs, were all hauled to market and sold as a bundle. Anyone who purchased pepper had to buy her eggs and oil. With extra cash on hand, they purchased several more chickens and ducks, which the older girls attended to. The girls gathered up the eggs every morning and carefully stored them away. Eggs brought cash and several new baby chicks and ducklings. That resulted in selling live chickens and ducks, and as people passed by on the public road, they read the homemade sign (written by Prem) nailed on the manicole siding advertising chickens, ducks, eggs, and vegetables for sale.

The high pepper price lasted several months, and with an abundance of chickens, ducks, and eggs, the family had an excellent stream of money coming in every week, and their diet improved significantly.

The 1949 rice crop was excellent, and with adequate income from the other sources, they sold most of the rice. The only problem was that Maloo was showing his age. He had served them well, and it was time for his retirement. Prem told them about the impressive steer that he had raised that would be an excellent match for Fineby. The animal's name was Redman, because he was solid red in color. He had unusually long horns. He was tall and refined, but most of all, he was tame, willing, and obedient. So the new team became Fineby and Redman. The now retired Maloo grazed about and came home in the evening, where he patiently waited for his treats.

Later that year, Finey, realizing that she was pregnant again, discussed with her husband the possibility of a bigger house where the children could have rooms of their own and she could get a nice kitchen. They went in search of a suitable spot, and within a week, they bought lots 143 and 144B at Number 67 Village. Within a month, Motilall hired some young men, and together, they went to Blackbush, where they secured several logs from hardwood trees called bulletwood. Within two months, after those logs were hued into support beams, the carpenters were hired, building materials were delivered, and before the rice planting season, the sound of hammers pounding on nails echoed in the neighborhood. As usual, Motilall placed a shiny shilling under the northeastern pillar for good luck and prosperity. Within four months, the new three-bedroom house was erected. It took a few more months to get all the finishing details completed, and in July 1950, Finey, with the help of the midwife and her sister, delivered her sixth child, another son, at the Number 65 house, then referred to as the old house.

Early one morning, as the carpenters assembled, Motilall, at thirty-five years old, walked toward the beach. He took a leisurely swim among the waves, watching as the birds dodged about along the shores in search of food brought in by the receding waves. He was floating on his back, admiring the acrobatics of other flying creatures that floated almost effortlessly on the ocean breezes. They reminded him that it was birds that planted his pepper garden some two years ago. He remembered being upset, asking for a miracle after his rice burned up. Then it dawned on him that his prayers were answered. He came to the realization that some mysterious power must have asked those birds to congregate on his newly tilled garden spot and seed it with the peppers. He sat on the beach and said his prayers of thanks. He realized that the high pepper prices with other commodities bundled together made them enough money to build a bigger and nicer house and a home for his expanding family.

Shortly after the baby came, Finey was walking about one day, beaming with excitement and dreaming about her new home with her new kitchen. Suddenly, she felt a prick on her toe and instinctively kicked out. To her surprise, a snake flew off her foot and into the air. Recognizing that it was a venomous serpent called a labaria, a coral snake, related to the pit viper, she ran to her sister, who sent a message to their mother to get a taxi and hurry to her house because they had to urgently get to the hospital. That they did, and by the time the doctor examined the injury, Finey was in a state of unconsciousness. The children found their father, and by the time he had bathed and cleaned up the mud that plastered him, the taxi brought Doormatie back with the bad news. They all returned to the hospital in the taxi except for the baby, who stayed with the older cousins across the road.

It was not a good period for the family as Finey lay on her bed, where she was expected to die. Her body was swollen, and she was semiconscious, drifting from quiet groaning to convulsions. Doormatie took the baby to her house, and Motilall and the children cried and prayed with the visiting pundit, who came over frequently.

At nights, friends and relatives gathered at the little house, offering their sympathy and their prayers. They all believed that she was dying. But she did not. In fact, after a month, she started to recover and was asking about her baby. Doormatie informed her that she had too many toxins in her body and must not attempt to nurse the baby. He was being bottled fed with Lactogen, a brand of powdered milk that came in a can, and with boiled cows' milk.

Finey recovered quickly, and as the months passed, she got her strength back and started packing her belongings and those of the family. Then one fine day, the family with their luggage on Colombia's cart and their animals moved into the new house at Number 67 Village on the Courantyne Coast. The year was 1951.

That year, they acquired more rice lands, and during the plowing season, Motilall realized that Fineby was no match for the new steer. Redman was a powerful animal with long, well-muscled legs that practically dragged the short-legged Fineby along with the plow. He was as obedient as a trained dog and performed all his duties with almost tireless energy. In the mornings, the kids occasionally played around him and climbed on his back as he sat in the pen chewing his cud, allowing Fury to lick his face. He was a gentle giant.

Motilall discussed the issue with Prem and tried to come up with a reasonable solution. Prem told his dabit that there was only one animal that could work stride for stride with Redman, and that steer was Brown. He was brown by name and by color, and most folks who knew of him referred to him as the broke (broken) handle (horns) steer. He was locally referred to as the "bruck handle steer." Brown was a fighter. He challenged anything that crossed his path. He chased and attacked people or any other animal, especially other male bovines. Through repeated fighting, he broke off both of his horns. On one side, the remnant three-inch malformed portion grew downward, and on the other side, just a two-inch stub remained, pointing upward. He was originally kept as a breeding bull because of his stature, but because of his aggressive nature, he was castrated and turned loose. He eventually wandered into the savannahs and turned into a wild beast. He was big and strong, and if he could be tamed, he would be the perfect match for Redman. They could become the envy team.

The vision of such a team added excitement to the discussion, but the idea of breaking such a beast was terrifying to both of them. Prem told his dabit that he was the only person who could turn such an aggressive beast into a working animal. After a lengthy discussion, they agreed to try with the understanding that if things did not go well, Brown would go to the butcher and Motilall would keep the money received from selling him and Fineby to buy another steer that would somewhat complement Redman. They talked for most of the day, and that evening, Motilall, excited about getting the animal for free, got on his well-oiled newer bicycle with straight wheels and pedaled northward to the Poonais' neighborhood. He went to recruit a few good cowboys who would be willing to bring the bruck handle steer close to home and tie him to a large mango tree. They would have to use a short and sturdy rope. That was a challenge for some of the younger cowboys, and after the fee was negotiated, they agreed to get the animal and tie him to the designated mango tree.

That weekend, men on horseback galloped into the sunset and camped with the ground crew, who took a pair of draft oxen, two dogs, and several lengths of rope. The horsemen brought additional supplies, and the evening found the group nestled along the bank of an irrigation canal, eating supper, telling stories, and inhaling smoke from their rolled tobacco. They paid no attention to the alligators that splashed into the water or to the noisy Canje pheasants or the curious monkeys. Those were common sights in the so-called back dam area, close to where the cattle roamed. With the setting sun, they went to sleep.

Before dawn broke, with the sound of barking dogs, the riders branched out in different directions with plans to meet at a designated spot when the sun was directly overhead. The rest stayed behind waiting for a messenger from the riding party. It took a while, but in the distance, one of the riders spotted a wild beast with its tail in the air, galloping away. He did not chase after the animal. Instead, he circled around a grove of trees and surprised the brown steer, who instinctively lowered his head and roared like a lion as he charged at the intruders. The skilled rider dodged about in an effort to verify his brand. With proper identification, he returned to camp, where the other riders were awaiting his arrival. It was Brown, he told the group, and they decided to get him the following morning. They went fishing and later cooked up several delicacies laced with hot pepper. They had a fun evening.

The ground crew with the draft animals and the dogs left camp early the next morning. The riders finished camp duties and cantered along to meet up with the crew. The riders circled around the scattered trees and bushes, and soon the roaring Brown took after one of the horses. The cowboy blew his whistle, and the group hurried toward the sound of the whistle. It did not take very long for the two dogs to perform their duty. They ran around and around the steer, barking in a vicious manner that totally confused him. When he chased one, the other was on his heels. While the relentless dog show was going on, the riders circled closer and closer in with lassos ready to be thrown. Before Brown knew what was happening, there were two ropes around his stubby horns, and he was being dragged toward the draft oxen, trying to avoid the pesky dogs. He was skillfully hitched between the two draft oxen as the dogs were called off. Then the oxen were turned loose, and they dragged the exhausted Brown toward home. The next morning, Brown was found tied up to the mango tree about a quarter of a mile from the Number 67 house. The cowboys collected their money, told several stories about securing the animal, suggested that the beast should be butchered, and departed to their respective homes.

Later that day, Motilall casually walked about the mango tree far enough so that he did not excite the exhausted Brown, who was resting standing up with his head down. Slowly, the man walked closer and closer until Brown caught sight of him, and the panic erupted. It must have been a spectacle as Motilall just stood there observing the twists and turns and all the charades that the animal performed. Eventually, the tired Brown lowered his head and stood there with rage exhaling from both nostrils and slobber drooling from his bellowing mouth. He was angry. It was the first time that Motilall had a close look at him, and he agreed that Brown was one of the most impressive animals he had ever seen and probably the most dangerous. Satisfied that the animal was not physically hurt in any manner, he slowly backed away and went home to discuss him with Finey.

The next morning, he took a pail of water and had Redman follow him to the mango tree. As they approached, Brown started his shenanigans. He even tried to climb the mango tree to which he was tied. As commanded, the obedient Redman stood to attention as Motilall boldly walked up to Brown. He reached out his hand to the animal, but Brown's excitement escalated. Then he told Redman to "get him," and the docile Redman walked up, placed his extra-long horns under Brown's ribs, lifted him upward, and dropped him. Brown fell down and quickly scrambled to his feet in total confusion. Motilall once again walked toward him with outreached arm, but Brown began the dance again. So once again, Redman was ordered to charge, and on that occasion, Brown took a beating and bellowed, not with anger, but with pain.

It was probably the first time that Brown had experienced real fear as he slowly stood up, trembling. The man once again reached out and scratched his ear as Redman was instructed to retreat. Every time Brown attempted to show aggressive behavior, Redman was called forward, and Brown trembled with uncertainty. After Motilall's scratching and petting, Brown was offered a drink from the pail. He drank. With an empty pail, the man and his obedient ox went home, where Redman was given an extra helping of bran and molasses and a good grooming. The girls were busy gathering eggs, and Fury's loud barks echoed in the village in harmony with other village dogs. Finey listened attentively to the stories of Brown's behavior. She understood her husband's ability to deal with such dangerous creatures and tried to convince him that he should sell the animal and use the money from the two to purchase a good, calm partner for Redman. But Motilall saw the stature of Brown and had visions of owning an enviable pair of oxen. He was determined that it was worth the effort to see what such a team could deliver.

Brown stayed tied up to the mango tree for over a week. He was given freshly cut grass and water and of course several handfuls of bran and molasses. As long as Redman was present, Brown remained calm and submissive, and one fine day, he was decorated with a nose ring. By the tenth day, it was obvious that he had lost a considerable amount of weight and seemed to be anxious when his food and water arrived. That evening, a few men gathered with lassos in hand as Brown was to be yoked to the right side of Redman. It took several attempts but with skills and some luck bundled with Redman's security, the two animals were tied together, Brown by the stubby horns and Redman at his neck using a bowline knot.

Brown, realizing that he was free from the mango tree, decided to gallop, but the anchoring Redman planted his powerful legs, which restrained Brown's aggression. When Brown got overly aggressive, Redman was given the command, and one of his long horns was all it took to remind Brown that Redman was the pain giver. So he quickly restricted his aggression. The group walked down the public road as Redman pulled and dragged the confused Brown. Neighbors stood by their windows, holding their breath, hoping that nobody got hurt. Mothers called in their children for fear that the beast could break loose and attack them. Everyone knew that there was a dangerous animal in the village and knew that the need for caution was an understatement. The commotion invited several barking dogs that ensured that the excitement went past their respective residences and then retreated and invited other dogs along the way to emerge. Redman knew the way home, and he dragged Brown toward the back of the house, where Brown was tied to a large tamarind tree. The men stood there watching and talking as cigarette smoke was exhaled with their discussions. More and more village men gathered, and they were to the point of betting on whether or not that animal could be tamed and turned into an obedient farm helper.

Time passed as darkness appeared and invited swarms of mosquitoes. The only happy creatures were swarms of bats that fed on the pesky mosquitoes. The group built a fire, added some green materials to it, and let the smoke drift toward the tied-up Brown. Redman knew that the smoke kept the mosquitoes away, so he stood next to Brown and shared his meal of freshly cut grass. Soon, other cattle appeared to share in the bug-free environment, and Redman stood there protecting Brown from any aggressive intruders. He instinctively understood his duty.

The next morning, the group congregated again to see how the master intended to tame the beast. They saw him feeding the animal with a handful of bran while Redman was being fed with the other hand. Then the grooming began. The man walked around, scratching and petting the steer under the watchful eyes of Redman. Brown seemed to like the attention. In the evening, they built the fire and again created smoke that drove away the mosquitoes. That routine continued for several days, and soon all the neighborhood cattle gathered there to avoid the mosquitoes. In the evening, men gathered there to view their livestock that congregated there and to drink rum and play cards with the aid of a kerosene lantern. They wiped their bodies with a mixture of DDT and kerosene to repel the mosquitoes. All those activities were good for Brown's temperament. As the days passed, he did not seem to mind the two-legged creatures that walked past and sometimes gathered there. He was well fed, and he began to expect his meals and water to be served. Neighbors still had their doubts about the beast. Most agreed that when he became freed, he would hightail it back to the savannahs and revert back to his bad habits.

The day came when Brown had to be released from the tree. Motilall waited until no one was watching, and after getting Redman into position, he yoked them together and turned them loose. Instinctively, Brown tried to run, but Redman held him back. Motilall followed them as the two eventually lowered their heads and started to graze. He went and got Finey, and the two of them walked about, admiring the two impressive animals as they grazed about. By four o'clock, the news was out that the beast was no longer tied up, so many hurried to the spot where Brown was tied up only to find the man and his wife sitting on two bundles of grass and each had a pail, one with bran and one with molasses. They greeted one another and waited.

Before long, they saw the most remarkable thing. They saw a pair of oxen yoked together approaching them. When they arrived under the tree, Redman did his feeding call, and the man went forward with a bundle of grass and a mixture of their usual sweet treat. Brown seemed calm. He lowered his head in rhythm with Redman and ate the treat. When that was gone, they moved over to the pile of grass and started eating. Eventually, at the man's command, Redman brought Brown to the tying spot where Brown was once again tied and groomed.

That routine continued until a sturdy pen was built, and in the evening, the pair was released there and given their feed. During the day, they were yoked together and turned loose. They returned by 4:00 p.m. with Redman calling for feed. At night, they slept independently in their pen, enjoying the smoke that drove the bugs away.

Finey did her various duties during the week and sold at the market on Saturdays. Colombia still maintained his agility with the cart and had a great social life because many folks wanted to breed their jenny to him on account of his perceived superior genetics. Motilall sold a few of Colombia's offspring to the high bidders and used the money to buy furniture for the house. He did not spend much time at the vegetable garden because Finey and the kids handled the weeding and harvesting duties. They still had an abundance of bird pepper, but the price had stabilized. Motilall peeled coconuts, and they made larger quantities of oil that they continued to sell at the market. In the evening, he spent time feeding and grooming his oxen and enjoyed the company of his new dog.

Fury died peacefully one night. He was now an old dog with bad legs, partially crippled with arthritis. It was sad to see him go. They dug a shallow grave in the backyard and did a ritualistic prayer. The parents assured the children that the mantras would send Fury to heaven to run about with no pain. That same day, they got a little puppy and named him Sacky. The children instantly fell in love with him, and they ran about the yard, calling to him in every direction.

One evening, a man named Reuben came to visit Motilall. He was a contractor who supervised bridge building. He explained that he heard that Motilall was a good swimmer and a diver. Motilall laughed and told him that he learned to hold his breath for extended periods of time when he was a kid. Reuben was curious and asked him why he did that as a kid, and the answer was to avoid getting beaten by his cruel uncle. He would submerge himself in the pond and could not breathe for at least two minutes. Reuben laughed and then explained that he was in the process of constructing a bridge by the savannahs and needed a good swimmer and diver to help guide and anchor the support beams. Motilall was about to turn down the offer when Reuben told him what the job paid. It was wages that most local men could only dream about. There was silence, and Reuben told him to think about the offer and to discuss it with his wife and that he would be back in two days expecting an answer.

The couple talked about it after the children went to bed. He sat on his chair, smoking a cigarette, and she sat on the floor, picking out defective materials from the container of raw rice that was to be boiled the following morning. He explained that with his high wages, she could afford to pay two women to help on a part-time basis in the garden, and the girls were capable of handling the chickens and ducks before and after school. He suggested that one of the village boys could be hired to peel the coconuts and gather bundles of fresh grass for the oxen and the donkeys. They agreed that he should accept the job until the rice-planting season arrived.

The next morning, a neighbor from across the road caught up with Motilall as he was securing the black sedge stem that he used for a toothbrush. Because money was scarce, most people there brushed their teeth with similar pieces of twigs that were cut fresh every morning with a cutlass and chewed into a brush. They could not afford to buy toothbrushes. The visiting man asked about the new steer and eventually came to the point. He was in the market for a different ox on account of the fact that his old ox was ill, and it was doubtful if that animal was capable of handling the heavy load of pulling a plow for the upcoming planting season. He wanted to buy Fineby. Motilall explained that Fineby was grazing in the savannahs, and if the man wanted to bring him home, they would discuss the details. The man agreed, and the next evening, he had Fineby tied up in his backyard. He was in excellent shape from being on vacation for several weeks. The two men discussed the details, and Fineby was sold. Once more, Motilall gave his wife the seventy-five dollars he received from the sale. He did not need Fineby anymore, assuming that Brown would become a manageable worker and a good complement to Redman.

The next day, he informed Reuben that he would accept the job with the understanding that he would work four days per week, five hours per day, until the rice-planting season started. He requested more money, and after some negotiating, they agreed on thirty dollars per week. He would get two half-hour breaks per day. That way, he would be swimming and diving for a total of four hours per day. They shook hands and discussed the project, and Reuben departed.

On Monday morning, his lunch was packed and placed into his shoulder bag with some sweets and fruits. With his cutlass securely fastened, he rode his bicycle on the earthen dam to Reuben's construction site. He worked there until it was time for his farming duties. Finey hired two women to help with the gardening on an as-needed basis, and they found an ambitious neighbor named George Bachun, who was willing to help with getting the bundles of grass and to peel the coconuts. The children did their respective chores as Sacky scampered about with them. He was an energetic dog that chased the yard creatures about, leaving flying feathers around.

George Bachun and his wife, Daisy, lived close by, next to the local cemetery. They were one of the few Negro families in the neighborhood. He was an unusually tall and slender man. Daisy was an unusually large woman. People commented that her behind weighed as much as most people's total body weight. She was a very nice woman, and the children in the village called her Auntie Daisy. If someone took an unusually large helping of food, the general comment was that eating that much would make you "fat like Auntie Daisy." They were good neighbors who did odd jobs. He did field work, and she helped households when women delivered babies and were locked up for the nine-day period. With families having eight to ten children, Auntie Daisy stayed employed fairly regularly.

Finey used some of the money to buy an upgraded sewing machine and kept the old one for the girls to learn how to sew on. She also had the local carpenter build benches and a table with four chairs. She bought four decorative plates that were proudly displayed on a rack in the living room. She made it very clear that those plates were not for use; they were for show. The children called them upstairs plates and understood their significance.

The year 1952 arrived, and in August that year, the family was blessed with their seventh child. They had another daughter, and that year, Prem got married. It was a spectacular wedding, and all had a wonderful time. After the wedding, they did their usual stuff that folks in that society did. They celebrated and welcomed the new bride to her new home.

Time was not wasted once the wedding details were accomplished. Motilall's priority was to ensure that Brown was trained to pull the plow and other heavy farm loads. By that time, Brown was not as aggressive as before, but most people still did not trust him, so he was always yoked to Redman when turned out to graze.

One fine morning, Motilall decided to put the wooden collar on the new team. It was gently lowered over Redman's neck, and then an attempt was made to do the same with Brown. That did not go well at all. As soon as Brown felt the pressure on his neck area, he instinctively tossed his head upward, and the collar went flying into the air and landed on the ground next to Redman. The process was repeated with varying results, none of which was productive. They broke two hames, but with replacement parts, the trials continued. Brown eventually got so tired of the repeated activity that he finally relaxed and allowed the collar to sit on his neck as the padded wooden hames were slowly slid into position. That completed, both animals were given treats, and the collar was removed.

Later that day, Motilall tried the collar exercise once more, and to his amazement, Brown gracefully accepted the equipment with minimal objections. Again, he quickly removed the equipment and gave the animals their rewards. That week, he gave Reuben notice that he was getting ready for field work and could not continue employment with him. With more available time, he spent countless hours with the animals, especially Brown. When the hames were finally tied securely, the team was taught the various commands and how to pull together.

Pulling light loads was just schooling. The true test was attaching the shaft to the collar and hooking the plow to the shaft. One morning, Motilall asked two neighbors to accompany him, as he was planning to do some plowing. Word spread fast. Soon, most of the village men were marching westward on the Side Line Dam, following the man and his oxen. The dog always went along. That day, stronger padded hames were used. They were more comfortable because Brown's shoulders were not tough enough to handle the heavy pressure imposed upon them from dragging the heavy load.

They arrived at the field, and the attempted plowing process started. Redman knew what to do, but Brown hesitated in the midst of the confusion. With Redman's help and a lot of patience, Brown started to walk stride for stride with Redman. They were going fast enough that the man pushed the plow to its maximum depth but was almost trotting as he stumbled along, pushing down on the plow handle. Things started well until it was time to turn. Brown did not turn to the right as commanded. Redman pushed as hard as he could, but the strong and stubborn Brown refused to turn. The screaming mob did not help as they shouted opinions from the sidelines. By the time they reached the third neighbor's field, Redman came to his senses and wanted to whoa, but Brown, with all his might, pulled Redman and the plow as the man was getting dragged along. Eventually, they came to a stop, and the three of them stood there huffing and puffing, totally covered in sweat under the tropical sun. Again, the command was given to turn right, and Redman wanted to obey, but Brown continued in a straight line. The obedient and angry Redman then stuck his long horn under Brown's neck, lifted Brown's front quarter in the air, pushed him toward the right as Brown pivoted on his hind legs about ninety degrees, and then dropped him. The mob was excited to watch an aging cowboy being the master as he trained the bruck handle steer. By noon, Brown and Redman were plowing and turning in a crude fashion. The exercise was a success. On the way home that day, the excited mob followed the man and his oxen, discussing their triumph. As they congregated that evening with a bottle of rum, the exaggerated stories became tall tales about how the team performed and the power they demonstrated, which could not be matched by any other team in the whole county. One man commented that that meant India also.

As the field work progressed, the man and his team worked almost effortlessly on the various farming duties. The heavy work was done at the break of dawn while the coolness of the morning minimized heat exhaustion. By midmorning, the animals were turned loose to drink and to graze in designated areas. Village boys too young to handle heavy field work brought along their fathers' breakfasts, and after the animals were turned loose, those boys kept an eye on them. Brown and Redman were now turned loose individually, and the boys were warned that in the event Brown would charge at them, they needed to run and stand close to Redman for protection. After a few close calls, the boys understood how to avoid the aggressive steer. Sometimes they dodged around the scattered trees and scurried upward to a high enough branch from where they called for help. Motilall was always close by and came to the rescue. Brown never chased him, and when he yelled at the beast, he would shake his ears, back away, and resume his grazing. Occasional visitors came to view the beast, only to find themselves running and screaming as the charging steer lowered his head and pawed with a loud, slobbery bellow and then took after any such visitor. Some climbed trees, some dived into the canals, and some ran behind Redman, but Motilall always came to the rescue and chased the charging animal away from the frightened visitors.

It was a good crop that year, and with Prem married and Finey too busy with the new baby and six other children, the family stayed busy. The older children went to school. During the off season,

Motilall resumed his employment with Reuben, building bridges and doing other construction projects that were mostly funded by the government. It was easy money for him.

Shortly after harvest, Prem came to visit and suggested to his dabit that he was acquiring more rice land. He mentioned that they had enough money saved to buy a tractor that would do many times the work of oxen, and tractors did not have to be fed. In fact, he said that one of his nephews also wanted to buy a tractor, and they were considering buying two David Brown tractors from the dealership in Georgetown. They were negotiating to get a discount for buying two. He asked about the oxen and was told that they were on vacation grazing in the savannahs. They agreed that getting a tractor was a great idea, and Prem left with a smile and rode his bicycle home to spend time with his new wife. At that time, they also were building a new retail store.

New Year's Day 1953 was a memorable day for that family. They gathered at Doormatie's house to celebrate the New Year and to talk about buying the new tractors. Several cousins attended, and they butchered a sheep and cooked a host of their favorite foods. Prem had enough to drink that day, and with every sip of rum, his voice escalated as he bragged and showed the cash that would be used to buy the tractor. He hugged his dabit several times, reassuring him that the day was coming when they would not have to walk behind oxen to get the field work done; they would be riding on four wheels. He would then imitate the sound of a tractor running at full throttle and did the bouncing dance as if he were driving the tractor. Everybody laughed at his enthusiasm. Motilall, being a dancer, put on some face paint and talcum powder, and as the mob sang and beat on pots and pans, he danced to the noise as Finey clapped and cheered him on. The relatives had never seen him behave in that manner before and laughed at his semi-intoxicated behavior. Eventually, they got tired, some passed out from overindulgence, and the rowdy party was reclaimed by tropical silence interrupted by an occasional barking dog and neighborhood roosters. It was a memorable event and all had a good time.

The day after the party, Motilall resumed his construction job. By then, he was doing such a fine job that Reuben would occasionally leave him in charge of the crew and wander off. The men assumed that he was being picked up by boat and going to town to party with some girls at a secluded establishment at Rose Hall. Later that day, there were some engineering concerns, and Motilall had to make the decision on how to best work through the difficulties. When Reuben returned in the evening and saw the changes, he was infuriated. He yelled and screamed at the crew and sent them all home except for Motilall. There was an argument, and Motilall told Reuben that if he had stayed and supervised like he was supposed to, the changes and disciplinary actions could have been avoided. He finally explained his logic for the necessary changes and why his plan was a good compromise. The angry Reuben told him to go home and return the following day for further discussion.

The next day, January 3, 1953, Reuben assigned work for the crew and told them that he was going to town to discuss the changes with the chief engineer. That day, they did not work on the bridge. They were assigned to cut some brush and trees along the walking path. Later that day, the crew saw a speedboat with its nose up in the air, parting the water as it approached and forcing alligators to scramble out of the way. Upon arrival, the workers saw the chief engineer, Reuben, and two other men. They asked for Motilall. He hid in the reeds, assuming that the bosses were there to fire him for changing the construction plans. Eventually, he was discovered, and Reuben informed him that there was horrible news. Reuben was almost crying, and the puzzled Motilall inquired about what was happening. He was told to get his lunch pail and his tools and get into the boat. As the boat raced away, he was told that Prem was killed in a tractor accident. Then silence prevailed as the speeding boat took them east in the Number 66 Creek. Motilall disembarked in silence at the public road. He hurriedly carried his tools home. Neighbors had already heard the news and watched from their windows as he sadly walked along wet and barefoot on the public road toward home.

Finey was at the rice mill gathering poultry feed. One of her daughters came limping from a foot infection and announced that someone had just notified them that Long Prem was killed in a tractor accident. She dropped her pail and ran home. She grabbed her baby and started running toward her mother's house. One of her nephews met her a short distance from home and convinced her to go back and leave the baby there, and he would take her on his bicycle. She then gave the older children strict instructions on completing their chores and taking care of the baby. Then her nephew pedaled her to the dead house.

*　　*　　*

Prem and his two nephews had gone to town and purchased two David Brown tractors as planned. Prem did not know how to drive very well as yet, so the other two drove the tractors toward home. To celebrate and to pass time, they started drinking. Under the influence, Prem insisted that they should teach him how to drive better because he wanted to drive into the village and into the yard, showing folks that he was capable. It took him a while to figure out the gears and how to release the clutch, but with some effort, he learned and started driving. As his confidence was building, so was his speed. He was warned repeatedly about his high speed and was told to slow down. He did not slow down. In fact, he became enraged and pulled the throttle wide open. The tractor weaved and bobbed along the public road until it hit a bump, and Prem lost control. The tractor bounced about and flipped into the ditch, and Prem was killed.

He was buried in the local cemetery. A rectangular picket fence was built around the site and painted white. The tractor was dragged home, parked in the corner of a shed, and never used again. Occasionally a rooster would perch himself on the rusting tractor hood and proudly crow away, and birds built their nests and raised their young there. The tractor became an ornament in the shed. The general consensus was that that machine was evil and should not be driven again. Many local farmers offered to buy parts from it, but the answer was always no. Eventually, it collapsed, and the pile of scrap iron rotted away above the pool of motor oil that seeped into the soil. Tragic!

With such tragedy, the family went through a period of depression. They did minimal chores and stayed close to other members of the family because loneliness evoked the need for companionship. So every evening, most members congregated at Doormatie's house, where they drenched the cotton sheets with tears. That family never recovered from the tragedy, and for the decades that followed, someone would always bring up the topic of Prem's misfortune. His wife returned to her parents' house. She eventually remarried and moved on with her life.

*   *   *

Before long, it was time to get the oxen and get things ready for the upcoming planting season. Brown and Redman were brought home, given their treats, and tied up in the backyard. Brown was much calmer than he had been the previous year, and when the team was harnessed and plowing commenced, spectators watched in admiration at that exceptional team of oxen that pulled in harmony with all their might and got work done in record time. As Motilall held the plow handle and directed his team, he would occasionally look up at the sky and talk to Prem about wishing that he was there with the David Brown tractor tilling the fields. Occasional beads of tears rolled down his dirty cheeks as he plodded along behind eight powerful legs. The droplets of tears and sweat washed down his cheeks, removing the soil particles that plastered his face like a little river gently cutting through dry sands and eventually evaporated in the wind. But the earth, with countless plows scraping at her skin, continued her programmed rotations and revolutions as she did for billions of years, as generations of earthlings wrestled with daily concerns.

Finey continued with her gardening and oil making. On Saturday mornings, while going to the market, the aging Colombia could hear her occasional sobbing in the sunrise as she grieved for her favorite brother. She continued her sewing and stayed busy making school uniforms for the children. She ensured that her mother did not stay alone at night, so the grandchildren took turns staying with her. They called her Nany. At nights when those grandchildren were too scared to be alone in her house on account of Prem's perceived ghost, she would set up a cot next to her bed, where they slept.

Occasionally, the children played in the shed where the David Brown tractor gathered dust and chicken manure, slowly rusting away. But if the old lady caught any of them climbing on the tractor, her screams could be heard across the entire village. She labelled the tractor as evil and did not tolerate her grandchildren climbing about on that piece of metal that she deemed evil and that had sacrificed her beloved son at the tender age of twenty-nine.

CHAPTER 16

Bananas and the Store

Every family knows grief, sadness, and tragedies. And just like families around the globe, the subject family members had their share of tragedies, distress, and grief. However, they had learned how to handle and manage their grief. They chose to be there for one another. Prem's accident was a major setback because he was an anchor in that family. He was a very likeable anchor who did things for others unconditionally. He was a giver with no expectations in return. He was hardworking, athletic, kind, caring, helpful, and cheerful. But he was also a fighter. Stories were told about him fighting injustice and usually coming to the rescue when someone in the neighborhood was being bullied. People did not want to cross him for two reasons: he was a good fighter, and he was a respectable young man with common sense who helped to solve issues, and he worked hard to settle disputes. When all else failed, he occasionally became violent and beat up on the bullies. He served his family and his community well, but most of all, he was always there to help Finey and Motilall and their children. He was a good man!

In 1955, Finey had another son, and in1956, their two oldest daughters got married. By that time, the new house had been painted white with a red roof. Brown and Redman were still the envied pair of oxen in the area. Brown was a much tamer animal, and after the day's plowing, the two older sons kept an eye on the pair while they grazed. During that time, the adults took a break, after which grass was cut and bundled for later feeding. In the off season, the team was kept close to home because more land became available and had to be cleared. Motilall spent countless hours chopping down trees with an ax, and the oxen were used to drag sections of the fallen trees to a burn pile. It was great entertainment for his two sons to help with tying and hauling the logs to the various little piles, and they ran about the bonfires as the intolerable flames danced about in obedience to that moment's breezes and reached upward during the calm moments. The warm ashes and smoldering logs served as slow cookers, where the boys roasted fish that they secured from nearby canals. Occasionally, they toasted coconuts in their shells, laced with a generous helping of raw brown sugar. It made them a good dessert.

One day, a man named Harry Armogan came to visit Motilall. Harry had a fair amount of land, and with middle age approaching, he had physical difficulties clearing and farming all his land. He proposed to Motilall that he was willing to rent him a small portion that was totally covered with trees, vines, and brush. He explained that it was good and fertile land but needed someone to clear and farm it. Respectfully, Motilall declined because he had land of his own to manage and did not think that he could do justice to an additional parcel. Harry told him to take a week and think about it. He explained that he did not want any rent for two years, and on the third year and beyond, all he wanted was two bags of rice in lieu of cash rent. Motilall suggested that he should find someone else, and Harry said that there was no one else who could do the quality job that he expected for his land. Motilall was the only person he trusted who had the work ethic and a team of oxen to get the job done to his satisfaction. They shook hands, and Harry departed, saying that he would return the following week.

Across the road from the Motilall family in a house lived the Thakur family. People called the man Mr. Nauth, and he had several children, including six sons. Nauth was a literate Brahmin man who read various magazine articles and the newspaper. He would then deliver the highlights of any worthy news to Motilall. That week, when Nauth came to deliver the news, Motilall told him about Harry's proposal. Nauth got very excited and explained that he had approached Harry several times to see if he would rent him that parcel of land. He explained that Harry repeatedly turned him down and refused to have any further discussion. Mr. Nauth suggested that Motilall should rent the land and sublease a part of it to him. He continued the discussion and said that the two of them, with the help of their sons, could clear that land in record time and turn that fertile ground into a productive farm.

That afternoon, Motilall went to Harry's residence and informed him that he had changed his mind and would be honored to lease the land according to Harry's proposal. Harry was excited to hear the news, and the two men shook hands, discussed further details, talked about the weather, and parted company. Motilall rode his bicycle home with a smile on his face.

The two partners stayed up late that night to discuss the details and timetable for getting the work done. They decided to remove the grassy ground cover, clear all the small clumps of trees, and leave the large trees for later. In that manner, they could start getting some produce in a short time. They agreed that after the vegetation was burned, they would plant sweet potatoes. Next to the sweet potatoes, they would plant cassava, and next to the cassava, they would plant bananas and plantains. Their calculations were that the sweet potatoes could be harvested in three months, and then the cassava would be harvested after six to nine months. The bananas and plantains would mature within two years. Such a banana plantation could produce large bunches for many years to come if properly maintained. The agreement was that although they would work together, each family would claim their section, and by the time the bananas and plantains were ready for harvest, they would become independent and would sell their respective crops as they saw fit. The excitement kept them up late that night as they sat on a wooden bench in a tucked under area of Motilall's house.

That area was called bottom house because it was at the bottom of the main structure, which was supported by bulletwood posts. Those posts rested on poured cement blocks for strength and stability.

Most of the bilevel houses in that county had a bottom house area. The spot was slightly elevated with packed clay and levelled. The women would gather fresh cow dung and mix it with dirt and then daub it over the packed clay, which, when dried, had the appearance of cement. That area was used for storing sacks of rice and some farm equipment. A hammock was usually tied to the pillars, and benches were strategically placed for catching the breeze. Babies were rocked in those hammocks, and children would swing to and fro, humming and singing their favorite tunes. Women would generally sort and clean their rice and other ingredients for the upcoming meals there.

So the next morning, the partners-to-be sat there sharpening their cutlasses and axes, and they chewed away on their pieces of black sedge stems used for brushing their teeth. After breakfast, they walked down the village Side Line Dam to survey their newly acquired rented parcel. Some of the boys went along, carrying their homemade slingshots. They ran about shooting at alligators when heads emerged from the water. Their aim was quite accurate, and they laughed and celebrated as the dried clay marbles propelled by the slingshots made contact with the alligators' heads. The reptiles would lower their heads into the water, and the boys would go off to other adventures. Birds were usually shot and carried along in a bundle. While the adults took their noon naps, the meat-starved boys built a fire and roasted the birds with salt and hot pepper. The dog always waited for any scraps discarded by the boys. Such fun made the almost three-mile journey exciting for the boys. They surveyed the parcel, made some preliminary decisions, and went home. The boys ate their roasted meat and scampered about in an eastern direction, seeking more adventures with their home-made slingshots.

It did not take them long to clear the scattered vegetation, and during the dry periods, flames engulfed the areas. With the high temperatures, most of the semidried grass and small trees burned, leaving relatively vast sections of open space. In the warm ashes, they planted sweet potatoes and cassava, but neither of the men had enough money to buy banana and plantain suckers. The men stayed busy digging irrigation and drainage ditches with shovels and cutting down emerging weeds with their cutlasses. They built a wooden frame that was thatched with coconut branches. That shed was called a *banaff*. In the center of the banaff was a firepit, above which they tied a long piece of heavy-duty wire to the rafters. On the hook of the wire, they hung a large cast-iron pot where they prepared various meals seasoned with hot pepper and salt and whatever was necessary for the day's meal. They made "cook up," pepperpot, and various types of soups and stews. Occasionally, one of the boys shot birds with his slingshot. Sometimes, they trapped a chicken-like creature, which they referred to as bush fowl. Those feathered creatures were cleaned, washed, and roasted in the fire or made into a pepperpot stew. They sometimes baked cassava and yams. There was always an abundance of hot pepper and salt to season whatever was being prepared. At the lowest part of the farm, they dug a pond that accumulated water, which they used for cooking and for washing the few wooden utensils that they carved during break time.

The banaff was a great place to relax. The flames danced at the base of the skillet, and the boiling of whatever created a rising steady steam pattern whose inviting aroma kept the crew salivating in anticipation of the tasty chunks and the broth. The food was good, and the stories that followed were interesting. Puffs of smoke from the pipe and cigarette mingled with the voices of the adult storytellers. The children listened attentively. One such story was about a man named Dr. Bhimrao Ambedkar, who was a poor untouchable from India. He surpassed all the odds and became a very prominent Indian subject. The story about his world travel and his attending major universities intrigued most of the children and planted the seeds of what could be possible for any poor child.

Most days, the men chopped down a few of the larger trees, and after school and on weekends, the boys used the oxen for dragging the wood away. Small pieces of wood and dried branches were piled over the stumps and burned, so there was always smoke arising from that area. The very large trees were left alone and were still standing some sixty years later. The smaller stumps were pulled out by the oxen. It was a test of strength to see how large a stump Brown and Redman could uproot. Those powerful legs and willing spirits pulled and tugged from all directions, and the boys were amazed at the strength of that team, which worked in harmony to accomplish unbelievable tasks. Motilall commented many times that Prem knew what he was talking about when he suggested matching up such a unique team.

The partners traveled about, asking neighboring farmers about getting some banana suckers. There were none available. Then one day, a woman stopped by and told them that her husband had started a banana farm up the Courantyne River. She explained that he got sick and could not manage that operation anymore. If they wanted to visit the abandoned site, they were welcome to take anything that they could use. But she warned them that there might be nothing there, seeing that the site had not been visited for almost a year and the weeds had probably choked out any young suckers that her husband had planted. She gave them proper direction where the site was located, and Nauth drew a crude map as the woman explained the location. Various landmarks were identified, and they used the river as a base from which to start. They thanked her, and she wished them the best of luck and departed, leaving both partners with some cautious optimism.

The next morning, the two men gathered some gunnysacks and rode their bicycles on the tar road past Skeldon. They went past Crabwood Creek to Road End and then down the dirt path. They were traveling south along the river. By noon, the bicycles could no longer go because of the excess vegetation that acted like a giant green umbrella of overgrown tree branches and vines. So, they parked the cycles and ate some lunch. Nauth smoked his pipe, and Motilall had a cigarette, and then they took a short nap under a shade tree before continuing their journey on foot, carrying their tools and supplies. Occasionally, they checked their map to verify that the landmarks corresponded to the drawing. It was almost dark by the time they found the site. They were not surprised to find nothing but weeds and wildflowers carpeting the ground. They made and ate supper, had a smoke, and slept using the gunnysacks as earthen mattresses and for blankets. The relentless mosquitoes were intolerable. Luckily, they brought small vials of DDT mixed with kerosene. The mixture, for the most part, kept the pests away, allowing the men to get some much-deserved sleep.

The morning fog hovered over the contour of the river, and the dew made everything wet. The partners gathered some wood, built a fire, and made some tea. Slowly sipping their tea from cups made locally from coconut shells and slapping sand flies, they wondered if there could be anything useful under that mat of wet vegetation. As the morning sun battled through the dew and fog, the barelegged partners walked about in search of banana suckers. Using cutlasses, they slashed and weeded small areas, looking for any sign of wide leaves, but did not find any. Desperate, they finally crawled on hands and knees, parting the vegetation at ground level. And there they were! Scrawny, dried-up suckers with almost no evidence of them being alive. They used shovels, and the mostly dead plants were dug up, washed, and placed in the sacks. They laughed when one commented that those puny things would be easy to carry. They collected a fair number of them, strapped the sacks on their backs with vines, and walked northward along the trail toward the bicycles.

With the loads on their backs, they battled the morning heat, the stinging bugs, and the biting ants. The good news was that it did not rain, leaving them a dry trail to walk on. It was midafternoon when they reached the cycles, and after strapping the sacks on wheels, they pedaled toward Skeldon. Those bicycles had no lights, and they wanted to get past the little town before dark. There was a police station in that town, and the cops arrested people who rode bicycles at night without lights. The strong south wind pushed them along, and into the darkness, they pedaled away. It was almost eight o'clock when they reached home, tired and hungry. Finey made her husband a plate of food, which he ate. Then he smoked his cigarette and lay down on the floor and slept. She snuffed out the cigarette butt, washed the dishes, covered him with a sheet, and propped his head up with a homemade pillow as he snored into slumber land. Finey and the boys untied the sacks and put the bicycle away, and then they all went to bed.

Before dawn, Mr. Nauth met his neighbor at the bottomhouse. Cutlasses and shovels were secured, and the sacks were again tied to the bicycles. The reinvigorated partners, full of hope and optimism, pedaled westward on the Side Line Dam toward the farm. There they dug up various hills of sweet potatoes, and into those holes, they planted the sickly suckers and watered them. They figured that in order for those suckers to survive, it would take some divine intervention, so they recited a few Hindu mantras as they loaded up some of the sweet potatoes on the cycles and pedaled home.

Every day, they visited those plants with hopes and prayers. Before leaving, they made sure the plants were well watered. The rest was left in the care of Mother Nature. Even though there were many other chores to do, the curious men inspected the plants and then gathered sweet potatoes and some skinny cassava and took them home. Such food was a welcome break from eating rice and vegetables all the time. Finey appreciated the substitutes because she did not have to make rice flour as often. To do that, she soaked the rice overnight and then pounded the grain into a wet mass, which she then dried in the sun on a piece of galvanized sheet. The dried end product was sifted through a fine mesh screen. She used the sifted mass, called rice flour, to make roti for the family. When the sweet potatoes and cassava arrived, making roti was optional, and she found creative ways to prepare meals from those produce.

Within a month of planting the suckers, Mr. Nauth one day announced to his partner that some of his suckers were showing signs of life. Daily, they were on hands and knees, straining their eyes to catch a glimpse of some slowly emerging, rolled-up green shoots containing chlorophyll that would jump-start the photosynthesis process and turn those puny suckers into healthy banana plants. Their optimism and prayers must have helped because in the weeks that followed, the plants adapted to the fertile soil and vigorously grew into healthy banana plants with wide green leaves. The men estimated that over 90 percent of the suckers survived. They also found a few plantains mixed in the lot, and just like that, it was mission accomplished. The banana farm got started. Various mangoes, coconuts, and other plants were inserted in open areas, and the partners then went about to plant their respective rice crops for that year.

During breaks and holidays and on weekends, the boys spent most of the time helping their respective fathers. It was fun time for them, and whenever they found a fruit that they liked, they saved the seeds and planted them in any open areas of the farm. Guavas, jackfruit, mangoes, pomegranates, sugarcane, ginnip, and various vines and berries found their way into that farm; and that spot was referred to as Farm, or as the dialect dictated, Fam. Coconut plants acquired from the local agricultural station were inserted among the various plants and eventually reached for the sky. As the years passed, folks could see those trees from long distances away as evidence of where Fam was located.

The family acquired some goats and sheep. Next to the ponds and under the neem tree, pens were built to keep the animals secured from wild dogs. The animals rapidly multiplied, and the family soon had a number of them. The boys took care of them and ensured that the gates were securely closed and tied at night, preventing dogs and tiger cats from attacking and killing the animals.

Early 1957 presented the family with another baby. It was a boy. The local pundit read his scriptures (Patra) and came to the conclusion that the baby was born under some mysterious planetary configuration and that he was subject to be easily possessed by certain evil spirits. So Finey had to stay confined in the bedroom for twenty-one days with the baby, and her husband was not allowed in that space. Motilall slept on the couch downstairs and spent time working his land.

About that same time, the man who lived next door, Mr. Ramdat, fell ill and needed medical attention. He had to pay the medical facility sixty dollars for treatment. The man did not have the money, so he approached Motilall and offered to sell him his only cow. She was a young pregnant cow, and he offered to sell the cow for sixty dollars. Motilall bought the cow and gave the man the sixty dollars plus two dollars to pay for his transportation to and from the hospital. The sick man thanked him and, with tears in his eyes, prayed that the cow would deliver several calves and plenty of milk to the new family. She was a gray cow with no horns, and within a few weeks, she delivered a nice bull calf. The cow's name was Bhoorie, and the calf was called Bully. Every morning, the family got half a gallon of milk, and Bully got the rest. The boys waited while their father milked the cow. Their job was to keep Bully away during the milking process. After eating her bran and molasses, Bhoorie led Bully away to pasture, and the boys got a good helping of warm raw milk. They turned the goats and sheep out, fed the chickens and ducks, ate breakfast, and went about the daily business like going to school.

By that time, the banana plants were getting into production, and the family found their bottom house covered with large bunches of green bananas. Motilall harvested them and loaded them into a canoe (*creall*) that he had bought, and as the ocean tide ebbed and the 66 Creek water rushed eastward, the man steered his canoe full of bananas, plantains, cassava, and some mixed fruits, propelled by the water current toward home. At the public road, he unloaded the cargo, secured the canoe, and walked home to get the bicycle on which he strapped the bunches of bananas and sacks of other produce and pushed it all home. When there was a large load, he used an old donkey cart, which he pushed and pulled, because by that time, there were no donkeys in their possession. Lorries and cars did most of the transportation.

Growing the bananas was probably the easy part. Marketing them posed a separate challenge. As the bananas ripened, the children were given large bowls filled with those ripe bananas, and they walked about the villages selling. Some bunches were hung along the public road where passersby would stop and buy some. But the bulk were sold to wholesalers who bought the green ones, ripened them, and sold them at the markets.

Still, there were too many ripe bananas that had to be disposed of simply because they ripen very quickly in the tropical climate. Bhoorie and Bully ate lots of overripe bananas. So Finey had an idea. They discussed it, and within a short time, the carpenters were called in. She had the vision that they should enclose a part of the bottom house and make it into a cake shop. There she could sell other things, but it would be an excellent way to sell the ripe bananas.

It took about a month to build, but there it was! A nicely blue-painted shop with shelves full of soda pop, candies, cigarettes, freshly baked bread and pastries, cassava, fresh fruits, and many large bunches of bananas that hung from the ceiling. Motilall bought a used icebox and an ice shaver. He got a recipe for a good syrup, which he improved upon. He sold the shaved ice with some syrup in a glass for two cents, and if the customers want to top it off with some sweetened condensed milk, they had to pay one additional cent. Most folks bought the cold and refreshing three-cent packages. Those same customers also bought bananas and took them home for their families to enjoy.

Twice weekly, the ice truck came and delivered a large block of ice, which was promptly covered up in the icebox. Next to the ice were bottles of soda pop. Families came for the cold shaved ice with syrup and condensed milk. Some wanted cold cream soda, which they mixed with evaporated milk. There were always Four Cows condensed milk and Carnation evaporated milk on the shelves. Soon, there were cans of sardines and cans of corned mutton on the shelves. Gillett razor blades found their way next to the cigarettes. Butter and cheese were available, and some folks would buy a small loaf of fresh bread and eat it with butter or cheese. They then washed it down with a cold bottle of soda pop of their choice. Pepsi, Coca-Cola, and 7Up were popular choices, along with locally made and bottled lemonade.

The little shop was a success, and the oldest daughter at home during that time did an excellent job working with the customers. In the evening, a gas lamp was lit and hung from the ceiling. That bright light soon attracted the evening crowds, who gathered to eat bread with sardines laced with hot pepper and a good helping of raw onions. Some just wanted a glass of cold ice and syrup, some wanted cigarettes, and some wanted a cold Pepsi or Coca-Cola. The interesting thing was that many stayed to visit, to play cards, to eat bananas, and to listen to the newly acquired Philips radio. The longer they stayed, the more money they spent, and many of them took bananas home for their families.

After two years, the reality was that the shop was too small and had to be extended. That enclosed the entire bottom house. It turned out to be a grocery store, a clothing store, and a store that sold a host of other things from various canned goods to matches, wheat flour, sugar, salt, split peas, numerous spices, pickled mackerel, tomato paste, salted codfish, buckets and pans, cooking oil and butter, kerosene oil, wine, vitamins, beer, and a host of other things. They made a paste from cassava, which was used for gluing paper into paper bags. They also bought a heavy-duty bicycle with a metal carriage in front above the small wheel. That was used for delivering groceries. It also worked well for transporting bananas. They named that bicycle Truck.

On Saturday evenings, the housewives came along with their baskets, and while they acquired their groceries, their husbands could stand by the counter in the original section and have a beer or something cold and keep up with the gossip or listen to the radio. If the baskets were too heavy, they would load them on Truck, and the boys pedaled them to the residence of the customers. Some customers did not come to the store; they simply sent their list along, and the children packed the items in the homemade paper bags and delivered the boxful with Truck.

There were numerous items in a large glass case that women generally gazed upon. It displayed various sewing items, types of lace, and buttons. There were always some blue and white boxes stacked up in the corner that the girls and women bought from one of the women who was attending the store. If the boys were the only ones there, the women would ask for Finey, who promptly came, got one of those boxes out, wrapped it in a paper bag, and collected the money. Finey told the boys that the boxes marked Modess contained ladies' handkerchiefs, and the boys always wondered what all the secrecy was about for buying handkerchiefs. Of course, it was a brand of sanitary napkins, which was not to be discussed with the boys.

One day, a family came in to buy their teenage daughter a birthday present. They looked at perfumes and other items but could not decide on a gift. So the number three son, watching Finey trying to come up with the right gift and not having too much luck, decided to help. He boldly walked to the glass case, opened the door, got a box of Modess out, and handed it to the mother, telling her that their daughter could really use some of "these." The silence was deafening as Finey quickly put the box away. The older sons were trying not to laugh out of respect. The family quickly bought a bottle of perfume and hurried home.

By that time, Motilall was a forty-something-year-old grandfather and stayed very busy with his banana farm and rice fields. Because there were many tractors in the neighborhood, he hired one of those farmers to do his tillage. Brown and Redman became semiretired and grazed about until they were needed for some light duties. The boys helped with the farming, and the girls took care of the store and the housework. Most of the children's work was done before and after school and on weekends. Truck was also used for hauling bananas. Motilall could pedal to the farm, check on his crops, transplant a few suckers, harvest a few things, and pedal the load home. But on weekends, the boys went to the farm and did some weeding and harvested several large bunches of bananas. They scouted and identified banana plants that were getting crowded with too many suckers that needed transplanting. Motilall had creative ways to load and strap the large cargo on Truck and walked along steering. The boys pushed and pulled and worked extra hard, especially up the inclines. If they got too hot, there were numerous canals along the way that they dived into to cool off and to keep up with their swimming and diving exercises. There was never a visible ounce of fat on those lads, and they were always hungry. They knew where the wild fruits and berries were along the way and would race to find what was suitable. They harvested and raced back to their father, who took a break and shared whatever the boys had gathered. They turned the work into fun and games.

During school breaks, the children weeded the farm, cleaned the ditches, harvested the rice by hand, and bundled it. The oxen were still used for hauling the bundles to the local kharyans, but the tractors did the threshing. The rice processing at the rice mill was the same, and Motilall, his two sons, and his two sons-in-law handled most of the work. Because the store and the various farms provided the family with their daily needs, the money earned from selling the rice could be saved or used to increase the stock at the store, which generated more profits. Most items were marked up some 20 percent, so the return on investment was quite good. To put it in perspective, most households earned less than twenty dollars per week. The Motilall family store earned on the average some fifty net dollars per week plus the income from the farms. In addition, they got all the groceries for free, and the children did not have to buy their treats. They had goats, sheep, chickens, eggs, ducks, and all the rice that they could eat. Bhoorie had a calf almost every other year, so there was no shortage of milk. Things were going very well for them, mostly because of the banana farm, the rice farms, and the store.

However, like most families, occasional tragedies did occur. One evening, as the oldest son, who was called Buddy at home, was in the process of lighting the gas lamp. He used a torch dipped in alcohol to heat the mantle and to get the lamp warmed up before the pressurized kerosene was turned on. During the heating process, he shook the alcohol can, informing his father that he had to buy some more alcohol. The fumes from the can attracted the flames from the burning torch, and there was an instant explosion. Buddy got sprayed and was engulfed in a ball of flames. He ran about the house screaming. By the time the flames were extinguished, he was badly burned, and almost immediately, a car arrived and took him to the Skeldon Hospital.

He spent almost a month in the hospital, during which time his father stayed with him at night. Finey and the girls handled the store and the housework. Their second son, with some minimal burns on his legs, had to handle some light field work, and he took care of the goats and sheep. A neighbor, Sonny, helped with the milking, and Mr. Nauth harvested and hauled the bananas. Motilall was always tired because he got a minimal amount of sleep during the night at the hospital.

It took Buddy months to recover, and he had the scars to prove the severity of the accident. His greatest shock was when he finally returned to school, he was informed that he had failed to advance to the next grade. He was forced to stay with the class of younger students in Standard Five. It was depressing for him because his friends and classmates were all promoted to Six Standard and sat on an elevated platform looking down on the lower grades. But he was determined to show the school personnel that they were wrong about him, so he buried himself in his studies and was the top student that year in the class. By year's end, his previous classmates wrote the school leaving exam and moved on from the New Market Anglican School. Buddy was promoted to Standard Six with his new classmates and sat on the elevated stage. He became obsessed with school and continued to be the top student in his class. One of his classmates nicknamed him DH because those were the first two letters of his name, Dhanraj. Soon, everybody was calling him DH, and as the years went by, he became known officially as DH.

At the end of the school year, he wrote his school leaving exam and went home. Not sure what he should do, his parents decided that he should learn a trade, and they agreed upon him learning how to be a tailor. So he took the sewing machine to the tailor shop in the village, which was owned by a man called Keaza. Most young men who wanted to be a tailor went to a tailor shop like the one owned by Mr. Keaza. At those shops, the boys were taught how to measure, mark, and cut the materials and then sew them into shirts and pants. Those garments that were not sold locally were sold by Mrs. Keaza on Saturdays at the Skeldon Market.

When the results of the school leaving exam were published, the message came that DH had passed. That was a big deal because it was a measure of a student's academic capabilities, and many of the students who passed went on to high school. When the news arrived, a friend of the family was visiting. The man's name was Jaffar Hussain, and DH hugged him, saying that the news meant that he could go on to school and not adopt a career as a fisherman. They were laughing when a car pulled up and stopped by the road. It was Mr. Keaza. He and some of his boys carried DH's sewing machine into the house. Mr. Keaza told Motilall and Finey that a boy of such intelligence had no business killing time in a tailor shop, that he needed to be enrolled in a high school. They all congratulated DH, bought several bottles of Pepsi and Coke, and celebrated the good news. It was during the excitement and soda pop celebration that the decision was made that the boy would attend a school of higher learning. It was a decision made by two functionally illiterate parents.

By 1959, more and more farm equipment were being brought into the village, and grain combines fitted and propelled by tracks could harvest rice even in the mud. Those machines almost eliminated the need for manual labor, and very few people used oxen to farm anymore. So, Brown and Redman wandered away into the savannas, where Brown resumed his bad habits of chasing and attacking people. As the complaints rolled in about Brown's behavior, Motilall knew that he had to do something about it. He justified selling them and used the proceeds to buy some heifers, but nobody wanted oxen. They had seen the power of the Massey Harris and Case combines and Ferguson tractors with various pieces of tillage equipment, and some small farmers sold or rented their land to larger farmers who continued to get bigger. The only option was to sell the pair of oxen to the butcher, and that was what happened.

Brown and Redman were sold for two hundred dollars each, and Motilall collected his four hundred dollars. His tears kept his broken heart company as he and his second son slowly walked home and gave the money to Finey. She could see the pain in her husband's eyes and remembered that creating such super workers was Prem's idea. She squeezed the purple twenty-dollar bills in her hands, which were clasped together as if she were praying for the animals, for her husband, and for her deceased brother.

Later that day, they opened up the enclosure under a small window located at the highest point in the living room. From his ladder, Motilall retrieved a small enclosed can, and they put the money in that can and then sealed up the area with a hammer and nails. Their emotions would rival those of any family that had to euthanize their pet. Many men gathered at the store that night as a memorial to those animals, and their stories lasted late into the night. It was a wonderful party to discuss Brown and Redman and all their achievements and to console a friend and a neighbor whom those two had served with all their might and their willingness to please their master. They were remarkable animals.

They all agreed that Brown had to go before he killed someone. They knew that Redman was getting old and would probably get stuck in some mud hole and suffer a miserable death. What happened was the right thing to do, in their opinion. It was their comforting message to a friend.

Early the next morning, Mr. Nauth came to the store and asked Motilall to go with him to the farm. They went. As they walked along, Motilall realized that the trip was more of a discussion than work. At the farm, they recalled the memories of the various heavy work that the animals did, and when they retired to the banaff for a snack and a smoke, he told Motilall that God had sent that pair to help not only Motilall but many others in the village. He explained that the butcher was the right choice because Brown was a danger to passersby, and those animals should not be allowed to get sick and die alone in the savannas. He put down his pipe and prayed for them. They prayed together and then walked toward home. Along the way, Motilall thanked him for the discussion and for being such a good friend. They were very good friends.

CHAPTER 17

Good Times

During the 1950s, British Guiana was starting the process of seeking independence from England. Dr. Chedi Jagan, a descendant of Indian indentured servants, was leading the charge by creating the PPP, the People's Progressive Party. He was a son from Port Mourant, and Motilall, having ties to that village, proudly and unconditionally supported him. Whenever Dr. Jagan was in the area, he sometimes visited the store and was given a hero's welcome and some cold refreshments free of charge. While he was there, in addition to his escorts, many gathered to hear what he had to say and to get answers for questions that seemed appropriate. Dr. Jagan sometimes played on their emotions about how cruelly the British had treated their Indian ancestors and talked about the achievements of Mahatma Gandhi and how Gandhi brought the British to their knees with his philosophy of truth and nonviolence. Dr. Jagan told the crowd about his trips to India after Gandhi's assassination and what the current administration was doing to keep down the violence created by the division of that nation and the creation of Pakistan.

Before the meeting ended, Motilall always made it known that both he and Dr. Jagan were born at Port Mourant and how proud he was to see his brother (Dr. Jagan) follow in the steps of Gandhi to put an end to the injustice and hardship imposed on their ancestors by those lying, heartless Englishmen. The crowd always stayed long after Dr. Jagan's departure, telling stories about the cruel treatment that their respective ancestors had received from the management at the sugar plantations and how many women were violated by those arrogant estate personnel in power during the indentured process. They told stories about the pandemic of 1918 and the deaths of many of their ancestors. They would justify the Sepoy Revolution of 1857 in India and praised the men who boldly led that revolution, referred to as the first war for India's independence. While there, most of them bought stuff from the store, and some drank beer. As their alcohol consumption increased, their voices escalated, and they would occasionally turn into an angry mob praising Dr. Jagan for his leadership to pursue Guyana's independence.

The Sepoy Revolution, the first war of independence that the group discussed further, ran from May 10, 1857, until July 8, 1857; and was a struggle between the Indian soldiers and the East India Company's army. That struggle involved men like Pyroo, who did many behind-the-scenes duties, especially raising money and doing some spying on the British while pretending to be their friend—and in Pyroo's case, their gambling partner. Motilall always reminded the group that Pyroo was his grandfather-in-law. He spoke about him with great pride and generally commented that men like Pyroo paved the way for Gandhi and ultimately many more like Dr. Jagan.

On many occasions, the name of Subhas Chandra Bose came up, with each man offering his opinion on what could have happened to that Indian national hero. Sometimes they agreed on a scenario. At such a moment, they would yell out their agreements, swallow some beverage, pause in silence as if grieving, and then wait for the next discussion. They had great respect for and loyalty to India.

After the group exhausted their political opinions, they departed one by one to their respective homes. Motilall was glad to see them go because after buying and drinking beer, some were intoxicated and used occasional foul language. He also had his evening chores to do and did not want his family members, especially the girls, hearing the unacceptable language that the men uttered. But he was happy to collect the money, as many bought cigarettes, borrowed someone's matches to light up, and puffed away on the wooden bridge toward home.

The Motilall family was one of the busiest families in the area during that time. A lot of the schedule was created by the parents, and the obedient children did their assignments without complaining. The only resistance came when it was time to take their medicine. They had a choice of castor oil or Epsom salt. The early-morning protests did not matter. It was imperative that they swallow the unpleasant-tasting liquids, resulting in heaving and vomiting. Everyone tried to keep it down because if it came up, there was another dose waiting. Then they drank some watery soup and waited for the stomach cramps and whatever followed. With maximum regularity and only one latrine, tension ran high. The two older boys generally headed for the woods and loitered close to a pond where coliform contamination was the least of their concerns. When they had to go, nothing else mattered. By noon, when systems somewhat stabilized, they were given a good helping of vegetable soup with scraps of boney pieces of chicken. After a brief rest, their normal schedules resumed, and the only sufferers were intestinal parasites that were common among many children in the neighborhood.

By 1961, the family's third daughter was married and moved away. DH enrolled at Tagore Memorial High School. Mr. Nauth's oldest son became a schoolteacher and had started a club at their bottom house. He later became Dr. Vic Thakur, professor and educator. Many of those sons became very educated. In fact, Dr. Rishee Thakur is still a professor at the University of Guyana. The club was for young boys and was referred to as GCYO, Gandhi's Cultural Youth Organization. There, the local boys met once weekly for debates, intelligent discussions about world affairs and current affairs, and geography lessons. It was a good place for the boys to congregate and learn a few things. DH and his brother always attended, and the group always adjourned by singing the national anthem of India.

Many of the children went to "night school." There, they were taught Hindi because many parents believed that the British schools brainwashed the children and made them recite Christian prayers. By creating the Hindi school at nights, the parents felt that their children were learning something about their heritage that would counterbalance all the perceived gibberish that the English school system was imposing upon their young minds. Most of the Motilall children attended Hindi school. However, on nights when the GCYO met, the boys were absent from Hindi school because the parents felt that there was more value there once weekly. Dealing with Hindi school, English school, GCYO, farming, animal chores, making firewood, operating the store and other domestic details, and occasional sports events, the Motilall children were always busy, and by bedtime, they were exhausted.

The two older boys shared a room. DH had a bed, and his brother had a homemade matress made from dried reeds stuffed in a large sack sewed together with bagtwine. His pillow was made from dried cattail flowers stuffed into a piece of cotton that was stitched on the sewing machine. His sheets and cover were made from imported wheat-flour sacks that were emptied at the store. They were washed and stitched together and used for various things like bath towels, sheets, and men's underwear. To keep the mosquitoes away at night, the entire house was sprayed with DDT from a flit pump that expelled the chemical as a fine mist. After the spraying, the house was locked, and all the tired family members went to bed inhaling the DDT fumes.

Mornings were busy because the milking had to be done; the store had to be opened; the goats, sheep, ducks, and chickens had to be taken care of; the meals had to be prepared over fire from the fireside; water had to be carried; the magenta-colored ice syrup had to be made; and the children had to get ready for school. The New Market Anglican School at Number 63 Village was about one mile away, and the children walked that distance twice daily to and from school. They carried their lunch along and left it at Doormatie's house, and at 11:30 a.m., the hungry children hurried to Grandmother's house and shared the lunch that Finey sent along that day. DH, being a high school student, did not have to walk anymore. He had a bicycle and usually rode home for lunch.

In November 1961, Finey delivered her tenth and final child. It was a boy, and Motilall bragged that he had planned it just right, having fathered five daughters and five sons. Finey confided in her youngest sister that she was somewhat embarrassed about the pregnancy on account that she was forty years old and had a few grandchildren. Her sister reminded her that their mother was forty-six when she was born, and she, too, was a grandmother many times.

Bhoorie was a good cow and had six calves. She had three bull calves and three heifers. The bulls were sold, and with the money plus some more from the sale of Brown and Redman, the family bought a few cows that roamed about in areas where there was no shortage of bulls. The cows continued to have calves almost every year, which provided more milk than the family could consume. So there was ample nutrition for the calves. Every year, the herd grew. Bulls were sold, and the proceeds went into the family savings in sealed canisters hidden under the little windowsill in the living room. Eventually, they bought several more cows.

Finey was a visionary and a dreamer. With the various sources of income, she started looking at diversifying. One Saturday as she walked about at the Skeldon Market, she noticed all the people walking about buying various things, including groceries. She realized that many of those people got paid on Fridays from the Skeldon Estate and had cash to spend on Saturdays. She stood there gazing at the various retail stalls and appreciated the speed with which transactions were carried out, especially at the grocery sections. She walked over to see Mrs. Keaza, who was selling clothes that were sewn at their village tailor shop. She was happy to have a friend to visit with between customers, and the discussion evolved into options for acquiring a stall and selling groceries at the market. There was a waiting list for the prime locations, and Finey added her name to the list.

She came home that day and made supper in a cheerful mood. After the children went to bed and the store was closed, Motilall sat on his favorite chair to enjoy his bedtime cigarette. As he puffed away, Finey sat close to him, informing him about what she had done at the market that day. Motilall told her that she was crazy because she had no vehicle to transport the groceries. She nodded and agreed but commented that they had money and probably enough to buy a motor vehicle. They looked at each other with glee and nods and stayed up late discussing their options.

Motilall always wanted to own a motor vehicle but never imagined that it was possible. One of his cousins owned a taxi, and one day, Motilall asked that cousin to teach him to drive. The rude cousin emphatically told him that if he wanted to drive, he should buy his own vehicle. From that day on, he would dream about owning and driving a motor vehicle, and that evening, Finey showed him that it was possible. He was elated and went to bed feeling like a king. He could not sleep, and neither could she. They talked about their humble beginnings. The possibility of owning a motor vehicle was beyond anything he could have imagined just a few short years ago. The tiring enthusiasm finally forced them to sleep.

For the next two years, their crops performed well, and with help from the sons-in-law, they kept labor costs to a minimum. Their fourth daughter took over the household duties and spent many hours in the store selling and keeping track of the books. They sold more bull calves and kept all the heifers. But the star of their operation was still the banana farm. That farm was in full production, and the two older sons kept busy with that farm and the various other farming operations at their father's direction. Things became easier with the introduction of commercial fertilizers and agricultural chemicals, especially herbicides and insecticides. Those new introductions and better equipment enabled them to become more efficient and to raise more tonnage and, in their perception, better products. All that spelled more money in the savings canisters.

In 1963, the management at the Skeldon Market notified Finey that a stall had become available at a prime location. She did not hesitate. Promptly, she went and paid the dues and hired a local carpenter to build a structure with a roof. The roof was necessary because it sheltered the various items from the weather and provided shade from the intolerable tropical heat. They made a list of what could be sold at their stall and had to decide on some introductory prices that would attract key customers. Finey was very familiar with the market because she had been selling stuff there for many years. But she had to learn a new type of selling for her new products.

One of the things that Motilall had perfected was a good blend of spices called garam masala. Most folks called it masala. At the store, customers traveled long distances to buy his masala, which they used for making their various curry dishes. He figured that if the masala was as good as he thought, it should be the lead item, and they had to get potential customers to try it. But the first thing was to determine and solve the transportation concerns.

It was time to get the motor vehicle. One of the sons-in-law worked for Bookers, the British firm that owned and operated the sugar estates. Bookers also owned the car dealership in Georgetown, and the company gave employees a discount when purchasing a new vehicle. So Motilall took that young man and Mr. Keaza to Georgetown and ordered a new vehicle in the son-in-law's name. Mr. Keaza drove his personal vehicle. They made a cash down payment and were told that the vehicle would arrive in a few months. Feeling as proud as a peacock, Motilall took the other two to a nice hotel to spend the night and had a good meal that evening at a Chinese restaurant. They ate fried chicken and chips and washed their meal down with cold bottles of Banks beer. The next morning, Mr. Keaza took them home.

After the market stall was completed to their satisfaction, Finey started taking a few items to sell on some Saturdays. She traveled with Mr. Keaza's car because they went there to sell clothes. Her goal was to introduce herself to potential customers and offer the packets of masala and the other goods at discounted prices. She took the time to talk with the folks who stopped by her stall and inform them that soon she would be selling a full line of products and would appreciate their future support. While DH monitored the stall, she scouted out the competition. When not on duty, DH walked about the market to get snacks and to check out the young ladies who either worked at the market or were just walking around looking for bargains. When they got home, he told his brother about his various observations, especially the two lovely girls who sold refreshments there. He especially like the older one and enthusiastically described her in detail.

Motilall and his two sons spent all their spare moments constructing a garage for the car. They had to build a sturdy bridge that spanned the trench from their yard to the public road. They harvested three large bulletwood logs and purchased some greenheart boards. With help from family members and from neighborhood carpenters, the bridge and the garage were fully functional by New Year's Day 1964. On that day, they butchered a sheep and gave the meat to the women to prepare. While the cooking was in progress, the men—the sons-in-law, cousins, nephews, and family friends, including the Dutch families—congregated to drink rum and eat mutton. Nanda generally attended the family functions, but his wife seldom did. Even when she visited occasionally, it was brief. Her presence generally created tension for the household. By the time darkness gathered, the celebrating lot were singing in the new garage and on the new bridge. Motilall could be heard bragging about the new vehicle that would soon be housed in the new garage.

The two Dutchmen did not have their original wives anymore. Rampersaud's wife was cheating on him while he was cutting sugarcane. Muna Singh suspected her of having affairs after seeing a man visiting the house quite often. One day, when he saw that individual sneaking in through the back door, he quietly came into the house and caught them in the act. The man grabbed his clothes and ran out naked, but the stunned and embarrassed woman stayed there. Muna grabbed her with one hand, and with the other hand, he opened his shaving razor. He slit the woman's throat and walked out. She did not die but had the scar to show for the incident. When she recovered, the two sisters went back to their parents' house and eventually remarried. Ramouthar did remarry, but Rampersaud never did. Muna Singh went to jail for two years.

The year 1964 was a memorable one. The first week of March, they were notified that their vehicle had arrived and that it should be purchased within a few days because there were several buyers shopping for such a vehicle. If the vehicle was not purchased and paid for by a certain date, their down payment would be refunded with interest, and the garage reserved the right to sell it to another party. Mr. Keaza was notified immediately, and he suggested that they go the following day to ensure that the dealership did not sell it to someone else. A message was dispatched to the son-in-law that he was being picked up at 4:00 a.m. to ensure that they made the ferry boat (Torani) on time and get to Booker's Garage before noon. Mr. Keaza said that he would bring his son along and that boy would drive the new vehicle home.

There was excitement and joy at that home all day. After supper, DH got a hammer, climbed up on a ladder, and pounded out the enclosure under the little windowsill. He tossed the money canisters to his father. Finey supervised. They opened the cans one by one and counted out the purple twenty-dollar bills. The children were amazed at how much money those canisters held. When they were satisfied that they had enough money, Finey folded the bills and wrapped the bundles with rubber bands. She took the pants that her husband and her son would wear to Georgetown the following day and put the money into the pockets. Then she pinned the pockets shut with safety pins. She warned them not to walk about with the large sums of money. There were bandits who were shrewd pickpockets waiting for folks from the countryside who went to town for business purposes. Those folks sometimes carried large sums of money, and the pickpockets, locally referred to as "choke and rob," were generally waiting for an easy victim. The dialect called the thieves "Chok 'n' Rab." The men were told to stay in Mr. Keaza's car for the duration of the trip, especially in the tightly packed ferryboat.

By 3:00 a.m. on March 5, Mr. Keaza and his son Arnold picked up Motilall and DH and drove to Albion to pick up Hubert, the son-in-law. They drove to New Amsterdam, caught the ferry, and crossed the Berbice River. Then they drove to Georgetown. Their only meals were the snacks and beverages that they had brought along, and they made one stop for a group bathroom break. They arrived at Booker's Garage before ten o'clock and identified themselves and their reason for being there. They could see transactions going on, but there was no sight of a new vehicle. They were told to wait for the next available representative.

In about a half an hour, a man dressed in a suit and tie emerged and introduced himself. He explained that he would be handling their transaction. The man could see the curiosity in their eyes and asked if they would like to see the vehicle. They followed as the man led them to a separate area where the mechanics were uncrating something. With excitement, they watched as the men carefully removed the packages and revealed an almond-green Series 6 Morris Oxford with white letters on the license plate that read "PO 902." She was beautiful.

While the men finished cleaning up the mess of cardboard and other packaging materials, the representative took the buyers back to his office, and Hubert, the son-in-law, bought the vehicle in his name and got the Booker's employee discount. It was embarrassing when two of them had to lower their trousers to unpin the money, but the representative had seen that before and took them to a private area where they lowered their pants and retrieved the stacks of cash. The various documents were signed, and the twenty-dollar bills were counted. After verifying that the sum was adequate and handing a receipt to Hubert, the representative suggested that they should go down the street to a restaurant and get some lunch while he took care of the details. As they walked down the street, they could see a shiny green car being pushed out to the street. Two technicians were discussing the details, and they saw the representative getting into a taxi going to the bank to deposit the cash. Mr. Keaza assured them that those were all standard practices, and they should not worry about such details.

They ate lunch at an Indian restaurant, compliments of Bookers, and rested there for a while, sipping on warm sweetened tea. Midafternoon, the representative came and notified them that the car was ready, and they could take it home at their convenience. He assured them that it had a full tank of gasoline and the mechanics test drove it and did a good final inspection. Mr. Keaza drove the new car, and his son drove their car toward the Berbice River. They crossed it on the ferry and disembarked at New Amsterdam. It was late, and after dropping Hubert home, they continued home. It had started to rain. The car was parked on the new bridge, and all went home to bed.

March 6, 1964, was their fourth daughter's sixteenth birthday. On that morning, as the sun crept out of the eastern horizon, PO 902, the new Series 6 Morris Oxford, found herself in the light, parked on the bridge at the Motilall's residence. The second son carefully dried the residual raindrops with carefully selected soft linen. By the time the cows were milked, many had gathered to view the shiny green Morris Oxford referred to as 902. The various chrome pieces reflected the morning sun, and neighbors took turns poking their heads into the windows and sniffing the aroma of a new vehicle. They all nodded their approval. Motilall told them not to exhale their smoke in his new car. He wanted to preserve the scent.

Their thirteen-year-old son finished the drying and polishing and asked if he could drive the car into the garage. Everyone knew that he was a semiskilled tractor driver but had never driven a car. There were discussions as the young man insisted on parking the car in the garage. Eventually, they agreed, and he was shown how the gear shift worked. He depressed the clutch pedal, pulled the gear lever forward and up as instructed, stepped on the gas pedal, and slowly released the clutch. The vehicle lunged forward, and before anyone could count to five, there was a hole in the lattice gate of the garage, and the car was stopped less than a yard from a large tree. Yes, he drove the car through the garage.

The only thing hurt was the underage and inexperienced driver's pride. The car survived without a scratch, and folks joked about the toughness of the vehicle as the embarrassed young man, the wanna-be driver, made his escape and walked away toward the tall coconut trees. The car was reversed and parked in the garage, which no longer had a back gate.

DH was eighteen, and he and his father got their driver's licenses. The family took several joy trips in the car, and occasionally they stopped and got ice cream cones on the way home. They went to the movie theater and to the beach, and on occasional Sundays, the car was hired to transport the bride and groom at some nearby wedding.

By May that year, the car found its main purpose. On Saturday mornings, it was loaded with bulk quantities of groceries and driven to market. They went early in the morning to maximize sales and to avoid the traffic congestion. By 7:00 a.m., the various items were unloaded, and the stall was organized. That operation was an instant success, and customers lined up with empty baskets and departed with various items. They loved the masala. They loved the prompt service and seemed to enjoy the discussions with their new supplier. The family members took turns going to various food and beverage stalls, but the two boys always meandered their way to the refreshment booth where the two pretty girls were. There, they bought sardine and bread sandwiches and cold soda pop, but the excitement escalated when one of the girls smiled and greeted them. Even more exciting was when there were no other customers, and the boys got a chance to have a brief chat with one of the girls. Needless to say, the boys loitered about, keeping a close eye on the counter area, and swooped in when there were no other customers. They would later compare with exaggerations how much time they individually got and what the girls talked about. Finey would laugh at their elated moods and gesticulations while having those conversations and probably told herself that boys would be boys.

By noon, 902 was parked in front of the stall, and all the unsold items were loaded up. Occasionally, some customers sent their order, and their goods were packed into a cardboard box and delivered on the way home. There was always a good lunch waiting at home, and after eating, the family counted the money from the day's sale at the market. Most days, they sold more groceries in a half day at the market than they sold all week at the store. The sales at the market were always cash sales, compared to the store, where customers charged their purchases, promising to pay after their rice harvest. Some never paid. It was always a reason to celebrate when the daily gross sales at the market exceeded three hundred dollars. With a 20 percent market markup, that was some sixty dollars in profit. That was good considering that field laborers were paid three dollars per day, and those families generally made less than twenty dollars per week. Some families made no money for weeks and relied on selling their rice after harvest. So between the store and the market, the Motilall family was doing quite well.

That year, Doormatie took ill and spent many days at Finey's house. One day, she had a spell, and everyone assumed that she had died, but suddenly, she recovered and told Finey that she had money hidden in her mattress and that money should be used for her funeral. She stipulated what she expected and told her daughter that any money left over was hers to keep. A few days later, she passed away at the age of seventy-nine. Her money was retrieved, and her burial wishes were honored. Finey shared some of the remaining money with her siblings.

Later that year, their second son and youngest daughter were admitted to Tagore High School, and the family had to pay tuition for three of their children. DH wrote and passed several subjects in the GCE exam administered through the University of London.

During that time, the government had developed agricultural schemes called Black Bush Polder, and many deserving families were given some land to cultivate and sustain a livelihood. Schools were built, and they needed teachers. So a few of the young people who were recently successful in the GCE examinations were offered teaching positions. The parents of those new teachers approached Motilall, suggesting that he should secure a teacher's position at one of those schools. He could drive 902 on a daily basis and transport at least four other teachers. With some behind-the-scenes discussions and some nepotism, DH was hired as a teacher and became the official chauffeur for other teachers. That way, he got his wages, and 902 was also making money for the family.

The following year, the fourth daughter was married, DH turned twenty, and his brother was fifteen. DH wanted to be an engineer and made hints that he would like to go to the United States and attend engineering school there. One of his dreams was to become the chief engineer on a project to build a bridge across the Berbice

River from New Amsterdam to Rossignol. Every time there was a heavy rainstorm, he observed the flow of the water from one pond to another. He then built a small wooden bridge that spanned the little streams. He would demonstrate his accomplishments to his brother as they watched the water going through the tunnel beneath the bridge. They made toy tractors from empty thread spools that were propelled by a wound-up rubber band and watched their toys as they drove themselves across the newly constructed prototype bridges.

Those two boys became the best of friends and spent their spare time at home with their father, working on the various farm duties. DH was concerned that his father was aging and would need more help on the farm as the years went by. So he decided that he enjoyed teaching and decided against going to the United States. Instead, he went to Teachers' Training College in Georgetown.

By the end of that decade, DH returned home after two years and secured a teaching position at Line Path School, teaching mathematics. His younger brother did well with the GCE exam and became a chemistry and science teacher at Tagore High School. Motilall was excited to have two teachers in his house. With his various endeavors generating money, he considered himself blessed. As the years passed, six of his children became schoolteachers. The other four girls were not given the opportunity to attend high school.

One Friday evening in 1969, as the two teacher boys had their weekend discussion over a bottle of rum and some spiced chicken that Finey had prepared, they talked about various things. DH asked his brother what his future plans were. The younger brother answered without hesitation that he planned to go to the United States and attend medical school.

Over the next several months, that boy went to Georgetown and secured a passport. He managed to contact a US college in the State of Minnesota and made an appointment with the American embassy in Georgetown, where he got a student visa. Tailors were hired and necessary items were purchased. A large suitcase was packed. His siblings were excited about their brother going to America for educational purposes.

On March 29, 1970, a large bus was hired, and all the immediate family members and a few extended family members congregated at the Motilalls' house. The family prayed, and the pundit did his usual rituals that were supposed to protect the traveler on his journey to the United States. That evening, more folks arrived. Among them was his uncle Nanda. He told the boy that he would not miss the trip to the airport because that trip meant a lot to the family. It was the first time anyone of that family was leaving Guyana since his father immigrated to that country from India.

By 3:00 a.m. on March 31, 1970, the large red bus loaded with various family members drove away from the Motilall residence at Number 67 Village, taking one of the sons toward a faraway land. There were plenty of food and various snacks as the red bus tooted its horn along the way in order to get the animals off the road. The bus and passengers crossed the ferry at New Amsterdam, and the rising sun found the family heading toward Georgetown. There were occasional stops for various reasons in the Georgetown area, and soon, the red bus was on its way to the airport.

Nanda sat next to his nephew soon to be leaving the country and had an emotional discussion about some family history. He talked about Kangal and Kalya. He talked about Desai and Mangrie and their stay with the Muslim woman, Naz. He talked about how proud he was to see his nephew moving on for educational purposes and said he hoped that the young man would always remember who he was and from where he came. Motilall sat close by, nodding and listening to his brother talking to his son. He said very little.

The British jet arrived on schedule as the passenger took care of his flight details. Satisfied that all things were in order, the family gathered for their farewells. Finey cried and told her son to remember to say his prayers and to travel in the name of God. She emphasized that her son must find a church upon arrival and pray. The siblings, except DH, did their hugs and kisses as passengers were heading toward the plane. Motilall was speechless. He stared his son in the eye and finally hugged him as if he would rather that he did not have to go. Then the tears came out, and he walked away, wiping off the uncontrollable gush of tears. His brother followed him. DH stood there like a rock, and when all the others finished their parting wishes, he walked toward his little brother and best friend. He was trying not to cry, but his eyes betrayed him. The two sons stood there, face-to-face, hand in hand, with eagle eyes as the rest looked on. Then DH spoke. He told his brother that he had always admired his courage and strength, and that courage and strength coupled with blessings from above would take him to heights that they could only dream about when they were kids. He wished his brother well and repeated a mantra, and then he spoke on behalf of their father. He told his brother that their dad was having a very difficult time with the whole thing because it reminded him of his father leaving India, never to return. He said that Ma was crying because her little boy was going away, and she did not know how to deal with the whole situation. Between the tears, they hugged, and DH said that he had nothing to offer except some advice. He told his brother that he should follow his heart but think with his head and that he should live life to the fullest but never live to regret anything. He gave his brother a green and white shirt that they stuffed into his bag. Then he walked away and stood between his parents, mother on the left and father on the right, with both arms wrapped around the parents' shoulders. Every other family member looked on.

The airport announcement was for all passengers to board the plane. The various noises from the jet engines were almost deafening. Finey told her son that it was time to go but not to look back until he reached the aircraft, and Motilall finally said his goodbye. The young man, with his duty-free rum bottles and a large briefcase, walked out of the airport shelter toward the plane. At the top of the stairs, he turned around, waved, and walked into the plane. He was seated in a window seat.

The engines roared, and the jet sped away from the airport runway and became airborne. The young man looked out the window and saw the dwarfed tropical forest, which appeared like a dark-green carpet below him being dissected by sediment-laden waters rushing toward the ocean. Then he realized that for the first time, he was on his own and all alone. He was soon above the clouds over the Atlantic Ocean on his way to the United States in search of whatever awaited him in that new land.

*   *   *

As the jet flew northward, the red bus was loaded, and the family went toward home. DH sat behind his parents next to Nanda as the tooting bus with its quiet passengers crossed the Berbice River on the ferryboat and stopped occasionally to let people off at their respective homes.

CHAPTER 18

Who Were Those People?

Now would be a good time to reflect upon who those people were. They were some of my ancestors. Radha, Lady, Kesha, Desai, Pyroo, Kangal, Kalya, Kumar, and Shanti were some of the roots that sprouted into our family tree. I was lucky enough to put some of the pieces together and recreate certain segments of their lives. Because many of those Indian indentured servants were basically illiterate, it was difficult to accurately narrate the details of their real stories. Even if men like Pyroo kept some type of diary, there is no record of such documents. The only sources are some translations from the archives and the stories told by one generation after another.

It has been over forty years since the first draft this book. The intent was to make it a factual description of the lives of our ancestors and what could have happened to them. After countless trips to Guyana (previously known as British Guiana), sorting through pages of documents, and asking many questions of anyone who could possibly have any notion of those people, I became even more inquisitive than I was when the process first started. A few good things came out of the investigations. The most important things were the consistent accounts of how many of the indentured servants were tricked into going to the various British colonies, the atrocities that they encountered, and the inhumane treatment that they were subjected to by the plantation management personnel and some of the field supervisors. It became obvious that the indentured servant process was a form of glorified slavery. After all, those people were replacements for the African slaves, who suffered tremendous hardships. What was even more shocking was that the so-called male authorities expected the women to be readily submissive to their sexual advances. The attractive women were preyed upon more often and were treated as hand-me-downs. That meant that the higher the man was on the totem pole, the greater priority he had. If a man with lesser authority wanted his respective chance with a particular female, he had to wait his turn. Women who resisted were treated poorly. They were given harder tasks, taunted, insulted, verbally abused, and, yes, beaten. Stories were told of the plantation personnel who would lift up the women's scanty dresses and beat them on their bare bottoms. One can only imagine the humiliation and embarrassment those defenseless women encountered. And for what?

Some years ago, it dawned on me that I do not have to have all the details because this is not a history book. The purpose was to tell the stories of a few people whose lives can adequately depict and represent the situations of their respective lives in India and what happened to them in British Guiana from 1838 to almost 1920 and generations beyond. It became my conclusion that these stories should be told, for the human race needs to realize and understand that although we claim to be civilized, we have not all evolved as far away from our animal cousins as we would like to think. But that is a whole different subject.

When I was growing up in Guyana (British Guiana) in the 1950s, my mother would occasionally send me to sleep at my grandmother's house. She was old and lived alone. Hence, various siblings and cousins took turn keeping her company after school was out for the day. Some of us stayed with her for short periods of time. I hated that! All the boys in our neighborhood were out playing cricket and having fun while I stayed a mile away with an old woman in a dark house. She was very smart, and in spite of her illiteracy, she ran a store. She was also an excellent cook. But by the time 7:00 p.m. came, we had already had supper, and it was her bedtime. The only light came from an old, dimly lit kerosene lantern that hung in her bedroom. But the biggest problem for me was that one of her sons (my uncle Prem) had recently been killed in an accident, and his room was left intact and was very dark at night. Many cousins and sisters who stayed there told stories of his perceived ghost dwelling in that room, and at the age of seven, I was scared that a ghost would rise up as a foggy mist and strangle me in my sleep.

Grandmother, whose name was Doormatie and whom we called Nany, recognized the concerns and allowed me to sleep in her room on a little cot next to her bed. To keep her from snoring and to keep myself company, I would ask her to tell me stories (*nancy*). She was not much of a storyteller, but her voice kept me from thinking about the ghost in the next room. The routine continued on those nights that I spent at Nany's house. For the most part, she was a sweet old lady who fed me well, gave me fresh oranges partially squeezed, and told stories. She was my grandmother, and apart from missing home and an occasional game of cricket, I eventually became fond of that old lady.

Then one night, she told a different story. She started to talk about her parents and grandparents. She went on and on and on until I fell asleep. The next night, she continued with the stories about how her ancestors came from India in boats and worked on the sugar plantations. She gave vivid details about how they lived and how difficult it was for her grandmother and talked about all the things that her mother had to cope with. She talked about the tragic lives of her in-laws and the difficulties and accomplishments of her orphaned late husband. But it took her several days to finish the details about her six sisters who died because she did not get to know any of them. She had no adult sisters who survived. That was difficult for her to accept, and in the darkness, I heard her sniffling and pouring out her grief to a kid not even ten years old.

At first, it was interesting to hear the stories. But after several months of hearing the same narrative over and over again, I started tuning her out, and after a while, as I got older, there was farmwork to do for boys like me. Some other person was recruited to keep the old lady company, and I did not have to listen to her stories anymore and did not worry about the ghost that dwelled in her house. But those stories became part of me, and in the early 1980s, while jogging, I began to question and try to make sense of the indentured servant process in British Guiana, Trinidad, Mauritius, and other parts of the globe. I questioned the situations of some 1.2 million indentured servants who were taken from India and shipped to various parts of the world to work on plantations owned by the British.

It was May 1983, and that lonely jogger on County Road 17 in Minnesota saw a cloud in the western horizon. It was a warm spring day as the constant hum of tractors filled the country air. An occasional pickup truck passed by, and the driver would wave or nod. The cloud was the shape of a man who appeared red from the reflection of the setting sun. That perceived figure planted itself there like a giant colossus, hot and inviting, with piercing eyes, and for some reason, that figure made me think about my grandfather. His name was Desai. The jog became a slow walk as I gazed at the image and allowed my imagination to lead me into obsession. It was that day that it dawned upon me that I needed to learn their real stories. Maybe I should write a book! I already had the first draft sketched for documentation purposes. The thoughts consumed me as large swarms of blackbirds that dotted the skies acrobatically flew from tree to tree with sounds that rivaled the diesel-powered tractors pulling the various tillage equipment and expelling black gases from their exhaust pipes. Darkness sent the birds to rest. The colossal figure in the horizon faded. The scattered tractors continued their humming, crawling along with flickering lights, mimicking distant fireflies. Thinking about the red image on that dark road, I hurried home.

The dawn abruptly came the following morning as the two WCCO radio announcers, Boon and Erickson, informed listeners that it was time to get moving. It was time to get to the office. There, reality overshadowed the image of Desai, at least temporarily, for various office duties took precedence.

That summer, I could not wait to get home and changed into jogging shoes so I could head west on County Road 17 and stare into the western horizon in search of Desai's hologram in the clouds. He never came back. The fall and winter months were no different. That provoking image stirred some deep emotions within as more and more childhood stories surfaced, and again, I decided that those stories should be properly documented and preserved for future generations. However, I was now a father and got promoted at my job. Many other daily survival routines somewhat dulled the burning passion of ancestral survival as the focus became life, family, and career.

It was not until the later 1980s that those old stories were again resurrected. By that time, my parents, Motilall and Finey, lived in Minneapolis. They came to be with family and for medical reasons. I lived on a farm by Waconia, Minnesota, and worked in a downtown Minneapolis office. A similar situation again occurred. I spent occasional nights with them partly out of concern for their loneness and partly because it kept me from fighting rush-hour traffic of driving west with the bright sun in my eyes. Besides, my mother catered all the old country foods, and Dad and I could sit with the brandy bottle enjoying the delicacies that Ma spent hours preparing. Needless to say, after a couple of brandies, Daddy's voice would start to amplify, at which point Ma would put the bottle away, complaining about Daddy's heart condition and the detriment of alcohol to his system. That spelled bedtime for all of us.

Then one night, we told a different story. It was the story about our ancestors. It was time to get a pen and notepad and start writing things. The stories were even more fascinating. We all knew bits and pieces. Ma told more about Nany's family, and Daddy talked about those on his side, especially his father, Desai, and his other relatives. He also talked about his maternal grandfather, a man named Kangal, and his grandmother, Kalya (Ramkulia). Then they told each other's stories, and we continued into the night. It was then that the visits with them became more and more interesting. I was discussing it from an adult's point of view now, and Ma did not remove the brandy bottle as early as before, for she was enjoying the discussions and making sure that I wrote things down exactly as she narrated. She was a good narrator, but Daddy was an excellent storyteller. He made the stories quite interesting with occasional pauses for confirmation from us and a sip of brandy and 7Up. After lowering the glass, he would lick his moustache, clear his throat with a quiet cough, and continue. He no longer smoked cigarettes because of coronary concerns. They got into some disagreements about how exactly things really were, but there were always compromises, and we filled in the gaps with some possible scenarios. Ma was generally embarrassed to discuss the details of the abuse of the women with me. But I insisted and reminded her that I was an adult and needed to hear the truth in detail. She finally told me. She sometimes stopped to blow her nose and wipe away her tears. The toughest story for her to tell was how her great-grandmother, Lady, had to lower her bloomers and take the punishment in the sugarcane fields. She would get all choked up and walk to the bathroom to compose herself. She cried for her grandmother, Radha, who witnessed such brutality during her tender years.

It all seems so long ago, and yet I can hear their voices and see their gestures as the keyboard on the laptop keeps spitting out these words as if it is on autotype. And the more I think about it, the clearer the affirmation is that their stories need to be told. So I'll leave the system on autotype and read what it can reveal as fingers effortlessly crawl over the keyboard and English words appear on the screen.

Year by year, the search and the writing process continued.

It would be impossible to choose one hero for this book because now they all seem like heroes to me. November 2010 came, and we had our first snow after some marvelous fall weather. The clocks were backed up one hour to accommodate daylight savings time and forced outdoor activities into basement offices as hibernation instincts would chat with artificial lights and encourage the fingers that walked over the keyboard. It still is not my intent to create heroes and villains inasmuch as they existed in the stories. The ancestors that continue to dance in my memory have long departed from life as we know it. But the obsession in my head about what I have learned forced me to continue.

Occasionally, I still scan the western horizon to see if Desai would care to make an appearance with a nod of approval. So far, there has been no trace of him. It is rather shocking that a cloud could evoke such emotions and reawaken thoughts that propel things into action. My only hope is that this writing can adequately depict the gist of his and other lives, and in some strange way, they can be immortalized and future generations will learn about the severe price that they paid in order for this family to survive and succeed.

It is 2016, and I'm still editing and revising. It can be difficult to create something from bits and pieces of information, but I concluded a long time ago that a somewhat creative nonfiction does not have to document all the details, and it was never my intent to write fiction with mostly invented names. In my opinion, that would be an insult to the subjects in this book, so it is written as based on true stories. I am convinced that the stories are true. The details have been buried and somewhat exaggerated with the respective generations. Yet some names had to be invented because nobody can remember their real names. So, I made up some names to identify who they were.

But to clarify, Doormatie, whom we called Nany, was the only surviving daughter of Radha and Pyroo. They were my mother's parents. Radha, therefore, was my great-grandmother. The classical dancer, Lady, was my great-great-grandmother. Shamlal was my mother's father. He would be my nana. Desai was my father's father, my grandfather. He would be my aja. Punit was Desai's father in India.

It is now New Year's Day 2021. The COVID-19 pandemic has temporarily paralyzed many activities, including business travel. In the dead of winter in Minnesota, options are limited during the pandemic. So, it is time to put the finishing touches on this book and move on. I am now seventy years old. The future is unknown. It's now or never. It is time to do one final edit and find a publisher. I am pleased to tell you, the reader, the stories about my ancestors.

CHAPTER 19

Reflections and Conclusion

It's almost midnight on December 28, 2017, as I sit here to write this final chapter. I am DH's brother who left Guyana on March 31, 1970, on my way to the United States. That was the last time I saw DH. With bittersweet enthusiasm, I departed from the airport in Guyana that day. I still miss him, and when I travel to Guyana on an annual basis, I take time to weed and wash his grave. Then I sit there talking to him and reminding him that he lives with me every day, even if only in my imagination. I tell him about his daughters and grandchildren who reside in New York. I tell him that people only die when the memories fade. I remind him that looking back at all the childhood things we did, there are memories to last several lifetimes and that he will not be forgotten as long as I live. Then I tell him that I still love him and do miss him and that I'll always remember what he told me at the airport about not living to regret anything. I have, for the most part, tried to live that way.

While at the cemetery, I would look over to Prem's burial site, which coincidentally is kitty-corner from DH's tomb and wonder what he would have become had he lived to full old age. Then I would walk to Doormatie's tomb, do a respectful greeting, and let her know that she has not been forgotten.

I am truly grateful for all the stories that I was told about our family history. I'm glad that on several occasions, their words were written as they were spoken to me. My uncle Nanda told me many stories about Desai, his father, and Mangrie, his mother. I only wish that I had asked him more questions. Yet I am thankful that he gave enough details to help construct that part of this written puzzle. I am glad that he told me about his grandparents in India and the circumstances under which his father left that country. There must be relatives of Desai generations later still living in India and probably still wondering what happened to that young man who mysteriously disappeared from the village, leaving the cattle he loved so much to roam about. I do intend to roam the villages in Agra in search of any such descendants of that family and those of Kangal and Kalya.

I am glad that my grandmother told me about her ancestors and how Pyroo and Radha's family came to the British colony. I wish that we knew more about Shamlal's parents, Kumar and Shanti, who died while still bound to the plantation and left their two young children at the orphanage at Ruimveldt Estate. I still intend to find out who they really were.

The years with my parents in Minneapolis were the final foundation for this book. Without their guidance and corrections, the stories would have been incomplete. They finally told the stories to me as an adult when I could comprehend things from a different perspective. They often used to talk about the difficult time they endured as a young married couple and the few years that followed. Their life story can be inspiration for the human race as affirmation that it should not matter where life started; rather, it should matter how things end up. That couple started with nothing except dreams and determination that escalated them into their humble comfort zone. They always said that there is no substitute for hard work and being smart about what you do. They said that as long as life is lived with honesty, sincerity, and integrity, it is worth living. They were people of faith, and faith had guided them through their difficult moments. They were good and respectable people, and I'm proud to have had them as parents.

I am thankful for meeting Mahindra, my father's cousin. He took the time many years ago to document the travels of ancestors like Kangal and Kalya. Meeting him was an exclamation moment. It has to be divine intervention that asks us to seek and find. I was seeking for a long time and eventually found enough from him. The search goes on.

It was never my intent to create heroes and villains in this writing. The primary reason for writing this was to document what happened to my ancestors and others like them who immigrated to British colonies and to tell their respective stories. At times, it was difficult to create something without any concrete information. In those situations, I had to use my imagination and the stories told and wrestle with logic and fiction, resulting in a kind of creative nonfiction. I do know that there could be some inaccurate and exaggerated depictions under some circumstances, but the gist is the basis of this narration.

Occasionally, I still look into the western horizon toward evening to see if the figment of Desai will show up, but so far, he has not. The conclusion is that his perceived image that once appeared in the clouds evoked some buried emotions in me that provoked something within to reveal his story and do whatever came after that. His perceived image had done its job and caused a state of restlessness within me. The rest was for me to decide, and this writing has partially cured some of that restlessness and evoked other emotions that will be decided and hopefully be solved in the future.

I have been asked the reason for the title *Marble, Grass, and Glass.* The title simply summarizes the generations. People like Pyroo and Radha's family had residences decorated with marble. The couple took Motilall's dreams to the mansion, which was made of marble. Generations of indentured servants lived in *grass* huts. In the United States and in other countries, many of their descendants now work in *glass* offices. The message is that things can change from generation to generation, but there is always hope during difficult times. Bad times never last forever, and neither do good times. The only constant is change, and the human race has the option to change situations that are unacceptable. Even in the darkest moments, we must maintain our powers and make every effort to right the wrong things, regardless of the consequences. We all know the difference between good and bad and that good will always triumph. And when in doubt, seek advice from a higher power. My parents taught me those lessons. Those simple lessons have served me well for many decades and continue to do so.

Although the stories in this book deal with my ancestors, there are numerous other people of Indian descent whose ancestors suffered similar fates. It is my hope that this book can inspire others like me to seek out what happened to their ancestors, and if they cannot find out anything, they can take comfort in reading this book and realize that the stories could be universal. It is our story. Many suffered the same fate during the indentured process, and we can all agree that what happened to most of those people was not fair. We should all feel for the women, some of whom were tricked into making the journey and were treated like chattel and violated by bullies in positions of power. We are not supposed to judge because judging belongs to some higher power, but sometimes it is hard not to do just that.

Today, it is all history. The tyrants who abused power and the abused victims are no longer here. Many good and innocent people in Guyana died prematurely during the indentured process from 1838 to 1917 and beyond. When those people were suffering in the hot tropical plantations, they probably prayed that their descendants would not have to suffer similar hardships. I do realize that today, many are living those people's dreams, and we should be thankful for that. We stand on their shoulders. If I could tell them anything, it would be, "Thank you for the prayers," and that they did not suffer in vain. I would further tell them that folks do not die as long as the memories live on. I can do my small part to remember their hardships and to tell their stories, which will ensure their immortality in words. And finally, I remind myself that survival is priority, and many people survived and, on several occasions, took time to celebrate their heritage. Our heritage.

It is difficult to conclude this writing because there are many other things to say, but the decision was made to conclude at this point because it started in India via Guyana and to the United States. I'm in the process of planning a trip to India to close the triangular path.

I would kindly ask all the brothers and sisters whose ancestors suffered and survived similar fates as did my ancestors to take a moment and recognize that sacrifices were made and to appreciate their respective freedom. And although there were varying degrees of suffering for those folks, they probably found time to bond and celebrate the joys of life and made the best of time even under bad conditions, even with limited resources. They did what they had to do. It is our duty to celebrate their lives by honoring them and demonstrating our achievements. On many occasions, when minor mishaps occurred in my life, I always tried to remind myself that I had nothing to complain about. I reminded myself that sacrifices were made to ensure my happiness and to deny my ancestors that satisfaction would be hypocritical.

Having lived in the United States for almost half a century, I understand that this country was, for the most part, built on immigration. Now with DNA testing, people have the opportunity to trace their ancestry. It is good to know who we are and from where we came.

The paragraphs that follow will try to summarize the indentured process from India. People were misled and taken to Fiji, Mauritius, Africa, Guyana, Trinidad, and many other islands in the Caribbean. They were taken from Orissa, Bengal, Bihar, Utter Pradesh, Awadh, Punjab, Nepal, Madras, Bombay, and other places. Some endured, and some perished. Some died during the ocean passage from sickness, diseases, depression, and malnutrition. Some committed suicide by jumping overboard. There was infanticide performed by mothers who were raped and did not want any physical reminders about the horrible experience and shame that they endured.

For all the atrocities that many suffered in silence, this writing honors them, and I hope that such things never happen again as long as humans roam this planet.

The Passage from India to Guyana

A Summary of the Indentured Process

This is just a brief background on how it all started. The introduction of sugarcane cultivation and the processing of sugar has been the biggest event in Guyana's written history.

Sugar was introduced to Europe from India by Arabs. After the rediscovery of the New World, the Portuguese occupied large areas in Brazil. At that time, the Dutch occupied parts of northeast Brazil. When the Dutch were driven out of Brazil in 1645, they brought their experience of cane production and settled along the Guyana coastal area. With the good land there and the strong demand for sugar, those early Dutch settlers managed to start small-scale sugarcane production. Initially, they used the native people to help with various duties at those early plantations. However, as production grew, the labor demand increased. Speculation is that they must have brought some slaves along when they fled from Brazil, but the labor demand kept increasing.

In the early 1500s, the Portuguese started the slave trade. For the next several years, the Dutch, British, French, and others battled for control of the transatlantic slave trade. It was a lucrative business at the expense of human lives and freedom. Many African people were kidnapped and sold as slaves to plantation owners in the western hemisphere. Guyana was no exception. Large-scale importation of slaves into Guyana started in in 1658 and ended in 1834.

After slavery was abolished in Guyana in 1834, there was a six-year transitional period allowing the plantation owners to secure an adequate labor force for the continuation of sugarcane production and the processing into sugar and other by-products. The freed slaves assumed that with such labor shortages, the British plantation owners would be forced to hire them at competitive wages. They were wrong. The plantation owners recruited people from various sources and eventually realized that people from India would be suitable for such duties. In 1838, the first group of people from India arrived in

Guyana on a contract basis. The first two ships were the *Hesperus* and the *Whitby*. The passengers were called indentured servants. They became known as coolies.

The time to complete the journey varied depending on what ship made the trip. Early sailing ships took up to four months to go from India to Guyana. Later, steamships completed the voyage in less than one hundred days. Most of those ships departed from Calcutta. They traveled down the Hooghly River into the Bay of Bengal and soon into the Indian Ocean. They stopped at selected ports for supplies and fresh water. Then they traveled toward the Cape of Good Hope. After circling the stormy waters of southern Africa, they proceeded into a northwestern route toward the Caribbean islands. Many of those people disembarked at the port of Demerara, Guyana. That was the route that my ancestors took. They settled in that colony. None of them returned to India. They all died in Guyana.

Many believe that the indentured process was more of a glorified enslavement process. The East Indian indentured people were shipped to various parts of the world. It is estimated that the British exported some 1.2 million from India. Their destinations were as follows:

British Guiana	238,909
Trinidad	143,939
Other West Indian Islands	10,000
Jamaica	36,412
Surinam	34,304
Natal	152,184
Seychelles	6,315
Fiji	60,965
Africa (other)	32,000
Mauritius	453,063
Reunion	26,507
Martinique	25,509
Guadalupe	45,844
French Guiana	19,276

These numbers may not be exact, but the point is that over 1.2 million East Indians were used in the process for enriching the wealthy planters. The sorry part is that they were not treated very well. The preceding chapters told some stories about the process. Today, it is only history. What has the human race learned from such atrocities? Can it happen again? Or when will it happen again? Where will it happen again? Who will be brave enough to stop it from happening again? Can future generations be smart enough to destroy such monsters in their shells and prevent them from hatching?

I have no advice for the future. My hope is that there will always be a Mahatma Gandhi with divine wisdom to keep such evil from destroying all of mankind.

The transatlantic journey must have been a nightmare for some, but some escaped from bad situations in India in search of a better life. There were atrocities and horrors on those ships, but some found the strength to gather together and tried to find activities that minimized the boredom. They sang and played whatever musical instruments were available. In life, most people do what has to be done in order to survive bad situations. It was no different for those passengers who bobbed along in small vessels that floated with the waves of the mighty oceans. Most survived the journey; some did not. No one can change what happened. We have moved on to better things. But we should not forget who we are and should be proud of our respective heritages.

To end on a positive note, it always pleases me to see Indo-Guyanese and other descendants from the indentured process who have made achievements beyond their ancestral dreams. Although a lot of suffering was endured, much good has emerged, and I hope that such goodness will continue. We can tell the stories and remember what happened, but we should not dwell on the past. We all have the choice to show what we are capable of and to be able to inspire future generations to become the best that they can be. We owe that much to the generations that paved the way for us and for generations to come.

I must say that I'm thankful to have lived in the United States for over fifty years. All alone, I initially endured university, immigration issues, corporate politics, and some ignorant human stupidity. Albert Einstein said it best when he said that the difference between genius and stupidity is that there is a limit to genius. We have choices. A lot has changed since I arrived here in 1970. What this country has done for me and my family cannot be defined in words. It is a true blessing. There have been occasional disappointments along the way, but that is life. Even a bed of roses can have thorns. I want to thank all the kindhearted citizens of this great nation who helped and encouraged me to be the best I can be. For those who were hindrances, thank you for allowing me to show what is possible in the United States. I want to say thank you to America for what she represents and for what she has done to help people like me to secure a comfortable lifestyle and to enjoy all the freedom that she offers. Liberty and justice for all. God bless the USA! Thank you!

It would be hypocritical for me not to honor India. She gave me my genes. Her teachings programmed me for life. Her wisdom, her music, her mysticism, her spirituality, her transplanted culture, her national heroes, her beliefs, her sentiments, her celebrations, her long history, her everything has helped to prepare me for life. Thank you, Mother India!

And what about Guyana? She brought me into the world. She nurtured me during those tender years. Many friends, relatives, and ancestors are buried there. For almost twenty years, she was the only home I knew. Guyana is the origin. She is still home. When I visit her and sit in the hammock, I am at peace. Dear land of Guyana, I love you too. Thank you for providing for our family and all that you offered us one generation after another. You have witnessed the struggles of our ancestors and now cradle their resting bones. You are home, sweet home!

England, she also played her part. She built schools for us to attend. She taught me English. In the big picture, she is responsible for my early education. For that, I am thankful. Above all, I praise the British abolitionists and sympathetic organizations that unconditionally fought for justice on behalf of the slaves and the indentured servants.

I am proud to be able to honor and sing four national anthems: "Jana Gana Mana" from India, "God Save the Queen" from England, "Dear Land of Guyana, of Rivers and Plains" from Guyana; and "The Star-Spangled Banner" from the United States. I often sing them all. I still honor them all. They are all parts of me, and I am part of them. Those anthems cemented the diversity within me. Each one is a pillar of my strength. I stand on all those pillars and view the world, and I can see what possibilities exist for the human race, for all my brothers and sisters.

Finally, thank you, Mother Earth, for sustaining life and continuing to give even when we are less deserving.

Most of all, thank you, God, for all your creations and your blessings that you continue to shower upon us and for doing so unconditionally for all Earthlings regardless of nationality.

EPILOGUE

Dear Reader,

It is New Year's Eve 2018. About a week ago, I returned from a trip to India. The flight went from MSP International Airport to the Netherlands and then to New Delhi. The scheduled driver took me from the airport to the Holiday Inn at 2:00 a.m. I was totally exhausted and jetlagged. I had two days to tour the sites of Delhi and to enjoy the food before going to a university to meet a friend. It has always been my dream to visit the land from which my ancestors emigrated generations ago. What is interesting is that I went there with the intention of finding evidence of my ancestors; instead, I found myself. I left India with a sense of satisfaction that my feet had finally touched the surfaces of villages where my ancestors walked a long time ago. It was great to tour the Taj Mahal and to see Agra and the Yamuna River and spend the night at the Trident Hotel. Agra is the place from which Desai supposedly escaped. It was satisfying to walk the ruins of Residency Park in Lucknow, one of the places where the Sepoy Revolution took place in 1857. Maybe Pyroo was there in some capacity. I visited cities and farms in that area and saw the Gomati River. I toured the 107-acre memorial of Dr. Ambedkar, the man whose achievements had inspired me at the tender age of ten.

I walked about in Varanasi and Moghul Sarai. It was a great satisfaction to know that it was from that area that Kangal and

Kalya departed, Kangal on the *North* in 1879 and Kalya on the *New Castle* in 1881. It was good to walk along the Ganges River in whose perceived healing waters my ancestors must have dipped themselves into spiritual trances. I felt at home in the company of the village people where the animals and people share a common domain. I drank tea, spiked with raw cane sugar and buffalo milk, with them and walked by their fields. My driver was overprotective and worried about the American casually walking about.

Staying at some less-than-desirable hotels was almost frightening. But with limited options, I made the decision to stay at such establishments and hope for the best. Viewing the various towns and the countryside was wonderful, and my driver and I sang old Hindi songs to avoid boredom on the way back to New Delhi. After returning to Delhi, I flew to Calcutta.

Four days in Calcutta was more than I expected. The staff at the JW Marriott was extremely helpful and made me feel like part of the family there. The cooks, the servers, the front office staff, and the daily drivers were all very pleasant. During the day, I toured various parts of that city. It was nice to see Victoria Memorial Garden. Here, the statues of the self-proclaimed Empress of India, Queen Victoria, tower vertically several feet upward. What really struck me there was the small, half-naked statue of Gandhi outside. I had to wonder about both of them coming to life with nothing and leaving their mortal bodies with nothing. And in the midst of that grand memorial, I stood there admiring Gandhi's little statue and thinking about all his achievements. Silently, I asked him to kindly find Pyroo and let him know that India had survived very well, and he should now rest in peace.

I found myself on the banks of the Hooghly River, a branch of the Ganges, in a place called Kidderpur. From that area, the ships sailed with the indentured servants to British Guiana and elsewhere. There, something happened. I could almost see the commotion and quietly heard the loud cries of the passengers about to embark on the ships that would be heading toward Kala Panni. The screams of the women were deafening with the vision of occasional souls jumping into the water. I watched as they eventually perished. I could see Radha's family pleading their case as the arkathies were screaming that all were leaving India voluntarily. One by one, I visualized all my ancestors, except Desai, being pushed and shoved onto the docks and into their respective vessels. I could see Desai's mighty body sweating. He was carrying and loading supplies into the *Lena* as his long hair blew in the wind. Finally, I could see the ships drifting away toward the Indian Ocean and disappearing into the distant fog that blended with the smog of Punjab. The screams from the hysterical mass confusion were fading, and I stood there motionless like a beach statue. And the waters of the Hooghly River waited for no one. The current obeyed its path as it had done for centuries. Passing vehicles honked their horns, but I noticed not. Finally, I walked to the edge of the water with painful joy.

There I stood, feeling alone among the crowd of people bathing and washing their clothes along the riverbanks. As the uncontrolled tears rolled off both cheeks, they gently kissed the waters of that mighty river. There, I realized that my tears were blending with those of so many who sailed away from there a long time ago. I found myself praying silently and talking to their departed souls. Then silently I told them that it was now time for them to go on to heaven because I finally came to see them ascend into eternity. I mentioned to them that our family was in good hands and that we had survived and were moving on. Through the tears and blurred vision, I could almost see their spirits as the ships disappeared into the smog that engulfed Calcutta. It was there that I realized that I had found myself. I realized that the search had made significant progress and felt a state of consciousness that words cannot describe. I was in this world with reality and yet out of this world's consciousness. My spirit blended joy with sadness, and somehow, with blurred vision, I could clearly see far beyond my mortal awareness.

I stood there blending tears with the waters of the mighty river as people walked past with questioning stares. One woman greeted me with "Namaste, sir. Are you okay?" I told her that everything was just fine and that I was really happy to be there. She left with a questioning look on her face. The driver must have been very confused also as he watched from a distance, patiently awaiting my return to the vehicle.

Sometime later, we drove back toward the hotel. I was looking for an address given as 8 Garden Reach, where the immigration information was issued. I found 28 Garden Reach. That area is now consumed with shipbuilding. Time, like the waters, has moved on.

The following day, I flew back to New Delhi and stayed again among friends at the retreat of the beautiful university campus. The next day, the twenty-two-hour journey took me back to MSP airport via Paris. My wife picked me up at the Minneapolis airport, and we came home.

For the past few days, my body has been in Minnesota, but my mind is elsewhere. I have seen so much and have so much to digest. I now realize that the triangle is fully connected—from India to Guyana to the United States and back to India. I now realize how blessed my life has been and understand who I am and from where I came. The mission is now partially completed. I have asked the ancestral spirits to move on because my generation has evolved. Today, we are just fine. I realize now that I made the journey for me and not so much for them. I went to India to find my ancestors and also found myself. That's a great joy.

It was wonderful to think about Lady, Radha, and Kesha; about Pyroo and Jahaj; about Kumar and Shanti; about Kangal and Kalya; and most of all about Desai. Those are the shoulders on which I now stand. I am living their dreams. I honor their sacrifices. I am very sorry for the abuses they endured. I want them to be proud of me. I want to be worthy of their prayers. It gives me great pleasure to learn about them, my ancestors, and my heroes. God bless their souls. I am so proud to be wearing their DNA.

Now it is up to future generations to seek and to correct any mistakes made during this initial search. I will continue to investigate and continue the search for information still missing. The intention of this book was to document the stories told about those who carried the genes long before my arrival on earth. I did the first leg of this relay and am now passing the stick to the next runner, whoever that might be. I'll be the cheerleader. This age of computers and search engines and the science like DNA testing will accelerate the search process. This book is only the foundation. Future generations curious enough can take the next leg of this relay and run into eternity. They can build upon this foundation and create mansions with glitter and paint. I am satisfied to have taken the initiative to build a narrative from stories about people who have long departed from this place. I am truly happy to be able to create this much over the past forty years. The future belongs to generations to come. I wish them all the best and plan to help them as long as I can. I'll challenge them to seek and find and to fit the missing pieces of our family puzzle in. I wish them all the best. This process may go on forever, still missing some details. But forever is a long time. Keep on searching, kids!

* * *

Dear Reader, I hope that you found this book interesting and enjoyed reading it. I told the stories as I saw fit. It can be hard to build something from nothing, but this was one of my life's missions. Thank you for being a partner in this process. The only thing I ask of you is to please stand up and help prevent injustice in this world. Together, we can create a safer world for generations to come—a world that can make even heaven proud. Let's create and sustain ongoing joy in the world!

Made in the USA
Middletown, DE
23 July 2023

35590789R00208